COLONEL CODY

THE FLYING CATHEDRAL

COLONEL CODY

THE FLYING CATHEDRAL

THE ADVENTURES OF THE COWBOY
WHO CONQUERED THE SKY

GARRY JENKINS

PICADOR USA

NEW YORK

B
CODY
S

For Thomas and Gabriella

COLONEL CODY AND THE FLYING CATHEDRAL: THE ADVENTURES OF THE COWBOY WHO CONQUERED THE SKY. Copyright © 1999 by Garry Jenkins. All rights reserved. Printed in the United States of America. No part of this book may be used or reproduced in any manner whatsoever without written permission except in the case of brief quotations embodied in critical articles or reviews. For information, address Picador USA, 175 Fifth Avenue, New York, N.Y. 10010.

Picador® is a U.S. registered trademark and is used by St. Martin's Press under license from Pan Books Limited.

The majority of illustrative material used in this book was provided by Jean and John Roberts.

Additional permission has been given for use of the following images:
Page ii © Science Museum/Science & Society Picture Library;
Pages 2, 30, 45, 68, 72, 75 © Autry Museum of Western Heritage, Los Angeles;
Pages 5, 53, 58, 168, 182, 184, 206, 209, 230, 237, 252 © Mary Evans Picture Library; Page 23 © Peter Newark's Western America; Page 99 © Newcastle *Evening Chronicle*; Pages 120/1, 137, 181, 245 © Reproduced by the permission of the Defence Evaluation and Research Agency, Farnborough; Page 267 © (British) Crown Copyright, 1999, Defence Evaluation and Research Agency, reproduced with the Controller, Her Britannic Majesty's Stationery Office; Page 167 © *The Mirror*; Pages 228, 250 © The Royal Aeronautical Society.

Library of Congress Cataloging-in-Publication Data
Jenkins, Garry.
    Colonel Cody and the flying cathedral : the adventures of the cowboy who conquered the sky / Garry Jenkins.
        p.   cm.
    Includes index.
    ISBN 0-312-24180-1
    1. Cody, S. F. (Samuel Franklin), 1861–1913.   2. Air pilots—United States—Biography. 3. Air pilots—Great Britain—Biography.   I. Title.
TL540.C64J45
629.13/093—dc21
[B]   00-036313
                                                                                                     CIP

First published in Great Britain as *'Colonel' Cody and the Flying Cathedral: The Adventures of the Cowboy Who Conquered Britain's Skies* by Simon & Schuster UK Ltd., a Viacom Company

First Picador USA Edition: August 2000

10   9   8   7   6   5   4   3   2   1

CONTENTS

PROLOGUE vii

1	The Great Imitators	1
2	A Pair of Shootists	31
3	Le Roi Des Cow-Boys	49
4	'A new and original act'	69
5	Man-lifting	89
6	'It's dogged as does it'	113
7	Second to None	129
8	Across the Greensward	151
9	A Clever Empiricist	169
10	The Flying Cathedral	187
11	Showman of Flight	207
12	The Arm of the Nation	231
12A	'Swift and sudden'	253

ACKNOWLEDGEMENTS 269

INDEX 273

Each frontier did indeed furnish a new field of opportunity, a gate of escape from the bondage of the past: and freshness, and confidence, and scorn of older society, impatience of its restraints and its ideas, and indifference to its lessons, have accompanied the frontier.

FREDERICK JACKSON TURNER,
The Frontier in American History,
1893

What is character but the determination of incident?
What is incident but the illustration of character?

HENRY JAMES

PROLOGUE

ON 11 AUGUST 1913, the British Army's headquarters at Aldershot witnessed a scene unprecedented even in its long and valorous history.

The first mourners had arrived in the English countryside, twenty miles or so outside London, with the dawn and the first trains from Waterloo Station. The flow of people – starched and steam-pressed in Bible-black – had continued unabated for the rest of the morning.

By early afternoon, according to most reliable reckonings, 100,000 people had positioned themselves along the aspen-lined lanes, from the village of Ash Vale in Surrey to the Military Cemetery at Thorn Hill, three miles away, across the Hampshire border. At the most popular vantage point, on a knoll overlooking the spot where a new grave had been excavated that morning, the crush was so dense a team of Army nurses had been requisitioned to treat the growing numbers of women overcome by the broiling heat.

The garrison's history was rich in pomp and pageantry. 'Never have so many people gathered together in Aldershot,' said one wonder-eyed witness nevertheless.

The ritual they had come to participate in began at 2 p.m. precisely, as a heavy oak casket emerged through the picket-fence gates of a large house on the edge of Ash Vale. The coffin was draped in a Union Jack and decorated with a single wreath of blue and white flowers in the shape of a broken steering wheel.

'. . . but a tithe of those who
wanted to come . . .'
Samuel Cody's funeral procession
on 11 August 1913.

The inscription on the card
had been written in a quaver-
ing hand. It read simply, 'In
Memory of My Dear Frank.'

The pallbearers placed
the coffin on a gun carriage of
the Royal Engineers, then fell
back into the cortège assembled behind them. The procession, too, was comfortably
the largest the home of the
British military establishment
had seen. Every member of
the newly formed Royal Flying Corps had volunteered to
take part. Every battalion of
every regiment stationed at
Aldershot was represented,
even though their numbers
reflected 'but a tithe of those
who wanted to come'. As a
team of six coal-black horses
eased the gun carriage into its
journey, the line of a thou-

sand men stretched back a mile along the neatly manicured roads.
The band and pipers of the famous Black Watch Regiment, and
the relentless dirge of Chopin's Funeral March, maintained them
in their slow, purposeful stride.

With the crowds standing two, three or more deep in places,

FUNERAL PROCESSION.

the procession's progress was slow. Only at the burial site itself, cut on a plateau in a tranquil corner of the cemetery, were the chief mourners left to grieve in some semblance of privacy. When, finally, the coffin was lowered into the grave, a solo piper played the traditional soldier's farewell, 'The Flowers o' the Forest'. As the final strains of the lament drifted into the late afternoon, and the mourners made their way home, only a blanket of floral tributes remained. 'He has won his wings,' read one. 'After life's fitful fever, he sleeps well,' read another.

By the time the trains arrived back in London that evening, the papers had already published their epilogues to the day's events. The *Evening Standard* caught the mood best. Its report began, 'On the top of a hill clothed with purple heather, looking out across the ground that was the scene of his struggles, his disappointments and his triumphs, they have buried Cody with all the honour they could render – the honour of a soldier's grave.'

For most of his forty-six years, 'Colonel' Samuel Franklin Cody's name had been synonymous with the epic and the melodramatic, the stirring and the unforeseen. Cattle-trail cowboy and bronco-buster, burlesque actor and sharpshooting King of the Wild West cowboys, dramatist, man-carrying kite maker and founding father of English aviation, even in an age of flamboyant pioneers, he had been the frontiersman supreme. Yet his life contained no more spectacular – nor improbable – a scene than the extraordinary funeral which followed four days after its sudden ending.

In October 1908 Cody had been the first man to fly in Britain. In the five adventure-filled years that had followed he had become what *Vanity Fair* magazine called 'the British public's chief and best showman of flight'. His death, in an air accident at Cove Common near Aldershot on 7 August, had provoked an outpouring of spontaneous grief. 'Millions who had never seen him felt they had suffered a loss, almost as if they had lost a friend,' wrote one who had known him. 'Not since King Edward's death has our country felt so deeply any one man's death,' ventured another, one of the hundreds moved to send letters of condolence to his widow, Lela, in the following days.

Edward VII's son and heir, King George V, had been among those to express their grief. Cody's friendship with the monarch extended back to his days as Prince of Wales. (It had been the King who had first referred to him as Colonel, a rank he had technically never earned. Cody had taken the compliment as some form of blessing and used the title freely ever since.) 'I have received with profound regret the news of the death of Mr Cody. I saw him on several occasions at Aldershot and always appreciated his dogged determination and dauntless courage,' the monarch wrote in a handwritten telegram, dispatched to Mrs Cody via the head of the Army at Aldershot, General Haig, from the Royal Yacht *Britannia* at Cowes. 'His loss will be much felt at Aldershot where he did much for military aviation. Will you convey to Mrs Cody and her sons my sincere sympathy with them in their sorrow. George RI.'

The King's message captured the public mood, and added new momentum to the campaign for Cody to be buried with full military honours. In the immediate aftermath of his death, his family had begun arrangements for a small, private funeral and an interment at a local church. Within forty-eight hours, General Haig and the War Office had offered Cody a plot within Thorn Hill, a site ordinarily reserved for officers and holders of the highest military honours. As far as anyone could ascertain, he was the first civilian to be granted such an honour. He was certainly the first Wild West cowboy to be laid alongside the heroes of Britain's glorious military past.

For most of his time in England, there could have been few less likely candidates for the tribute that he finally achieved. Only five years before his death, as his attempts to become Britain's first successful flyer floundered, Cody had been the butt of unprecedented vitriol. Large sections of the public regarded him as a laughing stock, a national joke made all the more amusing by the fact that he was an American. The final act of his life represented perhaps the ultimate triumph of his 'dogged determination'.

Yet if he went to his grave a hero, Cody also left the world an enigma. In life he had perpetuated the mystery surrounding his origins and his emergence as not just the most prominent flyer, but the most beloved adventurer of his day. In dying prematurely he had left the puzzle unsolved, and sealed his legend in the process.

'How was it that this boisterous son of a Western ranch, trick shot in music halls, and small lead in cheap theatres became one of the most daring and ingenious of English aviators . . . easily the most popular and picturesque of our flying men?' one editorial wondered at the time of his death. In 1913, the confusion of fact and fiction that surrounded Cody's life rendered the question all but unanswerable. The details of his work for the British Army remained protected by the Official Secrets Acts. Few, if any, knew the complex truth of his private life.

In the century that has followed, as his name and achievements have faded, so much of the material suppressed during his life has seeped into the public domain. Now, for the first time, his story can be seen in clear relief.

Cody's life turns out to have been a saga of invention – and frequent reinvention! – fortitude and occasional farce. Above all it emerges as a case study in the indomitability of the human spirit, an unlikely yet uplifting story set at the end of the pioneer age in which that disposition was allowed its freest expression.

CHAPTER ONE

THE GREAT IMITATORS

THE PROGRESS OF CIVILIZATION
THRILLING INCIDENTS IN ACTUAL BORDER LIFE
IN THE WILD WEST
THE GREAT DRAMA ENACTED BY FRONTIER HEROES

I N THE SUMMER OF 1888, ADAM D FOREPAUGH'S 'ORIGINAL and world famed Wild West show' lived up to the grandiose promise of its posters.

For a fifty-cent admission fee, audiences were treated to the spectacle of the legendary 'Doc' Carver, 'world's champion marksman', shattering a never-ending stream of flying glass balls with his Colt .45 revolvers, Forepaugh's son, Adam Jr, riding and driving a herd of thirty-one horses simultaneously, Round Up Bob, 'champion trick rider and roper of Texas', picking dimes off the floor in his teeth while remaining in the saddle of a galloping mustang, and – last but not least – a troupe of two dozen Sioux warriors re-enacting the blood-curdling events at the Battle of the Little Big Horn a dozen years earlier.

As a depiction of 'actual border life', of course, it was about as genuine as the pig's blood that oozed from Lieutenant Colonel Custer's corpse at the climax of his fateful Last Stand. Quite what

Adam D Forepaugh Sr

it had to do with 'the progress of civilization' was anyone's guess. If that mattered little to the hordes of eastern townspeople who packed Forepaugh's 10,000-seater arena twice daily that season, it was of even less consequence to the impresario then vying with Phineas T Barnum for the right to call himself the greatest showman in America, if not on earth.

Forepaugh's rise from small-time Philadelphia butcher to big-top impresario owed nothing to artistic veracity and everything to vaudevillian chutzpah. Four years earlier, for instance, on hearing Barnum's claim to have the world's only 'sacred white elephant' in his travelling show, Forepaugh had ordered one of his grey circus elephants scraped clean, whitewashed and rechristened Light of Asia. New York's yellow press had had a field day with the White Elephant War that ensued.

The stars of his travelling show were strangers to the truth too. While a New York variety artist called Louise Montague had reinvented herself as a dusky Indian Princess called Lalla Rookh, Doc Carver had obscured his true origins as a far-from-successful frontier dentist with a weave of stories so complex he often mixed them up himself. In a biographical sketch printed in the Forepaugh programme that season, for instance, Carver claimed to have played a crucial role in the bloody war fought against the Sioux and their chief Little Crow in Minnesota back in 1862.

'The defeat, capture and subsequent hanging of "Little Crow" was due largely to his courage, strategy and sleepless zeal,' Carver's publicist claimed with typical modesty in the notes. In the diaries that later formed his autobiography, however, Carver let slip that he had been hundreds of miles away at the time of

Little Crow's demise and only heard of the uprising in a city newspaper.

Their brand of brazen sensationalism was far from unique, of course. By 1888, with the prairies and cattle trails enmeshed in barbed wire and the golden age of the cowboy all but over, the last great frontier now lived mostly in the imagination of travelling burlesque players and dime novel writers. Most of them had been no farther West than Chicago. From their rumbustious, romantic and frequently preposterous version of the cowboy era, the most enduring and inaccurate of all American legends would take shape.

Yet as the Forepaugh circus worked its way along the railway routes of the 98th Meridian, at least one of its troupers seemed fit to be called a bona fide 'frontier hero'. Samuel Cody Jr had joined the show earlier that year. A former horsewrangler, mustang hunter and cattle-trail boss, he had launched a new career as a 'sharpshooter, cowboy and pistol shot'.

The apprentice showman had clearly learned much from watching and listening to the boastful and bellicose Doc Carver. Already a master of Carver's trick of firing at a hail of white, glass balls, fired from a clay-pigeon trap, Cody was applying his inventive, young mind to newer, more spectacular pieces of gunplay. Soon, for instance, Cody would perfect a heart-stopping stunt in which he could shoot an apple off a man's head while blindfolded. In his appearance and attitude, however, he had chosen to fashion himself after a frontiersman more famous than even Carver.

It had been with the dead-eyed dentist as his partner that WF 'Buffalo Bill' Cody had first whetted the American population's appetite for horse-thief lynchings and stagecoach attacks five years earlier. The 'Wild West, Rocky Mountain and Prairie Exhibition' they staged at a fairground in Omaha, Nebraska, had laid a trail which Forepaugh and a fistful of other, lesser entertainers were now extending to the eastern states and beyond. The partnership had degenerated into a series of court cases and public slanging matches in which both claimed to have sole use of the term Wild West. Carver's bitterness only deepened as the man he called 'The Great Imitator' acquired the rights to the title, then blossomed into the most famous Wild West cowboy in the world. In May of the previous year, 1887, Bill had even placed a thin smile on the face of Queen Victoria. His show at Earl's Court in London had drawn the mournful monarch into a public arena for the first time in the twenty-five years since her husband Prince Albert's death and made him a worldwide, living legend.

If Cody Jr's choice of role model was astute, it was also largely unavoidable. He was, even to those who had seen and known Bill, a doppelgänger for the older man. To accentuate this he had let his sun-bleached hair grow foppishly on to his shoulders, wore a thick, drooping walrus moustache and decked himself out in frazzled Codyesque buckskin from top to toe.

In the hotel bars and gambling halls of the east, the young sharpshooter did little to disillusion his public as to a genuine family connection. Anyone who asked was informed he was indeed 'a relative' of the great scout. Anyone who had the inclination could listen on as the garrulous young gun unfurled stories that proved he was also the tale-spinning equal of his 'Uncle Bill'.

The talkative Cody would spin the stories time and again in the years that followed, embroidering each episode, lending new and suitably dramatic denouements according to his audiences as he did so. Whether the tale was being told in Wilmington, North Carolina, or Wolverhampton, Warwickshire, however, the essential elements generally remained the same.

Cody Jr had spent his childhood in the small town of Birdville, near Fort Worth, Texas. He had been born there in March 1861 to Samuel Franklin Cody Sr and Phoebe Cody, descendants of settler families from County Antrim and Holland respectively.

'Birdville, I might tell you, was then a small village of seven or eight wooden houses, a small church, a prison built of rough-hewn logs, the boarders of the latter-mentioned establishment being few and far between on account of Judge Lynch,' he explained a few years later, unable as ever to resist adding a little colourful detail. (Judge Lynch, in fact, did not exist. The term had become a shorthand for instant justice since the activities of Colonel Charles Lynch, who punished those he considered criminals – or, worse, Tories – with hang-

The Great Scout.
An ageing Buffalo Bill.

ing in Pittsylvania County, Virginia, during the time of the American Revolution in 1780.)

In the heyday of the 1850s, the Cody cotton plantation and vineyards had provided a lifestyle befitting the grandest antebellum aristocrat. A small army of slaves picked, ginned and baled the cotton for the mills at Dallas two dozen miles to the east. The grapes were collected and dried in the arid heat ready to be sold in Fort Worth, nine miles to the west. The onset, shortly after Cody Jr's birth, of what was then called the War of Secession brought the idyll to an undignified end.

According to his son, Samuel Cody Sr was something of a local hero. 'He had distinguished himself in the Texan and Mexican war,' he explained proudly. 'His fellow citizens always accepted him as a leader and councillor when at war with the Redskins.' He had, naturally, taken on an officer's role in the Confederate Army. Like a million other men of the South, however,

Cody Sr had returned from the humiliation of the Civil War with his pride battered and his health impaired. 'He was the worst for wear,' his son once said.

To make matters worse, the soldier had arrived home to discover his land overgrown with weeds and his emancipated slaves now demanding wages he could not afford to meet. As the carpetbaggers of the North overran Texas, he and his family left the ranch to be reclaimed by the prairie.

The Codys accepted the lifeline offered to the north of Fort Worth in Wise County where, by now, the untended longhorn cattle that had drifted free from the ranches to roam the prairies during the War had multiplied into immense, half-wild herds. As the golden age of the West began, the grape growers became cowboys, and successful ones at that.

By the time he quit school at ten or so he was working as a nighthawk, tending to the herds after dark on ranches in Wise and Denton Counties. It had been on his return from his duties at a ranch one day in 1873 or so, that he witnessed the event that had shaped his young life.

Cody arrived back to discover the ranch besieged by a Sioux raiding party. The 'Redskins' had spent a day and night attacking the two log cabins in which his family and their ranch-hands lived. His account of the atrocity varied considerably over the years. In most Cody was saved by a gunshot wound to his thigh that had left him lying in a ditch on the edge of the ranch. He had managed to crawl his way to a safe spot, from where he had watched the war party raze the farm to the ground. In most accounts, the fateful moments of the raid happened at night.

'Whilst daylight lasted the cowboys were able to keep their foes at a distance, but when it became dark the Indians charged in a body, climbed over the palisade, and made the besieged beat a retreat into the log-house,' he recalled in one version. 'Here, finding it impossible to force their way, the Redskins got on the log-house, stopped up the chimney, piled up large quantities of wood on all four sides of the building and set fire to them.'

In some versions his family all perished. According to others, he later discovered that his parents and beloved sister Mandy had survived. In one or two accounts his family were spared any involvement in the attack whatsoever. Each telling of the story concluded the same way, however: with the wounded Cody dragging himself the nine miles to Fort Worth, being patched up in the town's army hospital and then striking out on his own for a life roaming the ranges and cattle trails of the Western frontiers. His adventures had taken him from the plains of Texas to the mountains of Montana and encompassed spells as a mustang and buffalo hunter, trail-boss cowboy and Klondyke gold prospector. It had been at the end of the legendary Chisholm Trail in San Antonio that his days in the saddle had been brought to an end, he explained. A scout from Forepaugh's show had heard talk of his exploits and offered him a job in the Wild West show. 'The rest is history,' he probably added.

The stories were as plausible as they were entertaining, especially given the impeccable cowboy credentials Cody displayed daily under Forepaugh's Big Top. In reality, they were laced with more than a few great imitations of his own . . .

C ODY'S VERSION OF HIS LIFE STORY REMAINED UNCHALlenged and intact throughout his life. There were, naturally, those who suspected his tales were as inventive as his aeroplanes, pieces of crowd-pleasing playfulness provided to add lustre to his reputation and steer the curious clear of a truth that was probably more mundane. 'His early life consists of a prolific mythology,' wrote one sceptic. 'I never knew whether Birdville was a joke,' puzzled another. In a gentler journalistic age, neither put much effort into adding substance to their suspicions, even though both would have been wise to follow their instincts. The story was fake – a mixture of myth and reality, hokum and half-truth.

Samuel Cody had in fact been born seven hundred miles or so to the north of the parched flatlands of Texas, amid the verdant landscape of the Great Plains and the city of Davenport, Iowa. His real name was not Samuel Franklin Cody, but Franklin Samuel Cowdery.

He had been born there on 6 March 1867, the fourth of five children born to Samuel Franklin Cowdery Sr and his wife Phoebe.

Many would have been happy to have claimed the heritage he had rejected. His American bloodline extended back eight generations and 250 years to the Pilgrim Fathers themselves.

The founder of the line, William Cowdrey, had completed the journey from Weymouth in the West of England to the windswept outpost of Lynn, Massachusetts, in 1630, the same year the first Governor of the Massachusetts Bay Colony, John Winthrop, led his four ships and 500 Puritans out of an intolerant England in search of 'a city of God'.

As well as a new spelling for the family name, the industrious Cowdery quickly established what would prove a lasting tradition for piety and public service. With his first wife, Joanna, he was instrumental in forming the settlement of Reading around 1640. He was, it seems, 'a most influential and useful citizen' serving at various times as a Deacon, Clerk of the Writs, Town Clerk, Selectman and Representative to the General Assembly of the Colonies. 'They found this spot a wilderness, they left it a fruitful field,' the grateful citizens of Reading wrote of the Cowdery family a generation later.

William Cowdery's heirs had continued to serve their country with humility and honour – and occasional heroism – throughout the century and a half that followed. In particular, the young Franklin Cowdery would almost certainly have heard of the exploits of his great-grandfather, Jonathan Cowdery, a sailor and surgeon in the embryonic US Navy at the turn of the nineteenth century. Aboard the frigate *Philadelphia*, Cowdery saw action against the French in the West Indies and the Barbary forces of North Africa in the Mediterranean. In Tripoli in 1803 he was captured and imprisoned for eighteen months by the Turks. Cowdery's memoirs of his time in a jail were serialised in an American newspaper and formed the basis for a sensational adventure book. Such was his resilience, he went on to become the oldest surgeon and indeed the oldest officer in the US Navy.

Jonathan Cowdery's eldest son Benjamin had refused to follow his father into medicine or the military, and had instead found prominence as a printer, publisher and editor. He set up his first newspaper in Angelica, New York, in 1819. Four years later he launched the first in Cattarangus County and later founded the *Ontario Chronicle*. He seems to have inherited a blend of his ancestor William's religiousness and his father's staying power. He was a leading figure in the revival that swept Rochester, New York, in the 1840s and, with his wife Amanda, campaigned tirelessly for the antislavery and temperance causes. He was, according to family lore, at least, the oldest printer in the United States at the time of his death, aged seventy-seven, two months after his grandson Franklin was born, in 1867.

Benjamin Franklin Cowdery died believing the greatest gift he had bestowed on his heirs was their good name, 'which though not highly valued by money changers is yet rather to be chosen than great riches'.

It would not be a view shared by young Franklin, however. The bleak, inglorious chapter his father added to the Cowdery family history may have been responsible for that.

Franklin Cowdery's father Samuel was the fourth of five children born to Benjamin and his wife Amanda Cowdery. He had been born in November 1831 in Rochester, New York. The turning point in his young life came with his mother's early death, at their then home in Oberlin, Ohio, in 1842. Afterwards Benjamin had been unable or unwilling to look after all his children and placed his youngest son, Jabez Franklin, then aged just seven, in an orphan asylum in the city. The loss of his only brother seems to have hit Samuel Cowdery hard. When Jabez later disappeared, presumed dead, after being 'bound' to a Shaker family in the city, his heartbroken older brother adopted the name Franklin on his behalf.

In fact Jabez had embarked on an adventure-filled life to rival that of any of his ancestors. He had run away from the Shaker homestead one morning, hopped aboard a canal barge bound for New York and begun a life as a 'buccaneer', first transporting molasses aboard the schooner *Mary Perkins of Cape Cod*, then on the *Carrington*. Jabez's adventures took him to the West Indies and Panama, Java and Shanghai. Back in San Francisco he spent time on the stage with the Bingham Theatrical Combination. From there he headed to Nevada and a spell as a gold prospector in the booming mining town of Downieville. By 1859, however, Jabez was practising law in the District Court. By 1861 he was elected District Attorney of the County of Sierra. By the time the Civil War broke out in 1861, the youngest of the Cowderys was ready to accept a post as the United States Internal Revenue Collector. It would be the beginning of a highly successful political career.

While his brother was travelling the world, Samuel had gravitated to the Great Plains and the burgeoning community of Davenport, Iowa, at the mouth of the Rock River in the Upper Mississippi Valley. Two decades after the first settlers had arrived there, Davenport and its neighbours across the Mississippi in Illinois, Moline and Rock Island, formed an important commercial crossroads in a rapidly changing landscape. While the Mississippi connected Davenport to Minneapolis to the north and St Louis to the south, the new railroads linked it with Chicago to the east. To the west lay the Great Plains, an untamed expanse consisting, as one of Cowdery's contemporaries recalled, 'of grass as far as the eye could see'.

In May 1857, Samuel married Phoebe Jane Van Horn, a twenty-four-year-old from Ohio. In February 1859 they welcomed their first child, Amanda, into the world. A second daughter, Martha, arrived in September of the following year. His expanding family apart, however, Samuel's life was singularly uneventful. While Jabez blazed a trail in California, and his sisters Martha and Sarah devoted themselves to the church – both were married to prominent Presbyterians – their elder brother seems to have drifted from job to job. Unusually, family histories make no mention of how he spent his early working life. In the Davenport city census of 1860 he left the column marked 'profession' blank. If he had been searching for a sense of purpose in his life, the outbreak of the War of Secession provided it.

A S EVERY AMERICAN FIFTH-GRADE STUDENT KNOWS, THE darkest period in the history of the United States began at around 4.30 a.m. on 12 April 1861 as Confederate troops under the splendidly named Brigadier General Pierre Gustave Toutant Beauregard opened fire on the Union-controlled Fort Sumter, in the secessionist Southern state of North Carolina.

In the wake of the attack President Abraham Lincoln called on an extra 100,000 men to join the Union army. Samuel Cowdery had been among the very first to respond to the recruitment posters and their call to 'vindicate the honor of that Flag so ruthlessly torn by traitor hands from the walls of Sumter'. He had signed up as a private in the 2nd Iowa Volunteer Infantry on 24 May at Davenport.

Samuel's joining up seems to have provided his family with the opportunity and the funds to buy their home, a weatherboarded house, built in the popular, Midwestern style, with a small parcel of land attached, at 1110 Gaines Street. Phoebe paid the area's main landowners, the Forrest and Dillon families, $200 for the property that August.

If Samuel Cowdery had entertained romantic notions of emulating his grandfather's glories, the squalid realities of the conflict he had entered soon put an end to them. From camp at Davenport, he set off on a riverboat to Benton Barracks four days down the Mississippi at St Louis. Over the following twelve months, Benton would grow into a camp capable of housing 30,000 troops. It would be much later in the war that its health and sanitary standards would catch up, however.

The Barracks quickly became a breeding ground for disease. One Iowan volunteer described how the situation was worsened by the swarms of 'bare-legged, dirty-faced boys and girls' selling 'baskets filled with what they called "Pi-zan-cakes" ', a confection which 'produced diseases as fatal as did the swamps and bayous of the Mississippi'. 'It has been said that these little urchins have slain more Iowa soldiers than were killed in all the battles with rebel armies in Missouri,' the soldier added.

Samuel Cowdery was assigned to C company, where he was given the role of wagoner or teamster. The only record of his activities in the first year of the war was of an expedition in which he led a wagon train from Bird Point in October. Instead his campaign was concentrated on Benton, where his prolonged stay produced predictable results.

According to his army records, Cowdery's medical problems began in late November when he began making a series of visits eventually put down to what doctors then called 'dysenteria'. Two weeks later he was admitted again, this time with bronchitis.

As a slow, shapeless war entered its second year, the 2nd Iowa Volunteers found themselves dispatched to the western front and the fight for control of the strategic lifeline that was the Mississippi. By now General Grant had begun planning what would be one of the key conflicts of the entire war, his assault on Vicksburg. Stung by the failure of a waterborne attack in June 1862, the Union leader spent six months trying to find a new route through the swamps and bayous into the Confederate stronghold.

Cowdery and the 2nd Iowa Infantry, by now based at Camp Montgomery, were among the pathfinders. In the first week of October, Samuel Cowdery set off at the head of his wagon on what his war record described as a 'foraging expedition'. Almost immediately, on 5 October, he and his company were overrun and, as his war record put it, 'taken prisoner by a guerrilla band'. He was chained and led into the garrison at Vicksburg.

Contemporary historians have compared conditions in the prison camps of the South to Auschwitz and Bergen-Belsen. Prisoners had to cope with overcrowding, polluted water, disease-riddled food, lack of medicine, and rats, not to mention the vicious habits of the guards and their bloodhounds. If tuberculosis, dysentery, scurvy, gangrene or yellow fever did not account for them, injury by beating, shooting, stabbing or hanging generally did.

It was Samuel Cowdery's good fortune that, under the Dix Hill agreement of July that year, both sides had begun operating a system of paroling and exchange. On this occasion Cowdery's time in prison in Vicksburg was short. He was back at Benton by the end of October, where he remained as an 'exchanged' soldier until February 1863.

That summer, with the war grown more ferocious and frenzied, he was soon back in action. Once more he was captured, however, near Corinth, Mississippi, on 7 July 1863. This time his luck failed him.

With the exchange agreement by now broken, he was taken to Richmond and the notorious Belle Island, where he arrived two weeks later on 18 July.

Belle Island, an oblong, mile-long tract on a desolate spit of land in the James River between Richmond and Manchester, was among the worst of the Southern prisons. Among Cowdery's fellow inmates there that autumn was GE Sabre, a lieutenant in the Rhode Island Cavalry. 'My first visit though the camp was a theme of the greatest horror,' he wrote in a diary. 'Around me were seven thousand men, human beings, massed, literally massed, within a space that was not sufficiently large to accommodate one half that number.'

Sabre's diary recorded how prisoners were forced to live off a daily diet of half-baked corn bread, an ounce or two of meat, and a pint of bean soup made up of 'a few wormy, hog beans, the more worms the better, a superabundance of James River water, and occasionally an imperceptible quantity of salt or saltpetre'. So appalling were the rations that prisoners had been known to skin rats and eat them raw. 'Cases have been known of Belle Isle prisoners vomiting up their breakfast and this afterward was eaten by others,' wrote another inmate, Frederick Bartleson.

Anyone straying into the 'dead line' ditch surrounding the camp was shot instantly. For the bulk of the inmates, sickness denied them even the strength to take this way out. Burial parties would scour the camp each day at noon asking any motionless men, 'Are you dead yet?' 'Anybody who did not answer went into a pine box for carting to the graveyard,' wrote Sabre. He regularly saw bodies twitching hopelessly as the lids were fitted to their coffins.

In this appalling place, Samuel Cowdery's sickness inevitably returned and worsened. For a while, at least, it seems safe to guess he would have been among the ranks of men to feel the butt of the jailers' rifles at noon each day. Somehow, however, he contrived an escape.

It is unclear quite how Cowdery managed to win himself a place at the Belle Island Hospital. He may well have resorted to bribery. According to Sabre, who himself paid $25 for a two-month spell 'invalided', 'greenback' was the only means by which the jailers could be induced into letting inmates into the relative safety of the medical block. Whatever the means, he not only talked his way into the sick ward but, by late September, on to the list of prisoners eligible for parole once more. At the end of the month he was taken to City Point, Virginia, at the conflux of the James and Appomattox Rivers, the main point of exchange for prisoners captured by the Confederacy. From there he was taken to hospital at Annapolis, Maryland. He remained there, 'debilitated', until 2 December.

His flight from Belle Isle was the most remarkable and heroic action of Samuel Cowdery's war. It was also the last. By the time he returned on parole to Benton Barracks he was, according to one family member, 'completely shattered' and 'so broken down in health from his terrible prison experiences that he was unfit for further duty'. He served six months more there. He was honourably discharged at Davenport on 13 June 1864.

B ACK AT 1110 GAINES STREET, CIVILIAN LIFE PROVED HARD. In the immediate aftermath of the war, Samuel and Phoebe produced three more children. In between his first son Charles, born in September 1865, and Lillie Elizabeth, born in 1869, Franklin Samuel was born on 6 March 1867. Yet the father the young Franklin grew to know in the following years was clearly, as he later put it, 'the worst for wear'. Like many of his wartime colleagues, Samuel returned to a North overrun with cheap labour, drawn predominantly from the new wave of European immigrant labour then arriving in the cities of the Midwest. He struggled to find odd jobs, mainly, it seems, as a carpenter and general labourer in the town. His humiliation was made complete by the demeaning nature of his illness.

'I have suffered from constipation and indigestion ever since I was a prisoner of war,' he said in a declaration for an increase in soldier's pension years later in 1902. 'As I grow older these complaints seems to grow worse. I have had to take medicine ever since the war to keep my bowels in order.'

The blend of resilience, resourcefulness and raw courage that had carried Samuel Cowdery out of Belle Island would manifest itself in his youngest son. In the broken figure of Samuel, however, the young Franklin was unable to see much of which to be proud. He would not, of course, be the first to reinvent his father's achievements, to mould them into something grander and more glorious than the truth. The temptation to paint over the past was, perhaps, all the more understandable, given the turn of events around his twelfth year.

Samuel and Phoebe Cowdery were divorced in 1879. Within the more pious sections of the Cowdery clan, the separation was never even acknowledged. (All mention of it was certainly excluded from the family history.) By 1880, Samuel had left Iowa and headed for California, where he was finally reunited with his long-lost brother Jabez, then on his way to winning the post of City and County Attorney of San Francisco. Jabez seems to have taken pity on his poor older brother. His weighty influence eventually secured Samuel a place in the Army Veterans' Home at Yountville in the nearby Napa Valley. He would remain there until he returned to Davenport, just a few months before his death.

(When Samuel died on 27 September 1902, his newspaper obituarist found little to say beyond the fact he had served in the Iowa Infantry and that 'all old soldiers are invited to attend' his funeral. His gravestone in Davenport's Oakdale Memorial Gardens made no mention of his children or his wife, even though, by then, she already lay in a brick mausoleum seven plots of land away. His headstone was marked simply, SF Cowdery, 'Co C, 2 Ia Inf'.)

Samuel Sr's departure left the family to fend for itself. Charles had already left home and had been working on a nearby farm since the age of fourteen, but the sisters rallied around their mother. Martha, married to a local carpenter, Frederick Meckel, in 1882, and Amanda, a nurse, stayed close to Gaines Street. It seems to have fallen to the youngest child, Lillie Elizabeth, to remain at home to provide her mother's main support.

The family's troubles seem to have had the most profound

effect on the young Franklin, however. By his early teens the root-less, restless spirit that would characterise his life was already apparent. No record remains of his schooldays in the city. (Later in life there would be a debate over whether he had learned to even read or write.) Like his brothers and sisters, he seems to have struck out into the working world at an early age. Unlike his siblings, however, he did so far from Davenport and its unhappiness. Instead, by the early 1880s, he had embraced the Cowderys' adventurer tradition, hundreds of miles to the west.

Only the final listing for him in the city register offered a clue to the life that had begun in the untamed territories of Montana. The entry did scant justice to the eventful existence he was already leading. It simply read, 'Cowdery, Franklin, horsetrainer'.

B Y THE AGE OF SIX, OR SO CODY CLAIMED, HE WAS ROPING dogs, calves and cockerels from the saddle of his pet pack pony. By the age of seven he was 'riding half-tamed bullocks at great speed'. 'In those days I felt that I could ride anything that wore hair. Buffaloes, wild steers, wild horses, wild elks – I've been astride them all,' he said, drawing disbelieving looks from his European admirers in the later years. 'No, I don't consider buffaloes hard to ride.'

No area of Cody's life is as poorly served by documentary evidence as his spell in the saddle – hardly a surprise. 'The conclusion that animals received more attention than men during the heyday of the range cattle industry is not unwarranted,' wrote the historian, William W Savage Jr. 'Cattle were worth more and could be sold for money: cowboys could be hired almost anywhere for a dollar a day.' Of course, the lack of hard fact eased the way for the mass mythologising of the Wild West that was to follow. Cody took advantage of this as much as anyone. Much of his account of his early days as a cowboy in Texas must, for obvious reasons, be taken with liberal sprinklings of salt.

'. . . sharpshooter, cowboy and pistol shot . . . ' Franklin Cowdery adopts a Buffalo Bill pose.

Yet his heroics on the back of charging elks, buffaloes and bullocks should not be dismissed too readily. What is indisputable, both in the light of later events and at least one contemporary account, is that Cody's career in the West was built around his quite extraordinary abilities as a horseman.

He may well have learned to ride before he could properly walk. It was far from uncommon for Iowan boys to be working by the time they were ten. One horse trader recalled how on his tenth birthday his father had given him 'a pony and a checkbook' and sent him out to complete his first deal. 'Plenty of boys became dealers that way,' recalled Leroy Daniels, a contemporary of Cody's from Adair, Iowa. By the age of sixteen Daniels was alone on a ranch in Montana with a herd of seventy wild horses to break. It seems Cody developed even more quickly than this.

Horses – and the horse trade – played a leading role in the commercial life of the Davenport of Cody's youth. His apprenticeship may well have been spent in stockyards swollen by herds of Colorado and Montana 'mustangs' bound for the great ports of the Mississippi.

Cody had almost certainly begun working even earlier than his brother Charles. By 1881 or so, at the age of fourteen, he had already headed west to Montana, where he was breaking in horses for stockmen in the western and central region of the territory, around the Crow Creek and Mussel Shell ranges. His ability to handle even the most temperamental mount provided a self-assurance and self-possession he would never lose. It also won him the respect of even the most hardened Montanan horsemen. 'He never knew what it was to fear anything and the least of his fears was a bucking horse,' recorded Jake Ross, a cowboy and horse tamer who knew and befriended the teenage Cody when he was working near the towns of Radersburg and Toston in the west of what was then Montana territory.

Ross, from modestly wealthy Montana stock, had left home to 'rough it' on the ranches. He worked for a prominent cattle family, the Sherlocks at Crow Creek, where Cody was also work-ing as a horse tamer. Ross went on to win a reputation as 'cham-pion rider of Montana', sealing his legend by taming the notorious 'Belgrade Bull', an unruly, 500-pound Holstein that toured state and county fairs at the turn of the century. Accord-ing to Ross, Cody was easily his superior as a rider — in fact, he was the best he had ever seen.

'I saw Sam ride a horse in the main street of Radersburg once, and he was a bad one too,' Ross recalled years later. 'Just at the moment when the cayuse was doing his best to separate himself from his rider, Sam calmly reached over and picked up an empty five-gallon oil can that was lying in the gutter, and threw it at a dog. He could reach down and pick up a pickle off the ground from a horse that was running at top speed and he never "clawed leather".'

For all his riding skills, Cody would have earned no more than the dollar-a-day rate that applied to most menial workers. As his teenage years continued, he improved his pay by graduating to the more lucrative cattle trails.

By the 1880s, with the Sioux and Cheyenne driven out from their ancestral grounds in the Black Hills, the vast open ranges of

Montana and Custer County, as its southeast corner was known, had become a magnet for the cattle barons of Texas and the southwest. With much of the prairies of Kansas, Oklahoma and Nebraska to the south now overgrazed and settled, Montana — and its connection to the markets of Chicago and the mining communities of the northwest — offered the flagging industry a new lease of life. Ranchers found that yearlings fed on Montana's rich pastures could weigh 200 pounds more at maturity. The 1880s heralded the beginning of Texas's march northwards. On what became known as the Long Drive, Cody became a fully fledged cowboy.

Cody's account of his cattle-trail days have, naturally, to be treated with caution. Yet his most oft-told story, about his participation in an epic drive from Texas to Montana, is credible for several reasons, not least the burgeoning body of evidence on the cattlemen with whom he claims to have worked, the 'hash-knife cowboys'.

The hash-knife brand.

In July 1882 the first herd of cattle to complete the 1,200-mile journey from Seymour, Texas, arrived at Box Elder Creek near the Little Missouri River. The range, along with a hay meadow and a horse camp, a ranch and a row of accommodation cabins, had been established by Colonel John N Simpson, his partner Colonel Hughes and their company, the Continental Land and Cattle Company, that spring. Each of the herd bore the company's distinctive brand, a mark based on the single-bladed implement used by bunkhouse cooks to make beef hash, the 'hash knife'. (The more obtuse the symbol, the harder rustlers found the job of converting it into other brands.)

With cattlemen able to raise herds wherever they pleased

under Montana's free-range laws, the Texas cattle companies required hard men to defend their hard-won lands. The 'hash-knife cowboys' who worked Box Elder Creek quickly won a reputation as being among the roughest and toughest examples of what one newspaper of the time witheringly called 'the cowboy specie'.

'They have ridden through the streets, whooping and yelling like savages and shooting their pistols at signs or anything that came in their way. They have made day and night hideous, and they make strangers think that there was neither law, order or decency in the country,' said the *Black Hill Times* two years after Simpson and his brand's arrival in the region.

The hash knife's reputation was cemented by the exploits of George Axelby, one of the first cowboys to drive a herd from the Pecos range in Texas to Box Elder Creek. Axelby and a group of others had quit Simpson's company to hunt buffalo. After losing an entire winter's worth of hides to an Indian raid they had set off on a killing spree. 'An Indian is Mr Axelby's detestation,' wrote one reporter as Axelby's murderous raids on the region's Indian reservations hit the headlines. Eventually the influential Sioux leader Young-Man-Afraid-Of-His-Horses persuaded the government to act and a party of federal lawmen were dispatched to 'exterminate' the gang. His escape from the so-called Battle of Stoneville in February 1884 fixed Axelby's legend among the Montana cowboys for ever. Neither he nor his most audacious companion, a young cowboy called 'the Kid', was ever seen again. It is unclear whether Cody actually worked with Axelby. That he and his exploits left a lasting impression on him is, however, certain.

Cody's precise position within the 'hash-knife' hierarchy is open to question. He claimed to have worked his way through the cowboy ranks – beginning as a dust-eating dragman at the rear of the herd, then progressing via swing man, pointer, top hand, then segundo until he finally landed the prize job of trail boss. His apprenticeship would have been a tough one. The successful cow-

boy was part mechanic, part carpenter, part navigator, part veterinary surgeon. Cody would have learned to fix anything from a jammed revolver to a shattered axle on a Conestoga wagon. Given his later life it is easy to imagine him passing each stage with flying colours. Even so, it is difficult to believe his claim that he had made this progression in time to lead one of the first drives to Box Elder Creek. At the time Cody would have been no more than fifteen. The ledgers kept at Box Elder Creek suggest Simpson's trail bosses tended to be at least in their late teens or early

Cattle drive arriving in Dodge City, Kansas, in the 1870s.

twenties. Yet intriguingly the trail-boss salary he claimed to have been paid, $125 a month, is precisely the rate recorded in the books Simpson began keeping in 1884, a season or two after Cody's drive.

What seems indisputable is that he followed a trail that became familiar to Simpson's herdsmen. Maps of the route taken by the 'hash-knife' herds have emerged in recent years. In most instances they accord almost exactly with the route Cody claimed he took leading an epic drive in the early 1880s.

Cody and a team of ten cowboys, a cook and a remuda of seventy horses collected their herd of 3,275 feeding stock in Wheeler County, on the eastern edge of the Texas panhandle, in the early part of spring. Over the next four months they would travel across five states, several major rivers and 1,200 miles of open country.

The romanticised image of the cattle-trail cowboy has glossed over the vicious and violent reality of the life. With herds worth in excess of $20,000, the pressures were immense. The ultra-nervous longhorn's tendency to stampede at the first thunderclap or coyote wail made sleep all but impossible. (The cowboy's campfire ballads were effectively lullabies to their cattle, not themselves.) By the 1880s, in addition to the traditional threat of rustlers and resentful Indians, trail bosses ran the gauntlet of settlers. With the domestication of the wilderness all but complete, homesteaders would poison, stampede or simply shoot at herds that encroached into their barbed-wired domain. As a result, by the time Cody arrived in the industry, cattle herdsmen were being forced to travel even more dangerous, circuitous and isolated routes to get their cattle north safely.

The early stages of the drive – through northern Texas, across the so-called Cherokee Strip into Kansas, then across the North Canadian and Cimarron Rivers – were, according to Cody's account at least, uneventful enough. Perhaps this is why he spiced the story up with tales of a setback in that most notorious of all cow towns, Dodge City.

Most likely Cody was drawn to Dodge's casinos. His passion for roulette, poker and the popular thirteen-card game faro in particular, may well have been an inheritance of his Davenport youth. His hometown had been the first in the United States to introduce casino riverboat gambling.

It is easy to imagine Cody sharing the same tables as Wyatt Earp and Doc Holliday. It is his account of how a colleague was dispatched to the infamous Boot Hill cemetery after picking an argument with the wrong man in a bar that rings false. Dodge City's position in Wild West legend is a largely inflated one. Even during the ten-year period when its streets were the liveliest in the whole West, only thirty-four men died within the city limits – and most of them through natural causes.

Wyatt Earp's Gunfight at the OK Corral and the murder of Wild Bill Hickock assumed legendary status mainly because they were such unusual events. Cody's habit of slipping gunfighting tales into his stories only adds to the dubiousness of the story. As well as being shot in Birdville, Cody claimed to have been hit in the leg during an argument with a red-bearded Irish railway worker during another cattle drive, this time in Wyoming. Such was the slowness and softness of the lead bullets used at the time, any direct hit generally left the victim bleeding to death from a hole the size of his fist. One, let alone two, wounds in the leg would have left Cody at best with a severe limp, at worst as a one-legged cripple. By all accounts, his gait remained jaunty until the very end of his life.

Less colourful but far more credible was the story of the troubles Cody and what remained of his team had encountered as they headed north from Dodge. The drive had moved on through the plain of West Kansas, into Nebraska, over the Republican River, towards the two forks of the River Platte. While leading the herd across the South Platte somewhere near Ogalala, one of the swing men was thrown into the swollen river. In the ensuing chaos eighteen cattle were lost. The cowboy perished too. The loss made the remainder of Cody's journey even more treacherous. With the North Platte River equally heavily flooded, he was forced to improvise a new route northwest, along the old Oregon Trail into Wyoming. From there, following the North Platte banks, he crossed the river twelve miles short of Fort Laramie at the Forty Islands crossing.

From there he had headed along the eastern border of Wyoming until the Big Horn Mountains loomed into his view. After 102 days, Cody issued the traditional order for his cowboys to 'let them go'.

Regardless of the part he played in the epic journey, the achievement was a formidable one. In sheer geographical – and climatic – terms the journey Cody completed was the equivalent of a march from Madrid and the heat of central Spain to the colder climes of northeastern Europe and the borders of Poland. At Box Elder Creek, Cody claims to have handed over a herd only seventy-four head smaller than that which had left Wheeler County, a more than respectable casualty rate given the length of the drive. Suitably impressed, Colonel Simpson's managers supposedly offered him a permanent position with the hash-knife brand. By now, however, his mind had turned to a fresh challenge.

By the spring of 1883, news of a new gold strike at Silver Bow on the Taku Inlet in southeastern Alaska had inspired tales of vast fortunes being made in the frozen far northwest of the American continent. That summer, according to Cody's own account, he set out for a territory where, as he later put it, 'the coward never started and the weak died on the way'. Once more it is impossible to separate fact from fiction in Cody's account. It is perfectly plausible that he could have joined the gold rush. He would, after all, have been following in the footsteps of his uncle Jabez. The details are predictably threadbare given the seemingly disastrous nature of the trip. Once more we are left to take – or leave – his word for it. He had, apparently, worked his passage by leading a herd of cattle to Wyoming, riding the 800 miles or so to Seattle and then heading for the new boom town of Juneau. By the time he arrived at the town the mines of the Silver Bow were already 'out'. He had headed northwards, through the Chilkoot Pass into the upper valleys of the River Yukon towards the biggest boom town of all, Dawson City. There Cody had spent a long hard winter holed up in a log cabin and living off sourdough bread on a claim somewhere between the Lewes and Pelly Rivers. Frustrated by the lack of success there, he had moved on to another supposedly lucrative piece of land towards the junction of the Yukon and Klondyke Rivers. By the time his first winter had come to an end, however, Cody was ready to admit defeat. 'I was glad to return with the spring of '84 and considered myself fortunate in having sufficient money to return to my old occupation of cowboy and horse tamer,' he said, succinctly, later.

It seems likely that Cody returned to Montana, where his name and reputation remained strongest. As the second half of the 1880s began, however, he had moved south and begun his final Western adventure, as a mustanger.

The capture of the mestenos, the wild, cream and buckskin-coloured horses that had emerged on to the Great Plains from Mexico had been an important – if perilous – part of the Western economy for more than a century. The untamed stallions weighed on average 800 pounds and possessed a survival instinct so ferocious they could attack and kill their hunters with ease.

In his battle of wits with the horses, the mustanger had developed a repertoire of hunting techniques that bordered on sadistic. In the most common, the 'round-up', a team of riders would herd the horses into vast corrals built on the edge of the prairies. Once inside, the panic-filled horses were left – often for weeks – until they tired themselves out. They were then lassoed and rendered immobile by hobbles or clogs – strong, forked sticks about two feet long which were attached to the front legs. 'Within a few weeks the entire band would be freed of encumbrances and could be driven in any direction desired,' recalled one mustanger, James H Cook, in his memoirs.

A second method – euphemistically called 'walking down' – involved a team of three riders working in relay to keep the mustangs on the run for as long as a week. A third and even more barbarous approach was known as 'creasing', and involved the mustanger grazing the nerve cord running along the top of the horse's neck with a rifle shot. Even the most hardened hunters were reluctant to resort to such cruelty. 'It was very easy to break the neck of the animal or to give it a slight wound or a bad scare,' admitted Cook.

If Cody's accounts of his mustanging years are to be believed, he worked with a team that favoured 'walking down' its prey. His greatest feat on horseback, he once said, had been riding 112 miles in ten and three-quarter hours. 'I covered the distance with a single horse,' he added. 'Real hard work', he called it, for once veering towards understatement.

Even Cody admitted mustanging was real dangerous work too. 'Indian thieves used to rob me repeatedly, and we had a number of sanguinary encounters with them,' he told a rapt European audience years later. 'Yes, we killed a few.'

His closest shave came in an encounter with a particularly

wilful horse. 'Well, I'll tell you, it was like this,' he said, settling into a telling of the story during an interview with the English magazine *Chums* in 1903. He went on:

I had had saddled one of the largest mustangs that had ever been captured and we drew lots as to who should ride it. Luckily or unluckily, the topping of the broncho fell to my lot, and I confess that I regarded myself as fortunate. He was about sixteen hands high and a stubborn, sulky beast – far more treacherous than a wild mustang. After playing all the tricks he could to unseat me, he eventually threw himself back on me, and while I was endeavouring to release my left foot which was in the stirrup, he regained his foot and galloping off about twenty yards dragged me under him. Fortunately I had my revolver with me and just as I was thinking that I was done for I fired three bullets into the brute. One of them entered his heart and he dropped all of a heap on to one of my ankles, still holding me a prisoner until assistance arrived. This was one of the numerous occasions on which I have blessed Colts for inventing the most useful weapon which bears their name. I had decided that my goose was cooked.

Whatever the truth about Cody's teenage years, it seems clear he emerged from them feeling fortunate to be alive. 'I've had many a narrow squeak,' he confessed later in life. He once confided to his friend Jake Ross that he did not believe he would live beyond the age of twenty-one. His chances of survival were improved by the demise of the industries in which his daring skills had been so saleable.

The mustanging business would continue in a small way for much of the remainder of the century. But by 1888 the cattle industry was in terminal decline. The beginning of the end had come in 1884 when beef prices began to drop. On top of this the cattlemen had overestimated the northern and central ranges' ability to sustain the huge herds they had led there. The terrible winters that battered the Great Plains from 1885 to 1887 finished them off. Around 50 per cent of Texas cattlemen went bust between 1883 and 1887. In Montana, a 90 percent loss of herd was normal in what cattlemen called simply the Big Die-Up.

By the time the blight hit, however, Cody had begun displaying a foresight that would serve him throughout his eventful life. He had given Jake Ross an inkling of the way his mind was working years earlier as he spent long hours practising a flamboyant repertoire of lasso tricks, or 'fancy roping'. Cody told his friend it might prove useful if he ever went into show business.

By the spring of 1888 Cody had duly joined the steady flow of cowboys drawn by the prospect of a new career with the Wild West shows of the East. In early April he became a member of Forepaugh's combination at his headquarters in Philadelphia. At the end of the month he climbed on board the show's train bound for Salem, New Jersey, and the opening night of that season's tour.

If the sights and sounds of the industrialised East seemed alien, at least the rootlessness of the life he was soon leading did not. The Forepaugh spectacular began its tour in Salem on 30 April. Cody's first six weeks with the show would take him through five states and forty-two cities.

Adam Forepaugh's Greatest Show,

✲ 25TH YEAR. ✲

HIPPO...

CIRCUS,

MENAGERIE,

ADAM FOR...

SOLE PROP...

ADAM FOREPAUGH, Jr., - Manager D...
CHAS. H. BROOKS, - Treasurer C...
C. A. DAVIS, Manager Publications
R. C. CAMPBELL, - General Agent
R. S. DINGESS, - Route Agent
M. COYLE, - R. R. Contractor
S. H. SEMON, - Contractor
JUDD C. WEBB, Master Transport'n
HARRY EVARTS,

PERMANENT ADDRESS:

4-PAW'S G...

1612 GREEN ST.,

OFFICIAL ROUTE

OF THE

GREAT FOREPAUGH SHOW

SEASON 1888.

Day.	Date.	Town	State.	Popul'n.	Railroad.	M...
Monday	April 23	Philadelphia	Penn.	846,984	P. R.	
Tuesday	" 24	"	"	"	"	
Wednesday	" 25	"	"	"	"	
Thursday	" 26	"	"	"	"	
Friday	" 27	"	"	"	"	
Saturday	" 28	"	"	"	"	
Monday	April 30	Salem	N. J.	5,516	P. R.	
Tuesday	May 1	Bridgeton	"	10,065	"	
Wednesday	" 2	Camden	"	52,964	"	
Thursday	" 3	Mt. Holly	"	4,021	"	
Friday	" 4	Norristown	Penn.	13,064	P. & R.	
Saturday	" 5	Chester	"	14,996		
Monday	May 7	Wilmington	Del.	42,499	P. R.	
Tuesday	" 8	Lancaster	Penn.	25,769	P. & R.	
Wednesday	" 9	Columbia	"	8,341	"	
Thursday	" 10	Lebanon	"	8,786	"	
Friday	" 11	Pottsville	"	13,253	"	
Saturday	" 12	Reading	"	43,280	"	
Monday	May 14	Allentown	Penn.	18,063	P. & R.	
Tuesday	" 15	Easton	"	11,943	D. L. & W	
Wednesday	" 16	Trenton	N. J.	34,386	P. R.	
Thursday	" 17	New Brunswick	"	18,254	"	
Friday	" 18	Elizabeth	"	32,110	"	
Saturday	" 19	Newark	"	152,988	"	
Monday	May 21	Jersey City	N. J.	152,518	P. R.	
Tuesday	" 22	Hoboken	"	37,721	D. L. & W	
Wednesday	" 23	Paterson	"	68,973	"	
Thursday	" 24	Newburg	N. Y.	1,813	N. Y. L. E. & W	
Friday	" 25	Kingston	"	18,342	West Shore	
Saturday	" 26	Albany	"	90,903	"	
Monday	" 28	Cohoes	N. Y.	19,417	N. Y. & H C.	
Tuesday	" 29	Troy	"	56,747	"	
Wednesday	" 30	Hudson	"	8,779	"	
Thursday	" 31	Poughkeepsie	"	20,207	N. Y. C. & H. R.	
Friday	June 1	Peekskill	"	6,930	N. Y. C.	
Saturday	" 2	Danbury	Conn.	11,600	N. Y. & N. E.	
Monday	June 4	Waterbury	Conn	20,260	N. Y. & N. E.	
Tuesday	" 5	Ansonia	"	3,833	N. Y., N. H. & H	
Wednesday	" 6	Bridgeport	"	27,643	"	
Thursday	" 7	New Haven	"	62,882	"	
Friday	" 8	Meriden	"	18,340	"	
Saturday	" 9	New Britain	"	16,087	"	
Monday	June 11	Middletown	Conn.	11,781	N. Y., N. H. & H	
Tuesday	" 12	Hartford	"	42,533	"	
Wednesday	" 13	Springfield	Mass.	37,577	"	
Thursday	" 14	Holyoke	"	27,904	C. R.	
Friday	" 15	Palmer	"	5,923	B. & A.	
Saturday	" 16	New London	Conn.	10,529	N. Y. P. & B.	

CHAPTER TWO

A PAIR OF
SHOOTISTS

I am a roving Cowboy,
I've crossed the Texas trail,
I've shot the shaggy buffalo,
I've heard the kyates wail.

I've slept upon my saddle,
And covered with the moon,
I think I shall return to this,
Before I meet my doom.

For the cowboy's name is butchered,
By the papers in the East,
And when he's in your City,
He's treated like a beast.

But in his native country,
His name is ever dear,
May God watch and protect,
O'er the Western pioneers.

— Attributed to Cody, circa 1896

T HE NEW LIFE SOON LOST ITS LUSTRE. FOR EVERY EAST-erner enthralled by his frontier personality, Cody discov-ered another ready to treat him 'like a beast', and often with good cause.

Forepaugh's circus travelled with a small army of scam artists, pickpockets and petty criminals in tow. (The showman's notori-ous 'vest pocket' swallowed most of the criminal proceeds. He charged staff $100 for 'grifting rights' to each town's washing lines and even took 90 per cent of the alms collected by a blind woman on his payroll.) When the train suddenly changed itinerary with-out warning, Cody quickly learned, it was generally because Forepaugh's advance guards had spotted a lynch mob or tar-and-feather gang lying in wait farther down the line.

Only within the confines of the sawdust-filled arena could Cody rely on a civilised welcome. His early act seems to have blended two-handed trickshooting with flamboyant displays of what the playbills and programmes liked to call 'fancy roping' and 'rough riding'. Cody would charge into the arena on horseback, firing at assorted targets with a shotgun and pistol as he went, before pulling his mount up at an instant, spinning around and repeating the routine all over again. From New London, Con-necticut, to Pottsville, Pennsylvania, the crowds lapped it up.

For the early months of his performing life, at least, Cody remained in the shadow of 'Doc' Carver. Carver had resisted Forepaugh's exhortations that they form a partnership – 'Let's run the Great Imitator into the gutter,' he had begged – and was form-ing a company to tour Europe and, ultimately, Australia. He remained the star of the show until mid-September, when he made his farewell performance at the town of Suspension Bridge, New York. Cody may well have been one of Carver's protégés. In his memoirs Carver talked of having trained two members of Forepaugh's troupe, California Frank and Wild Horse Harry. Throughout his life Cody's intimates referred to him as Frank. If it is unclear whether he was this particular Frank – nicknames often had no connection to their owner, so the 'California' is no guide – it is certain that Cody based his subsequent act on Carver's repertoire of long-range target shooting and high-speed gunplay.

Cody maintained that, after Carver's departure, Forepaugh elevated him to the title of Captain Cody: King Of Cowboys. This is not borne out by the posters or playbills of the time, none of which single him out as being a star of the show. (Besides, the sobriquet actually belonged to a prodigious sureshot from North Platte, Nebraska, called Buck Taylor, whose exploits had already formed the basis for a stream of dime novels by the prolific Colonel Prentiss Ingraham.) The credibility of the claim is dented even more by the fact that, rather than pledging his future to Forepaugh, Cody seems to have tried his damnedest to break free from his company.

Shortly after his first season with Forepaugh came to an end a few weeks before Christmas 1888, Cody joined a new production company formed by Annie Oakley. Her phenomenal target-shooting performances before Victoria in London in 1887 had made Sureshot Annie by far the most famous female name in American vaudeville and a serious rival to Buffalo Bill as the most popular performer in the entire Wild West world. Relations with the fractious Bill had driven Annie and her partner Frank Butler to strike out on their own. According to Cody he joined them in *Deadwood Dick or The Sunbeam of the Sierras*, a revue produced by the leading Broadway figure Tony Pastor.

The drama's promise of 'Bold Border Boys – Bad Bucking Broncos – and Masterless Mexican Mustangs' seems to have been strong on alliteration and little else. *Deadwood Dick* was not a hit and closed by the end of January 1889, leaving Annie to swallow her pride and to rejoin Bill and his partner Nate Salsbury in preparing for a new European tour and Cody to once more hitch his wagon to the Forepaugh show. His view of stage life at the beginning of his theatrical career was probably what it was at the end, a decade later. 'I am not much in love with acting,' he would often complain.

In April 1889, Cody climbed off the Forepaugh train sure, for once, of a warm reception.

When the show and its traditional preshow procession had arrived in the town of Norristown, Pennsylvania, the previous May huge crowds had turned out to see what one observer called the 'glittering array of handsome wagons, fine looking horses, rare animals, beautiful women and gallant knights on gaily caparisoned horses'. As the show returned, hundreds gathered to watch the spectacle once more. Cody's most heartfelt smiles would have been reserved for only one of the throng, a pretty brunette from the Spring Mill Heights neighbourhood, Maud Maria Lee.

Later in his life Cody confided the unromantic reality of his saddlebound youth. 'The real cowboy', he explained, 'must be a good shot, a good roper, able to mount any horse, act as veterinary, blacksmith, tailor, wash his own linen, wear it unstarched, cook his own food and last, but by no means least, he must consider womankind nonexistent.'

No doubt there were encounters: his good looks, sturdy physique and imposing personality earned him female admirers all his life. (Even in his forties he was capable of inciting genteel European women to most unladylike thoughts. 'So big, so strong, so recklessly brave,' swooned one admirer.) In Maud Lee, however, he had undoubtedly found his first serious girlfriend.

Since her mother, Phoebe's, death, Maud had lived with her English-born father, Joseph, and her stepmother. When she met Cody in the spring of 1888 she was just seventeen to his twenty-one. Against the odds, the romance had lasted beyond the circus's one night in Norristown. It may well have been Cody, a studious sender of postcards throughout his life, who kept the flames burning. By the time Cody reappeared in Norristown, the young sweethearts' minds were made up.

On the morning after the show Cody and Maud, accompanied by her father and stepmother, appeared before the clerk of the Montgomery County Orphans' Court. Five minutes after Cody was granted a licence, he and Maud exchanged their wedding vows.

The only other witnesses to the event seem to have been reporters from the town's newspapers, where word of the quick-fire nuptials had spread.

Joseph Lee, who had given his permission for the licence, seemed approving of the match. Cody and his daughter had become 'kinder thick' the previous year, he told the newspapermen. His blessing had almost certainly been guaranteed by the fact he believed Cody was a relative of Buffalo Bill.

Inside and outside the courthouse, Cody stuck to his guns, reeling off his by now well-drilled confection of untruths. On his marriage certificate he gave his place of residence as Birdville and his parents as Samuel and Phoebe Cody. His age, twenty-two, was, at least, accurate. Afterwards he reassured the curious reporters that he was, indeed, a 'relative' of Buffalo Bill.

He did not loiter long enough for a more detailed interrogation. Maud had decided to join him on the road with Forepaugh. Later that day the bride and groom boarded the train bound for the next scheduled destination, Chester, Pennsylvania.

Maud soon took to what her stepmother called 'life in the sawdust ring', becoming her husband's assistant. Away from the Big Top Cody appears to have passed on the tricks of his trade, teaching Maud both to shoot and become a target-holding accomplice in his act. Within six months or so, her time with the Forepaugh show was over, however.

Adam Forepaugh died in New York during the influenza epidemic of January 1890. His status as Barnum's greatest rival was acknowledged all over the East. Even the *New York Times* carried a lengthy obituary. In the aftermath of his death, the company he had built was sold off to rival circus companies in America and England. Adam Jr was appointed to make sure his father's show – and the name – lived on.

Cody and Maud did not sign up for the new season that spring, however. The money they had made with the previous tour had gone into buying two one-way passages across the Atlantic. They set sail for Europe, London and what they hoped would be a more appreciative audience later that year.

B Y THE 1890S, THE ENGLISH VIEW OF THEIR RENEGADE colonial cousins had softened only marginally in the hundred years or so since Samuel Johnson famously called them 'a race of convicts, and ought to be grateful for anything we allow them short of hanging'. Americans talked in what even their country-man, Henry James, called a 'helpless slobber of disconnected vowel noises', suffered in general from what France Trollope called a 'want of refinement' and were generally characterised by a lack of background and an overreaching greed. 'The youth of America is their oldest tradition,' wrote Oscar Wilde summing up the first trait after his visit there. 'In America there are no ladies, except salesladies,' was Langdon Mitchell's pompous précis of the latter. Fortunately for Cody, however, he belonged to the one breed of American that Englishmen and -women found irre-sistibly fascinating.

The passion for all things Wild West had only increased since Buffalo Bill's triumphant tour of three years earlier. A piece on the Texas cowboy, written by W Baillie Grohmann in the *Fort-nightly Review* at the time, typified the popular impression of its distant, discordant landscape. 'The Texans are unrivalled – the best riders, hardy and born to the business, their only drawback being their wild reputation,' Grohmann wrote before cautioning his readers. 'The bad name of Texans arises mostly from their excitable tempers, and the fact that they are mostly "on the shoot", that is, very free in the use of their revolvers.'

On the streets of the capital Cody must have seemed the embodiment of this most dangerous and appealing of all Western men. He still dressed in the buckskin, Buffalo Bill regalia of his Forepaugh days. No one would have been able to place the origins of his baritone drawl in Iowa rather than Texas. Almost immediately, it seems, he found work in a new show being planned at the Olympia exhibition centre in west London by the English impresario, Albert Newton Ridgeley.

Ridgeley's show offered a taste of the kind of spectacular – if silly – entertainments to which American audiences had become used. In addition to stock acts like a horse-thief lynching and a raid on the Deadwood Stage by a Red Indian war party, Ridgeley had hired a troupe of roller-skating mustangs! In comparison, Cody and Maud's trickshot double act was a piece of near-classical drama. By now husband and wife had developed an entertaining routine, Maud holding the ubiquitous glass balls ever more perilously close to her body and head while her husband fired shots over his shoulder, between his legs or even by use of mirrors. The fact that the trick was exactly that, a trick, seemed to matter even less in an England where guns and gunplay were a mystery to all but a small, elitist minority of the population. (It was Buffalo Bill, who had also incorporated Carver's act into his own, who let the glass-ball secret slip. Asked once, how he managed to shatter the spheres every time, he smiled and whispered, 'Bird shot in the shells.')

The Olympia show was a sellout success, packing in 7,000 people nightly. Ridgeley's decision to advertise his show as a 'Wild West burlesque' soon brought unwanted attention, however. On 15 April 1890, he was served with a writ by Buffalo Bill's London solicitors, Jenson, Cobb and Pearson. Bill, through his agent in England, Lewis Parker, had heard of the show and had objected to his use of the two words to which he claimed he owned all rights. Days later a browbeaten Ridgeley signed an undertaking not only to halt the show but never again to use the term 'Wild West'.

The closure must have been a hammer blow to Cody and Maud, who were forced to fall back on their work in the musical halls. They were soon driven into a miscalculation that cost them dear.

As well as working for Ridgeley, Cody had signed up with Frank Albert, a 'dramatic and musical agent' based on Waterloo Road on the fringes of the lawless Lambeth Marshes, south of the River Thames. Albert seems to have been instrumental in finding him work at local variety halls like the Washington Musical Hall and Gatti's. Soon after the closure of the Olympia show, Albert was approached to supply acts for a large outdoor variety event being held on Whit Monday in the grounds of the Half Moon pub on the Thames in Putney. Among the other attractions was Professor Charles Baldwin, an 'aerialist' whose act involved his leaping from a 100-foot gantry before inflating a parachute to break his fall. Albert added Cody and Maud's name to the bill.

Soon he was pasting up the posters Cody had seemingly already been carrying around England with him. The billboards offered Londoners their first glimpse of an intriguing new act: 'Captain Cody and Miss Cody: Buffalo Bill's son and daughter'.

Elsewhere, Cody and Maud could have expected to get away with their deception. Few in the provinces of England would have known Buffalo Bill's only son Samuel had died as a baby, and that his only daughter, Irma, was in fact only nine years old. In a London where Bill's pan-Continental paranoia had displayed itself only weeks earlier, however, the move seemed to be an invitation for trouble. It arrived soon enough.

Whit Monday itself was one of the wettest on record and the show was rescheduled for the next day. The postponement did no harm as Cody attracted some welcome press coverage. The theatrical newspaper, *The Era*, greeted the new act's appearance with a characteristic piece of Victorian vagary. 'The joker was abroad on Tuesday last at the Half Moon Grounds, Putney,' its correspondent wrote. '"What is the difference between Professor Charles Baldwin and Captain Cody and his sister?" asked a wag. "Give it up, eh? Well one is a parachutist and the others are a pair of shootists".'

After the show, a colleague, John Cannon, recorded at the time, Cody was in buoyant mood. He and Albert were talking animatedly about extending the act to include Cannon in a lengthier dramatic 'sketch' Cody was already mapping out in his head.

The optimism swiftly dissipated. Within a fortnight, perhaps as a result of *The Era* publicity, a letter bearing the imposing livery of Messrs Jenson, Cobb and Pearson arrived at Albert's offices on the Waterloo Road. It wasted little time in getting to its point:

> Our clients, Colonel Cody and Buffalo Bill's Wild West Co. object to the use of the term Wild West in the programme of the entertainment given under your direction at Putney on 18 May and to a person being called Captain Cody and also to a person being called Miss Cody and described by implication as a daughter of the great Buffalo Bill, such persons having no right to either the names or the description.

The solicitors' main interest lay in finding the man passing himself off as Buffalo Bill's 'son'. With a letter doubtless already drafted for service on his clients, Albert was ordered to 'furnish the present address of the persons calling themselves Captain Cody and Miss Cody'. He, in turn, was ordered to 'give an undertaking not in the future to use the description Wild West, Captain Cody and Miss Cody again'.

Buffalo Bill's reputation was enough to scare most of his

adversaries. In Cody and Albert, his London solicitors found themselves up against frustratingly canny, not to mention elusive, opponents.

Cody and Maud seem to have vanished into thin air. Meanwhile, on 12 June, the morning after seemingly promising he would not contest the case, Albert arrived at the High Court to find Buffalo Bill's briefs absent. Seizing his chance, he not only fought his corner but successfully applied for the plaintiff to pay his costs. The agent's cheek only incensed Buffalo Bill further. Lewis Parker, in Leeds preparing the opening leg of the Wild West's latest tour of the provinces, and Charles Wyndham, doyen of the theatrical establishment in London, were drafted in to add gravitas to the case.

Wyndham's speech was particularly forceful. Captain and Miss Cody's act was 'calculated to deceive the public', he proclaimed grandiloquently.

As the case dragged on even Albert was forced to swear an affidavit. He gave away little beyond the fact he did indeed represent Cody and his sister as 'champion pistol and rifle shooters'. Beyond that, however, he stuck to his story that he had organised neither the show nor the offending programmes. Affidavits from Cody and his wife were never sworn, however. Throughout five months of legal manoeuvring they remained nowhere to be found.

Eventually, Buffalo Bill found it impossible to lay a legal glove on Albert. On 2 November, in the continued absence of Cody and Maud and with months of court time effectively wasted, Mr Justice North ordered that 'all further proceedings in this action be stayed'. The ignominious performance of Buffalo Bill's solicitors was completed when the judge ordered their client to pay Frank Albert's costs in full.

For Cody, however, there was little cause for celebration. As it turned out, Buffalo Bill's lawyers achieved their aim. They could hardly claim any credit for the fact that the 'son and daughter of Buffalo Bill' did not grace the music halls of England again, however.

P RECISELY WHY CODY'S MARRIAGE TO MAUD COLLAPSED is a mystery. Perhaps she married Cody believing he really was Buffalo Bill's son. Certainly the disastrous start to their English adventure could only have placed a strain on their relationship. To judge by the way events unfolded within months of the marriage's ending, however, by far the most plausible explanation is that Cody had fallen in love with another woman. Less than two years after the 'son of Buffalo Bill' case, he had returned to the London stage – this time as the male half of a new pair of shootists.

Regardless of which version of the story he was telling, the beginnings of Cody's love affair with Lela Blackburne Davis, the daughter of the leading English bloodstock agent, John Blackburne Davis, invariably bore all the ingredients of the most ardent, Victorian, romantic melodrama.

In the most colourful account, he had met her in Montana, of all places. Quite what she was doing there was never explained. Instead Cody concentrated on telling how he had beaten off a pair of rival suitors to win her hand.

Cody had not been 'the only pebble on the beach', wrote one interviewer beginning his reconstruction of the romance.

> But he happened to be the favoured admirer, and this fact inspired two of his rivals to challenge him to mortal combat. They settled that the fight should be of the triangle kind, and a day was fixed for the duel to the death. But Mr Cody didn't relish the idea of not being able to shoot at the man who was aiming at him, so instead of turning up at the trysting place, he arranged with the lady that they should elope – or at any rate go and get married – which

they did while the two disappointed suitors were cooling their heels and using early American language because of the non-appearance of the successful lover. Mr Cody assured me that it was not cowardice that kept him away, but he would rather that morning get married than go shooting.

Later this tale was supplanted by a slightly more credible version of events in which they had actually met when Cody had begun making regular trips to London, shipping horses from San Antonio to England on Blackburne Davis's behalf. The two had met in Chelsea and gone riding along Rotten Row in Hyde Park. They had married in England, then moved to Texas where they had welcomed their first son, Leon, into the world. A second son, Vivian, had been born back in England, where Lela had returned while Cody had attempted to make his fortune in the Klondyke.

Again the truth was murkier and much more complicated. Leon and Vivian were, in fact, the youngest of the four children produced during Elizabeth Mary Blackburn Davis's marriage to Edward King, a 'licensed victualler', from Chelsea, whom she had married, at the age of twenty-one, in January 1873. Leon and Vivian's oldest sister, Lizzy or Liese, had been born in December 1873, their big brother, Edward, two years later in October 1875. Leon had been born in London, in September 1879, Vivian in Brighton in August 1882.

The true beginnings of Cody and Lela's relationship are unclear, although it seems safe to guess that a love of horses may have brought them together. Despite her tiny stature, Lela was an accomplished horsewoman. What is certain is that by 1891 or so, a year after her father's death, Cody had replaced Edward King in Lela's affections.

The couple made the most unlikely of matches. Apart from being fifteen years Cody's senior, Lela could claim a pedigree that included connections into the Royal Family. According to some

Clockwise from top left: Vivian, Lela, Cody, Leon and Edward.

her father had provided horses for the Royal Stud. In 1890, after twenty years in the monarch's service, her sister Mercedes' husband, Robert Glassby, had succeeded Sir Joseph Edgar Boehm as official Sculptor to the Queen. (It seems Victoria was not amused at her sculptor's sister-in-law's decision to leave her husband for a Wild West cowboy. According to one family member, she refused to meet Cody and Lela on one occasion because of their unmarried status.)

Yet to anyone who came across them it was soon obvious that, in Cody, Lela had met the great love of her life – and vice versa. Over the next two decades she would provide the reliable, occasionally matronly, rock on which his remarkable career was built. He, at the same time, would remain a devoted, not to mention decorous, partner. From the beginning until the very end, he generally referred to her as Madame Cody. 'They adored each other from the moment they met,' one family member recalled once.

Lela's boys seem to have felt equally strongly about Cody. The thirteen-year-old Vivian and ten-year-old Leon were soon spending every spare moment practising their shooting skills with their mother's American boyfriend. Vivian, in particular, displayed an eye that impressed even Cody. Cody was also close to the teenage Edward King, an aspiring actor and dramatist. No one could have been more excited than he was when, in 1892, his mother and brothers joined Cody in forming a new stage act.

SF Cody and Family, Champion Shooters of America, made their modest debut on the bill at London's Royal Aquarium that summer. The act was a far cry from the blood-and-thunder reviews of Buffalo Bill and Forepaugh. The posters promised that: 'For the benefit of the ladies and children present, we use American wood powder making little noise and no smoke'. With young audiences in mind, the boys played a prominent part in the entertainment. While Leon had learned to fire accurate shots while hanging from a trapeze, Vivian had been coached to fire at

Champion shooters.
Two early posters introducing
'The Great Codys'.

a target while Cody held him upside down by his ankles and swung him 'like a clock pendulum'. Along with a pair of boxing kangaroos, a troupe of musical-instrument-playing baby elephants, and Dan Sullivan, an Irish strongman whose act climaxed in his lifting 'a Cob, Cart and Four Persons' with his teeth, they offered little more than an amusing support to the main attraction of the day, a trio of divers who, 'health and circumstances permitting', ended each evening with a leap from the roof of the auditorium into a five-foot pool of water a hundred feet below.

Star billing was not long in coming, however, for Vivian in particular. Lela's youngest son's reputation as one of the more unusual acts on the London stage soon won him bookings as a solo artist. At one stage he was dividing himself between the Aquarium and the Alhambra Theatre in Leicester Square. As his first fifteen-minute performance with the Codys came to an end at 5.15 each evening, he would be rushed across central London in time to share the Alhambra bill with the grand dame of the English music hall, Marie Lloyd. After completing the climax of his act with a display of long-range shooting from the Dress Circle, the youngest member of the troupe was rushed back to the Aquarium in time for his family's second show at 9 p.m. According to Vivian, his wage of £20-a-week was supplemented by the five shilling pieces slipped into his stockings by admiring ladies. Soon Cody was featuring him on his posters as 'Little Vivian: The Youngest Pistol and Rifle Shot on Earth'.

Cody's 'Doc' Carver–style sharpshooting remained a centrepiece of the family show. Each night he would bring the house down by hitting a single glass ball from the back of the auditorium, a distance of at least 300 feet, at the Aquarium. The act also allowed him to display the natural inventiveness for which he would later become famous. He introduced an item in which he would unleash a salvo of bullets at a bank of metallic plates he had placed inside a sturdy wooden case, forty feet or so away from him. To the crowd's delight, as the bullets flew along the line a familiar series of notes rang out. Cody had calibrated the plates to reproduce what he called 'a correct representation of the noted chimes at the House of Parliament'.

Cody had also constructed a gleaming metallic case, into

which he had cut a silhouette of Lela, or 'Little Sunbeam: The Girl Rifle Expert', as she had been rechristened. The outline was surrounded by twenty glass balls. Night after night, Lela would climb into the case, then stand implacably still as Cody fired twenty shots in twenty seconds, each of them within a whisker of her body. The bullets were 'sub-charged' so that they would drop harmlessly to earth a few feet past their target. They were potent enough to scorch Lela's skin nevertheless. 'Grandma used to wear blood-red tights, so that if she was grazed it did not show,' her grandson, Samuel, revealed many years later. 'And Grandma got a lot of grazes.'

Audiences found it hard to decide who was the coolest. A reviewer from the *Morning Advertiser* could not get over the way Cody fired at his 'wife' 'with the utmost sang froid'. Others were simply astonished at Lela's faith in her accomplice's unerring accuracy.

No one needed have worried on Madame Cody's behalf. Years later, a veteran of even more amazing acts of faith, she claimed she had never once worried at what might go wrong. In Cody, she confessed, she had found a man who made her feel immune from danger. 'He had once said, pointing to a camp fire, that if he told me to walk through that fire I would do it – and I would willingly too,' she said on one occasion. 'I never knew fear when I was with him. He told me it was safe, so I knew it must be,' she added on another.

CHAPTER THREE

LE ROI DES COW-BOYS

AT THE END OF 1892, CODY, LELA AND THE CHILDREN crossed the English Channel en route to Paris and a debut at the spectacular Casino de Paris. The change of scene produced an almost immediate change of fortune. 'Absolutely colossal,' Cody called the audience's reaction as the Great Codys shared the bill with a troupe of yelping cancan dancers. Soon rival cabarets like the raucous Ba-Ta-Clan club were vying for his act. Four years after leaving Forepaugh and America, Cody could enjoy his coronation at last: *Le Roi des Cow-Boys*, his Parisian promoters were soon billing him.

It was no surprise that the Paris of Toulouse Lautrec and the new Moulin Rouge, Manet and the brothers Melieres took Cody to its heart in a way London never had. Brash and voluble, exotic and irresistibly *pittoresque*, he fulfilled Zola's credo that life should be 'lived out loud' and personified the French's ultraromantic idea of the Cow-Boy. 'Tall, tempestuous and solid; he reminds us of D'Artagnan,' was one, far from untypical, impression of him in the flesh. In *belle époque* Paris, too, his unconventional relationship with Lela would have barely raised an eyebrow. Freed from the prejudices of Victorian England, the family prospered, taking up lucrative bookings all over France. If the story later told by

Vivian was true, the money did not remain in Cody's grip for long, however.

T HEIR PARIS SUCCESS HAD BROUGHT AN INVITATION TO play the pier at Nice in the summer of 1893. According to Vivian, Cody had spent all his spare time at the adjoining casino, where he became obsessed with perfecting a 'mathematical system' for playing roulette. When the family moved on to an engagement at Monte Carlo, the experiment produced its predictable conclusion. Vivian later recounted the story of how in the small hours one night he found his father sitting on the edge of his lodging house bed 'white-faced, looking as I'd never seen him look before, as though the bottom had dropped out of his world'. Cody had returned from his first night at the Monte Carlo casino having turned 2,000 francs into 3,000. This time, however, he had lost 'practically all the money he possessed', 28,000 francs. As well as the Cody name, Vivian inherited his adoptive father's flair for occasional fabrication. His ending of the story is worth recounting, nevertheless. His stepfather had eventually risen from his bed and made a solemn promise to Madame Cody. 'I shall never gamble again, at roulette,' he apparently told a silent Lela. 'And he never did – at roulette,' said Vivian.

S URE ENOUGH CODY REVIVED HIS FORTUNES WITH A wager, this time one he was sure of winning.

Back in Paris that autumn, a café conversation with a group of gentlemen turned into an argument about the relative merits of France's transport à la mode, the autocar and the velocipede, or bicycle. Such contretemps were far from rare in a Paris obsessed with science and technology. ('Impossible is not French,' was the popular phrase of the day.) Two years after the pioneering engineers Panhard and Levassor had set a world record for a long-distance journey by travelling from the Avenue d'Ivry to the Point du Jour, a distance of six miles, the jury was still divided on whether their internal-combustion-engine-powered carriage had a future. (It would not be until 1894 that a car reached the then unthinkable speed of fifteen miles per hour.) The doubts had deepened as the velocipede had begun to win the official backing of the French military as their preferred form of transport. 'The velocipede has come as a useful innovation in army circles. Regarded with diffidence when first introduced its services have now been recognised as being of the highest utility,' reported *Le Figaro* in the wake of an impressive performance at exercises to mark the centenary of the Battle of Valmy in 1892. 'A circular from the Ministry of War has advised all officers in command to make the fullest possible use of it.'

Cody, it seems, rated neither invention terribly highly and had shot straight from the hip, declaring that even the fastest two-wheeler would be no match for him and a good horse. Within weeks, on a chill October afternoon, a crowd of several thousand Parisians had gathered within the perfectly manicured grounds of the Hippodrome du Trotting Club in the smart suburb of Leval-lois-Perrot determined to see him eat his words. Over the following three days, Cody, equipped with a small stable of horses, was to take on one of France's champion cyclists, Meyer of Dieppe. The winner would be the man who had completed the greatest aggregate distance. To the victor would go a prize of 10,000 francs.

The genesis of what would prove an important turning point in Cody's life was doubtless more subtle and convoluted than this. Cody's claims that the idea was an original one should certainly be taken lightly. He — or, at least, Lela and her children — would almost certainly have heard of a bicycle-versus-horse challenge taken up by two former members of Buffalo Bill's troupe, 'Bronco' Charlie Miller and Marve Beardsley in England in 1887. Their challenge to the English cyclist Richard Howell and the

Philadelphian WM Woodside had taken place at the Agricultural Hall in Islington, north London, over six days. Yet there can be no denying that Cody's contest was touched with genius, in the sheer perfection of its timing in particular.

In the London of the late 1880s, Miller and Beardsley's challenge had failed to capture the imagination. In the *fin-de-siècle* Paris of the 1890s, however, the challenge instantaneously touched a nerve. The modern bicycle may have owed its existence to two Scots – Kirkpatrick Macmillan, who had devised the treadle-operated machine in 1839, and John Boyd Dunlop, who had developed the pneumatic rubber tyre in 1888 – but it had been the French who had all but invented cycling as a sporting and social phenomenon. The first recorded bicycle race had been held over a two-kilometre course in Paris in 1868. By 1893 thousands packed the 'velodrome' of the Parc des Princes and lined the countryside to watch road races from Paris to Trouville, Dieppe and even St Petersburg. (Within a decade what would become the world's most watched sporting event, the Tour de France, would begin.) Even the fashionable middle and upper classes regarded cycling as *très chic*. On Sundays the Bois de Boulogne was alive with men and women in the couture houses' latest 'cycling outfits'. In this atmosphere, '*Le Match Cody–Meyer*' became an instant *cause célèbre*.

Cody responded to the considerable media interest in characteristically forceful fashion. On the eve of the race, in a profile in the cycling newspaper, *Le Velo*, he spun a selection of colourful tales from the West and claimed various feats of horsemanship, including a record supposedly set in 1880 in which he rode twenty miles on twenty horses in fifty-eight minutes! The fact that dates, names and places had slipped his mind mattered little. *Le Velo*, like other publications, found him irresistible even though they gave him little chance in the challenge that lay ahead.

In Meyer, a tough, stern-faced young Dane, Cody had taken on a formidable foe. His wins included the Paris-to-Trouville race

'Le Match Cody—Meyer'

and another contest from Amiens to his home town, Dieppe. As the first race got under way, few saw any great cause to change their opinion that man and machine would comfortably triumph over man and horse.

Cody had made a swift selection of horses from a livery stable in the city. His first mount allowed him to establish an early lead but his second proved a handful, first refusing to break into a trot, then vainly attempting to throw Cody on to the track. 'Kicks of the head and tail, diverse leaps, nothing could throw the intrepid cavalier,' wrote one admiring eyewitness as Cody gave a display of his bronco-busting prowess. He was eventually forced to give in, however. 'After losing a minute and a half of debate, Cody took the wise course of action and mounted another,' recorded the witness.

Cody quickly regained the lost ground. Over the next three hours, despite saddling another horse so lifeless that one observer thought he was 'ripe for the abattoir', he drove himself and his horses to the limit to build a comfortable lead. 'Nothing could deter the ferocious American,' wrote one witness. By the end of the four-hour challenge, Cody had registered a convincing win, travelling 124 kilometres and 375 metres to Meyer's 112 kilometres and 220 metres.

The defeat left Meyer's – and Paris's – pride severely dented. Yet even with Cody once more struggling with his motley collection of horses, the challenger could not reduce the overall gap in the second race. This time, at least, Meyer matched Cody almost kilometre for kilometre, racking up the same aggregate distance of 112 kilometres as his rival in the four hours. By the time the third race day arrived, a sense of disillusionment and disappointment had set in at Levallois Perrot, however. Some sections of the crowd vented their anger by booing the upstart American for humiliating one of their most famous sporting sons with such seeming ease. '*Oh triste et stupide public,*' lamented one writer afterwards. ('Oh, sad and stupid public.')

As the end of the contest drew close, nothing could dampen Cody's delight. He sealed his triumph with a piece of flamboyance that supposedly took even Lela by surprise, pulling up a lap short of the end to rein in an extra horse and crossing the finishing line standing astride both animals. (He later admitted he had never tried the stunt before.) At the reception afterwards he overindulged on champagne and, according to Vivian, turned boisterous. He had to be restrained before he started 'shooting up' the Paris gaslights as he rode triumphantly back into the city in a landau.

By then such behaviour would only have endeared him even more to the Paris public. 'Cody's performance was simply marvellous for the qualities of energy, endurance and equestrian science deployed by the celebrated cowboy,' wrote one journalist. 'When shall we see another duel so exciting and so truly sporting?' wondered another.

The answer came six weeks later in Bordeaux, where, a week before Christmas, a 3,000-strong audience packed the Esplanade de Quinconces to watch Cody take on another champion, this time a homegrown one, Henri Loste.

Cody had taken greater care in choosing his horses this time and won the first race comfortably enough. After the first hour, he had travelled 27.9 kilometres to Loste's 26.9. He stretched his lead through the rest of the race, travelling almost three kilometres farther in the second hour, four in the third hour. By the end his overall distance of 84.9 kilometres was more than 17 kilometres farther than Loste's.

The Frenchman came back strongly in the second race. At the end of the first hour he had clocked a remarkable 31 kilometres to

Cody's 30.3. Cody was only marginally ahead an hour later. It was only in the third hour that Cody put clear distance between them. Cody travelled 88.6 kilometres to Loste's 86.5. His winning margin at the end was just over two kilometres.

Sensing Cody's winning streak was about to end, a record 5,000-strong crowd turned out for the third and final contest. Once more Loste set off fast but this time Cody stuck with him. After one hour he was half a kilometre ahead; after two hours he was over two in front. In the final hour Cody pushed himself to the limit and matched Loste's phenomenal hourly run of 31 kilometres. By the end his winning margin was emphatic. Over three days he had clocked up 264.1 kilometres to Loste's 251.5. His average speed throughout the race had been a remarkable 29.33 kilometres an hour.

By the time Cody arrived back to Paris, where the stage act had been once more booked at the Ba-Ta-Clan, he was one of its most celebrated citizens. '*Le roi des cow-boys est un homme exceptionnel*,' *Le Veloce Sport* concluded in its detailed report of the match afterwards. Cody claimed he would regularly be stopped in the streets by Parisians shouting '*Vive, Le Roi des Cow-boys.*'

His fame spread overseas. In London, the *Daily Sketch* carried a cartoon of the race under the caption, 'Captain Cody Gains A Victory'. In the Paris edition of the *New York Herald*, the columnist Le Coq Heron reported that Cody was being 'pestered by some half a dozen show managers'.

'I'm going to have a rest,' Cody reassured the *Herald*. In reality, his mind was working overtime. Soon Cody was using the columns of *Le Veloce Sport* to issue a challenge to all comers. The handwritten note was the equivalent of a glove to the face of the entire sporting nation. It read,

To my friends the French cyclists. I certainly glory in your spunk, but nevertheless I shall attempt to put you in the shade occasionally.
Yours as ever, SF Cody Jr.

To my Friends the French cyclists I certainly glory in your spunk, but nevertheless I shall attempt to put you in the shade occasionally

Yours as Ever

S. F. Cody Jr

With the proceeds from the first two races boosted by his winnings on side-bets, Cody began assembling a small stable of horses of his own. Soon he, Lela and Edward were organising a tour that would take them all over France. By now Edward had become an indispensable part of Cody's life. Lela's eldest son had been so taken with Cody's French *nom de plume* he had adopted it himself, becoming Edward Leroy rather than King. (For the sake of avoiding embarrassing questions, he had already become Lela's nephew rather than her son.) He seems to have overseen much of the organisation and promotion of the racing, and acted as an official starter and referee at many.

His involvement allowed Cody to concentrate on training his horses specifically for the demands of the races, teaching them to come to a sudden halt and bolt off again at full speed as they would need to do during the crucial changeovers. Cody was soon convinced he could produce whatever result he pleased – and bet accordingly. At the same time he ensured that his challenges produced enough drama to satisfy his audiences.

I N THE WAKE OF THE MEYER AND LOSTE RACES, CODY accepted a challenge from a champion French walker, a Monsieur Gallon. Gallon reckoned that, over a fifty-hour race, with Cody restricted to the same horse, he could outdistance the American. When the race got under way in Paris, however, the challenge quickly descended into farce. According to Cody's version he had gained such a huge lead over the walker that the crowds had begun to lose interest. Cody had chosen a particularly malleable horse and contrived to have it throw him. His sons carried him theatrically back to a tent, where he lay prostrate for hours while Gallon slowly made up his ground and overtook him. According to Vivian's characteristically colourful account, the walker was within minutes of recording a win when Cody picked himself off his sickbed, clambered on to a horse muttering, 'I must go on', and added enough distance to his total to emerge victorious.

'Un homme exceptionnel'.
Cody photographed in France
in the 1890s.

It is unlikely Cody was quite the master of his own destiny he claimed. He certainly lost a race against the top tandem riders, Fournier and Gaby, and was also soundly beaten when he travelled to England and Blackpool for a challenge. What is in no doubt, however, is that, for the following two years, his eternally entertaining exploits made him a popular hero not just in France, but across the Continent.

Cody vanquished many of the best-known riders in Europe. Early in December 1894, in Milan, for instance, he beat the Italian champion Buni, covering 335 kilometres to the Italian's 319 in just ten hours. A fortnight later, in Brussels, he took on the Belgian champion Van Cromburgge. His arrival anywhere by then constituted something of an event. In Brussels the magazine *Le Soir Illustre* welcomed him by devoting its entire front page to a lavish lithograph of the man they called '*L'extraordinaire* Yankee', the '*Tombeur des velocipedistes*' ('thrower of bicyclists'). Ten days before Christmas, Van Cromburgge was duly overthrown as Cody emerged from the three races victorious, covering 128 kilometres to his rival's 124.

His progress around Europe brought its customary quota of dramas, of course. In one story, later told by Vivian, while travelling through the Black Forest, Cody had inadvertently set up camp in grounds belonging to the German Emperor. Against Lela's advice he had shot a rather magnificent stag with a small-bore rifle while hiding in a pine tree. As the woods filled with the sound of approaching bloodhounds, Cody displayed some of his old cowboy cunning, first cutting up and salting the best bits of the carcass and burying it in the ground, then spreading powerful horse embrocation around the camp perimeter to confuse the approaching hounds. His quick thinking saved him from a public beheading – the statutory punishment for hunting the monarchs of the Imperial forest. Even Cody had been unable to evade the law in Berlin a few weeks later, according to another story. He fell foul of a city magistrate when he challenged a horse owner to a street race for the ownership of a magnificent stallion called Goldschlager. (Cody won the race and the rights to the horse, of course.)

His races took their toll, too. In Brussels a contrived fall backfired and he broke his arm. '*Grave Accident au Velodrome, Cody Blessé*,' announced the city's *La Feuille Illustre*. Even Cody's absence failed to bring the show to a halt, however. While Edward acted as a manager, Vivian, Leon and Lela took part in races themselves. Lela, in particular, proved a hardy competitor. Her only defeat in France had come on a muddy circuit unsuitable for horses. 'The track was so bad that my horse sank up to its knees, and therefore it was almost impossible to race at all,' she explained once. Her gravest moment came in Hamburg when her saddle slipped and she was left hanging by her stirrups as her horse cantered on. 'I met with fearful injuries,' she said later. 'And it was at first thought that the bones of my leg, which was broken in two places, could not be set right again.'

By late 1894, however, even her appearances on horseback were reduced. That summer she had broken the news to Cody that she was pregnant. In February 1895, in Basle in Switzerland, she gave birth to a son, named Frank after his father. With Lela now approaching her forty-third birthday, he would be Cody's only child. While Cody continued his travels, mother and son remained recovering in Switzerland for much of the year.

In the early summer of 1896, Cody dropped anchor on the island of Malta. With Lela and the boys he settled into the Flag Ship Hotel in Floriana, a few miles from the capital, Valletta, where he was due to take up a series of challenges.

By now his horse-versus-cycle spectaculars had begun to wane in popularity. There had been more notable triumphs. In June 1895, for instance, he had won a sizable prize of 1,000 marks in gold by narrowly beating the German champion Gebruder Bokh in Nuremberg. At the same time, with fewer serious sportsmen willing to take him on, he had been forced to veer towards more vaudevillian ventures. In Rome he had accepted a chariot-racing challenge in which he had been required to dress theatrically in centurion's armour. (Cody had wanted to stage the race in the Colosseum but discovered its arena littered with masonry.) Leading the race and only yards from the finishing line, his chariot had broken loose from its team of four, almost propelling him into the path of his rivals. It had been all he could do to hang on as the other chariots robbed him of a valuable win.

His adventures had left him far from destitute, however. Unhappy with the Maltese sports grounds earmarked for his races, the British Garrison's St Clement's Parade Ground and another open area called the Marsa, he nonchalantly announced he would begin looking for land where he could build a new track specifically for his races.

On 16 May in a letter to the editor of the *Daily Malta Chronicle* from his rooms at the Flag Ship Hotel, came the news that he had found a site on the outskirts of the town of Sliema. 'The men are already working upon it and I expect it will be ready in a few days. I shall therefore be pleased to accept all challenges for races on foot, cycle or horseback that there is any chance of my winning,' he joked.

Suitable challengers were thin on the ground, however. First Malta's official champion cyclist, an Englishman called Arthur Harding, lost control while practising for his £20, ten-mile challenge, 'injuring himself severely' in the process, or so he claimed. (Cody all but accused him of feigning the injury to avoid a beating.) Then, as he struggled to drum up worthwhile challenges, he made the mistake of being far too generous with his handicaps. Challenged to a one-and-a-half-lap, man-versus-horse race by a middle-distance runner called Light, Cody gave his opponent a half-lap start. The runner won the £10 bet easily as Cody's mount struggled to get up a proper head of steam in time.

Soon Cody was reduced to taking up any challenge he could think of. One week he was a strongman, offering £10 to anyone who could 'perfectly repeat' his weightlifting performance of Sampson Redivivus, the next he was a wrestler, taking on — and seemingly beating — two men at a time. 'Mr Cody can be said to have muscles of steel,' said one impressed observer.

By the middle of June, there was almost an air of desperation about the show as he augmented the races at Sliema with a series of short 'sketches of life in the Far West' put together with Edward and Lela. The revue was as far from a Buffalo Bill–style spectacular as could be imagined. What it lacked in scale, however, it clearly more than made up for in theatricality. By now Edward had become the company's stock redskin while Lela had developed a penchant for damsels in distress. Cody meanwhile rode in on his white horse Bergamo, firing shots off in all directions as he did so. The Maltese audiences were enthralled. 'The best event was the Wild West sketch, it contains all the essential elements of a nice little novel,' wrote one reviewer. 'Seldom if ever has Malta been favoured by such a novel and clever exhibition of skill and daring.' The performance seems to have marked a turning point.

By the end of the summer, Cody had left Malta for a brief spell in Tunis, where he had been invited to take part in another oddity, a national chariot racing competition. (Malta did not easily forget his brief stay: for years afterwards the area where his track had been built was known as Codyville.) The years of constant touring had by now taken its toll on even Cody. To make matters worse he had contracted a fever while travelling back from Tunis to Marseilles. According to Vivian he had feared the worst and 'thought he was going to die in bed with his boots off'.

By the time he arrived in France in January 1897, Cody had decided he would make one last sweep through the country that had been so good to him. From there he would head back to England and London. A farewell tour called *Adieux de Cody et sa Famille* began at the Velodrome Libournais on 17 January 1897. As well as horse races between Leon and Vivian, and a 'Grand Match' between Cody and a new three-man bicycle ridden by his old adversary Henri Loste, and two others, Alix and Ratineau, the bill featured an expanded selection of 'scenes from the Wild West'.

As he bade farewell to France, it was clear Cody had reached a crossroads in his life. In February of 1897, the French journalist Jehan d'Arsimpre wrote an article in the *Gazette Béarnaise*. France's love affair with Cody had clearly not lost its ardour. 'He is constantly asked to be "a fearless creature, a loyal friend or a fierce and dangerous enemy", Cody is all of that. He only fears two things in life: God when he thunders, and illness, a coward and a traitor when it affects his children rather than himself,' wrote d'Arsimpre in his sentimental tribute to Cody, '*Le Tireur*', ('The Gunman').

Yet even to d'Arsimpre's adoring eyes, Cody now seemed a displaced and strangely disillusioned figure:

> You can't help but be affected by the feminine softness of his eyes, the look has a strange mobility; the smile is soft and generous. In his private life he is a dreamer, filled with melancholy as are all of those who have seen the infinite horizons of the Orient and America. He longs for his roots and to go back to his native land. He is ill at ease in the circuses, so let us go to him: the enthusiastic bravos, laboriously won, are his reward.

The escape he clearly longed to make was still a long way off, however.

After six peripatetic years, England came as a welcome relief to Lela and the boys in particular. Cody too found work easy to come by still. With the capital planning a spectacular series of celebrations to mark Queen Victoria's Diamond Jubilee, he was asked to appear as part of a huge spectacle called the Last Days of Pompeii at the giant Alexandra Palace pavilion in north London. As well as trickshooting he performed a chariot-driving stunt in which he drove himself and his four horses into a lake. (Apparently the stunt was performed at night, thus allowing Cody to swim himself and the horses to safety under cover of darkness.) He had more pressing business in mind by now, however.

Of all the inventive devices Cody had added to his act during his tour of Europe, he was proudest of the rapid-firing handgun he had devised and built himself. Cody had been aware of the revolutionary machine gun invented by his American compatriot Hiram Maxim in England and had set out to make a more practical, lightweight version suitable for his sharpshooting act.

Vivian later recounted how Cody had become increasingly obsessed with the idea while on tour in Belgium. He had finally cracked the problem while staying at a pension in Antwerp, where he had emerged one day with a series of meticulously detailed drawings. He had gone on to commission a Berlin gunmaker to manufacture the barrel and breech, and an engineer in Liege, Belgium, to make most of the moving mechanisms. For secrecy's sake, he had made the final elements himself. Vivian later recalled how he had 'thrown his stetson high in the air' when he had tried the gun out, successfully firing a magazine of eight cartridges at a brick wall in one blinding, bullet-spitting flash.

Soon after arriving back in London, Cody wrote to the War Office offering the gun to the British Army. He was duly summoned to a demonstration at a firing range at Aldershot, where the assembled officers were, in his words, 'staggered' by what they saw. They probably were. Cody arrived astride Bergamo, dressed in his Stetson, leather boots and Mexican spurs. At the given order he proceeded to give a display straight out of his Forepaugh repertoire, firing at and hitting a variety of targets.

No official records of the trial seem to have survived, yet there are two reasons for believing Cody's account of the events that followed. His feat of discharging a volley of up to sixteen shots in three-fifths of a second and with deadly accuracy would be replicated time and again in the years that followed. So too

Father and son. Cody and his only child, Frank.

would the blend of scepticism and barely concealed scorn with which he claimed he was treated by the War Office.

According to Cody's later reminiscence, the War Office expressed an interest in subjecting the gun to technical trials. When Cody outlined his terms – £1,000 on delivery of the gun and a further £4,000 plus a royalty on every model, if it was accepted – they dismissed the idea of doing business with him immediately.

Cody could not resist firing back. In the weeks and months that followed he staged a series of impromptu displays with the gun for the press. 'It will discharge bullets at the rate of 1,500 per minute, though I am bound to state that it has never been tried to that extent for the mechanism wouldn't stand the racket, so to speak,' wrote one impressed observer on seeing what Cody called his 'toy gun'. The writer added,

> It has a penetrating power which sends its missiles
> through a four inch plank at 1,000 yards but its terrible
> talents could be best utilised at short distances. Mr
> Cody . . . thinks when an officer, or even a private, gets
> to close quarters with the enemy, that one magazine
> would precipitately stop the coming foe. At any rate,
> it would make his body look like a porous plaster.

He, like most others, found it hard to understand why Cody's handiwork had not been taken up by the War Office. 'Mr Cody offered the patent to the British Government for £1,000 but it has not been accepted,' he concluded, suggesting that Cody had subsequently dropped his price. Cody left the reporter in no doubt why he thought he had been rejected. 'The patentee thinks he did not measure the right quantity of red tape to guarantee a favourable reply.'

Cody should have been able to take solace in the fact that his gun remained a crowd-pleasing element of his act back at the Alexandra Palace.

His marksmanship remained as awe-inspiring as ever. Among his feats that season was a routine in which he shot at gas-filled balloons three hundred feet in the air and another in which he fired tiny holes in a hail of pennies and sixpenny pieces thrown skywards by Vivian and Leon. 'The bullets seem to be bewitched. They seem to obey him. He does not seem to take aim at all, merely to look towards the object, and sends a bullet through it,' wrote one observer.

The English's relish for red tape soon put a dampener on his successful return, however. A stern letter from the Home Office forced him to abandon the sixpenny shooting routine. It warned he would face a 'severe penalty' if he continued 'defacing coins of the realm'.

THE KLONDYKE NUGGET.

BY S. F. CODY.

"Think! Rosy, try to recall the past."

CHAPTER FOUR

'A NEW AND ORIGINAL ACT'

B Y THE SUMMER OF 1898, CODY'S ACT HAD EVOLVED
into a series of energetic and imaginative, if at times grisly,
tableaux. The show began sedately enough with quaint re-
enactments such as 'crossing the immense prairies of Texas', 'the log
hut and Post Office', 'the dinner' and 'the departure of Col. Cody'.
By the second half of the show, however, the mood had turned altogether darker. The final sequence featured 'the approach of the
negro horsethief and assassin', 'the theft', 'the murder of Mrs
Cody', 'torture of her son', 'stealing the horse', 'the flight', 'pursuit
and capture by lasso', 'trial and execution by Judge Lynch', 'the
funeral of Mrs Cody' and, as a suitably Grand Guignol finale,
'Cody's shot which brings down the hanging nigger spy'.

In an arena set in the grounds of the Alexandra Palace that
summer, audiences watched on with a mixture of shock and sheer
amazement. 'We do not envy the feeling of the "hanged" nigger
thief when the cabin is in flames, nor would we care to experience
his repeated journeys at the end of the lasso, with Col. Cody on his
gee-gee at the other end,' winced a visitor from the *Gentleman's Journal*. 'A very uncommon and exciting show,' he called Cody's exhibition, recommending it wholeheartedly to his readers, nevertheless.

Such praise only stiffened Cody's determination to steer the
act into new and even more dramatic territory.

Cody had been restless to move on from the ill-fitting formula of cycle races and stock Wild West scenes since the final days of his grand tour of Europe. With the backing of the Alexandra Palace's manager, Cecil Barth, with whom he had become friendly, he had begun constructing an elaborate series of sets on the stage of its main theatre. The log cabin, underground gold mine, frontier saloon and courthouse would be the setting for what he called 'a new and original act', *The Klondyke Nugget*.

Spectacular new discoveries in Alaska had made news around the world the previous year. Rather than returning to the land 'where the coward never started' he decided to mine theatrical gold instead, effectively amalgamating his outdoor tableaux into an hour-long melodrama in three acts.

As the outdoor show continued to play to enthusiastic audiences through the summer of 1898, Cody spent every spare hour and a small fortune, £280, re-creating the spectacular Klondyke landscape. By August of that year he was ready to offer a sneak preview, and invited a reporter from the *Daily Graphic* to the Alexandra Palace.

The newspaperman had needed no second invitation. By now Cody's face was a familiar sight in London newspapers, as much for his marksmanship as his showmanship.

In March that year he had been hired to demonstrate a revolutionary new automatic pistol, the Borchardt, at the Moore and Grey's grounds in Neasden, west London. The pistol seems to have been a more successful close cousin of his own 'toy gun'. (The suspicion that his invention may have been a mere variation on the Borchardt cannot be dismissed.) With newspapermen watching on, Cody had landed seven out of eight bullets within a four-inch circle on a moving target in a third of a second of fire. The popular magazine *Land and Water* was so impressed, it got Cody to reproduce the display, then printed a reproduction of the bullet-peppered bull's eye for the benefit of disbelieving readers.

At first the *Graphic* journalist seemed more interested in why the ace marksman was not in Cuba, where the United States had just gone to war with the Spanish, following their sinking of the USS *Maine* in Havana harbour. 'Why ain't I in Cuba? Well I'm busy right here just at present and must leave the war to the other Cody.' (The 'son of Buffalo Bill' episode still played on Cody's mind, it seems. By now no interview passed without his issuing a disclaimer to any blood ties. 'He isn't in our family Bible,' he told the man from the *Sketch*.)

As Cody led his visitor to the main stage inside the building, he revealed the reason behind his failure to do his patriotic duty. Cody outlined the storyline of the play in which he intended taking on a leading role himself. 'I take the part of the villain,' he explained. 'Though I haven't as black a heart.'

With evident pride he pointed to scenery comprising 'rocky mountains, a savage ravine and a settler's hut'. Cody claimed to have painted the backcloth, said the *Sketch* man, 'with his own hand' and based the landscape on his own experiences in 'the wild region of Alaska'. (For some reason, he had begun claiming his father had been among the 'first of the white settlers' there too.)

With a well-practised sense of drama, he then climaxed the tour with a preview of the show-stopping highlight of his drama. His assistants led one of the team of horses from his Wild West show to the upper level of the set where his carpenters had constructed a wooden bridge into the painted mountain scenery. As the horse made its way across the structure Cody gave a signal, the bridge collapsed and the horse fell fifteen feet, clawing at thin air as it disappeared from the audience's view. 'That ought to make an effective scene,' smiled Cody.

THE EFFECT WAS PREDICTABLE ENOUGH WHEN CODY unveiled the show a week or so later. Cody's most spectacular addition had probably been inspired by his old mentor Doc Carver, whose Wild America show had enjoyed huge success in

Australia with a stunt in which a horse dived from a platform into a pool below. Victorian London proved less tolerant as it watched the bridge explode. Inspectors from the Society for the Protection of Animals arrived at Alexandra Palace brandishing letters complaining about the 'alleged cruelty' being visited on the horses and with members of the London press in tow.

This time Cody was more than ready for a run-in with officialdom. *The Klondyke Nugget* programme was soon carrying a 'spe-

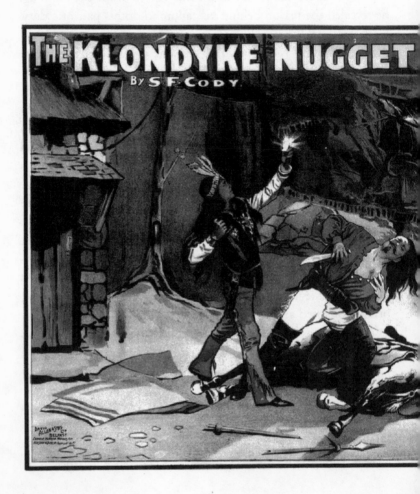

cial notice' reassuring audiences that the SPCA's 'Superintendent and two other representatives of the Society were present several evenings at the Alexandra Palace Theatre and witnessed the performances on the stage and expressed their opinion that there was no danger whatever and the entire performance throughout was free from any cruelty'.

A newspaper columnist let slip the secret Cody had shown the SPCA men. 'Although from the front of the theatre they appear exceedingly dangerous, as a matter of fact, there is absolutely no risk of danger, nor any cruelty whatever involved,' he reported. 'The horse which falls from the bridge has about five or six feet of straw and bedding to drop on to which is not seen by the spectators.'

The publicity proved priceless. The packed houses and thunderous applause that filled the Alexandra Palace each evening encouraged Cody to press on with his plans to develop *The Klondyke Nugget* into a full-blown, five-act play.

By the night of 5 December 1898, a full house attended the St George's Theatre in Walsall near Birmingham to see Cody leading Lela, Edward, Vivian, Leon and his company of players through the premiere of the full-length *Klondyke Nugget*. The posters left no one in

A frontier melodrama.
An early poster for Cody's debut
as a dramatist.

any doubt of Cody's status. 'The world renowned SF Cody' was billed the play's producer, star and, most intriguingly, its author.

The Klondyke Nugget would be the first of several dramas to bear Cody's authorial stamp, yet it is highly doubtful that he was its sole creator. Cody's literacy, or lack of it, was the subject of much speculation during his life, and has remained so ever since. Later testimonies would claim with some certainty that he could not read or write at all. They would cite as evidence the fact that he took an eternity to sign his autograph, did so in huge, balloon-like script and, in private and public, relied entirely on his family to read to him. Yet the large amount of Cody correspondence that has emerged in recent years suggests a different and, as usual, less straightforward story.

There is a curious inconsistency to the scribblings he left behind. One diary in particular, from 1901 or so, could have been written by an overreaching primary school pupil, so full are its pages of strange, strangulated sentences and elementary mis-spellings. Yet other Cody correspondence, penned by what appears to be the same hand both before and after this date, conveys an impression of impeccable spelling and grammar. The likeliest explanation for the discrepancy probably lies in Cody's frequent description of Lela as his amanuensis. Her job may simply have been to tidy up the deficiencies of Cody's Davenport education, his frequent impatience or maybe even a form of mild dyslexia of which the diary may have been a rare surviving example.

In the case of *The Klondyke Nugget* the arguments are all but meaningless. The first great Western melodrama of the English stage could not have been produced by the imagination of anyone other than Cody himself.

The action took place in the hills near the Chilcoot Pass in Alaska and at Dawson City, by now world-famous as the boom town of the region. At the heart of the story was the love triangle formed by an exiled English gentleman called Joe Smith, his

Scenes from the frozen north.
A tantalising glimpse of Cody's spectacle, circa 1898.

sweetheart Rosie Lee and the 'black-hearted' villain of the piece, George Exelby. The play opens with Exelby discovering that Rosie's heart is with Joe rather than him. A series of dastardly deeds ensue: first Exelby blows up a bridge as his rival crosses on horseback, then he hires an Indian war party to kidnap Rosie and kill Joe, then finally he sets Joe up for the murder of another man. The drama climaxes with a courtroom scene in which Exelby's plans are thwarted by Joe's loyal Indian guide, Waco.

Oscar Wilde it was not. Instead Cody played on the melodramatic mythology of the Wild West shows and filled his Alaska with 'desperate characters' and even more desperate dialogue. Far from an untypical line was that delivered by Exelby to Waco. 'If I have any more of your black looks I'll stick six inches of cold steel into your nigger carcass, do you hear?' Villains were referred to as 'curs', 'scoundrels', 'darned skunks' or, if they were French, 'frog-eaten spalpeen'. Phrases like 'snakes alive' and words like 'tarnation' and 'geossifax' abounded.

Yet amid the dime-novel doggerel, *The Klondyke Nugget* contained a faint but intriguing seam of autobiography. Anyone who had chosen to look carefully enough would have discovered Cody had studded his drama with a series of subtle – and sometimes not so subtle – nods to his past. His main family, the Lees, for instance, shared the surname of his estranged American wife and in-laws; his 'black-hearted' chief villain was named after his old 'hash-knife' cowboy colleague George Axelby. If the fact that Cody took on the role of Exelby (and his alter ego Sam Deats) himself deepened the impression that it was a self-portrait, some of Exelby's lines only added to it. At one point, for instance, Exelby admits his weakness for faro and other card games. 'My only bad habit is gambling,' he says.

On top of this his lovelorn speeches to Rosie Lee were filled with a streak of sentimentality curiously at odds with the rest of his melodrama. 'Women are said to be merciful in matters of the heart. Find some pity for me, some forgiveness for the past,' he

7.0. Theatre. Grand Re-production of New and Sensational Sketch,

"THE KLONDYKE NUGGETT."

Written and arranged by S. F. CODY.

SAM DEATS (alias George Exelby)	-	MR. S. F. CODY.
JOE SMITH (in love with Rosie)	-	MR. F. W. MUSSETT.
JUDGE MATHESON (of Dawson City)	-	MR. JOHN MACAULEY
WACO (true as steel)	-	MR. EDWARD LEROY
TOM LEE (an old Trapper)	-	MR. J. HUDSPETH
TED LEE } (Sons of Trapper)	-	{ LEON CODY
VIVIAN LEE }		{ VIVIAN CODY
JIM WILSON (Sheriff)	-	MR. GEORGE AUBREY
BILL SYKES (Sam Deats' Pal)	-	MR. HAROLD MARSHALL
RAVEN (Indian Chief)	-	MR. A. MORTON
NIGGER	-	MR. ROBERT SANDS
USHER OF COURT	-	MR. R. EPSOM
ROSIE (Tom Lee's Daughter)	-	MISS LELA CODY

Supported by 20 Auxiliaries as Indians, Miners, Emigrants, &c.

THREE SPECIALLY TRAINED HORSES,

Who will perform in their respective Scenes:—

BRIDGE SCENE	-	The Chicago Favourite	*McKinley*
COURT HOUSE	-	An American Mustang	*Bergamo*
FINAL SCENE	-	A Russian Cossack	*Bijou*

Also Five Highly-bred Horses and Five Mules.

Gallery Free. Reserved Seats, 3d., 6d., and 1s.

Alexandra Palace programme, September 1898.

asks her at one point. 'Do you forget the many happy hours we spent in old days?'

Cody placed the most thought-provoking words of all into the mouth of his hero, Joe Smith, however. In his first major speech he proclaims his love for Rosie. 'I sought to find complete extinction and now the world believes me dead. I then tried to make a name for myself – in that too I was successful,' says Joe. 'I am in search of a woman who will love me not for my name but for myself alone.' Was this Cody's reference to his own transformation from Franklin Cowdery? Was the second a hint that Maud really had believed she was marrying a cousin of Buffalo Bill?

Cody's annotated scripts remain intact but, unsurprisingly, reveal no real clues. Their concern is maximising the audience's enjoyment rather than mining deep and meaningful truths about its author's melodramatic past.

Cody's showman instincts were by now as finely tuned as those of any vaudevillian in England. He packed his scenes with spectacle – from a trickshot exhibition in which he, Vivian and Leon reduced dozens of white balls to a blizzard of snow to a scene in which Edward, as Waco the Indian, jumped through a fake glass window on horseback. He and Edward also spent hours practising the climactic knife battle. There were breaks from the breathless drama too. Cody hired Ern Clifton, a popular Irish music hall comedian, to play the scatterbrained Dr Paddy O'Donoghue, landlord of the Eldorado saloon. Clifton's gag-filled interlude was augmented by the voice of Maud Marsden, as the bar's singing barmaid. From the first night, it provided an entertainment the likes of which few in Victorian England had seen before.

'The drama is full of highly sensational incidents, and affords opportunities for the introduction of some very effective scenery and for the Messrs Cody to exhibit their skill as crack shots,' wrote the critic of the *Walsall Observer*, seemingly the only scribe in attendance. Cody's performance as Exelby, predictably, stole the praise. 'Mr SF Cody plays with much force, and gives a pictur-esque personality to the part.'

The press reaction was the same as the play went on to tour the rest of the Midlands, the north of England, Scotland, Wales and London. At the Grand Theatre in Newcastle, the house was crammed to capacity, 'even in the exclusive parts whose forte is not melodrama'. In Llanelli in West Wales, 'the theatre was so crowded on Monday evening that hundreds had to be turned away'. By the time they arrived at the Elephant & Castle Theatre in London in August 1899, the family had formed a formidable combina-tion. Lela played 'with self possession', Edward supplied 'a lithe-looking and energetic Waco', Cody 'in speech mannerisms and truculent bearing . . . was an excellent and life-like study of the roving desperado of the Far West.'

R EGARDLESS OF WHETHER HIS OWN ILL-FATED VISIT TO the Klondyke was myth or not, Alaska had finally allowed Cody, in the new vernacular of the gold rush, 'to strike it rich'. For the next five years *The Klondyke Nugget* would remain one of the most popular touring productions of its era.

There were setbacks, as ever, most notably when the show's producer, author and shining star almost burned alive in mid-October 1899. Cody had been summoned from his bed to be told a fire had broken out at the Theatre Royal in the town of St Helen's in Lancashire. By the time the town's emergency services had arrived, he had made one successful dive into the building to emerge with a box of equipment. 'But the police restrained him from any further effort although he informed our representative that he was confident he could have saved the greater portion of the dresses and properties which are of a very special kind and somewhat expensive,' reported the *St Helen's News*.

He was soon back in business, however. Typically Cody offered a variety of estimates about the money he was making. 'My average income arising from my theatrical enterprises was £1,800 a year,' he said in a sworn affidavit at one point. On another occasion Cody inflated this to £50 a week, or £2,500 or so a year, at the time a lavish wage. With Edward Leroy, he began writing more Western-inspired melodramas. *Nevada*, *Viva* and *Calamity Jane* failed to match the sheer energetic authenticity of the *Nugget*, however, and none proved as big a commercial success.

In all likelihood, the later plays were either written or co-written by Edward, or Teddieboy, as Cody called him. While Vivian and Leon seem to have been uncomfortable on stage – adjectives like 'quaint' and 'acceptable' were the best critics could usually offer in praise of their performances – Edward's genuine abilities as an actor had by now begun to shine through. He would often stand in for Cody as Exelby, and had clearly turned the character into a *tour de force*. One reviewer called him a 'scowling, bronco-bestriding villain, whose Mexican haberdashery conceals an arsenal of awesome weapons'. 'Mr Edward Leroy is consummately tigrish,' the critic went on, 'and plays up to the last ounce of energy.'

As *The Klondyke Nugget* established itself as something of an institution, Edward's talent as his understudy made it easier for Cody to take a more peripheral role in the show at times. Often he would stride on stage to introduce the show beforehand, at other times simply join Leon and Vivian in a sharpshooting display. His drift away from the stage was, by now, inevitable. In truth Cody remained 'not much in love with acting', and by 1899 he was becoming increasingly obsessed with a new – though no less dramatic – venture.

It was probably around the early months of 1899 that towns up and down the country began witnessing a curious sight. Dressed in their distinctive, Wild West outfits, Cody, the boys and a group of helpers would arrive on the largest available open space where they would spend hours laying out what seemed like miles of ropes and wires, then assembling a mass of bamboo and canvas into vast, box-shaped kites. The crowds would thicken as, one by one, the huge constructions were allowed to catch the winds. To the onlookers' astonishment, Cody would climax the show by climbing into the basket attached to the last of the kites, bark his customary instruction to 'let her go', then begin climbing imperiously into the air.

I T HAD BEEN THE FAMOUS, IF FAINTLY FOOLHARDY, EXPERI-ments of Cody's grandfather's namesake Benjamin Franklin that had revived the Western passion for kite flying. In a field in

Philadelphia in 1752, the eternally curious Franklin had sent a simple kite into a thick thundercloud and proven lightning was, just as he suspected, another form of electricity. By the late nineteenth century hordes of enthusiasts were experimenting with kites as aids in meteorology, photography and, naturally, warfare. Each of them followed Franklin's advice to 'keep the ends of the lines dry' so as to avoid a lethal voltage from on high.

In reality, the new kite flyers were merely attempting to rediscover arts learned 2,000 years earlier. Despite Western claims that the first kite was built by a fifth-century-BC Greek mathematician called Archytas and that the Cretan legend of Icarus was inspired by even older man-carrying kites, few really dispute the fact that the first flyers were Chinese soldiers.

By common consent, a General Han Hsin had come up with the idea while laying siege to a palace, as long ago as 2,000 BC. He had floated a simple kite towards his enemy's battlements, used the length of the paid-out line to gauge the distance between the fortress and his forces, then dug a tunnel of the same distance under the palace walls. By the time of the Han Dynasty, around 200 BC, Chinese soldiers flew kites fitted with bamboo 'hummers' at night-time. Spies inside the camp would spread rumours that the kite's disembodied moans and screeches were the voices of the gods predicting death and defeat. The enemy armies often left the field before daybreak.

It had been the Japanese who took the invention a step further and allowed a man to fly. Like the Malays and the Maori, the Japanese believed in the mystic powers of the kite. They developed a series of representational symbols: a crane or turtle for long life, the dragon for prosperity, and other shapes to frighten away evil spirits and help fertility and good fishing. According to the most famous Japanese kiting legend, a thief called Kakinkoki Kinsuke built the first man-carrier in order to breach the defences of the great Nagoya Castle. Once inside he stole the gold fins of a fabulous dolphin kept under guard there. (Presumably the dolphin became the criminal profession's good-luck symbol from there on.)

In the century and a half or so since Franklin's experiment, kiting had developed at a steady if unspectacular rate. It had been the work of an English-born Australian, Lawrence Hargrave, that had prepared the science for its greatest step forward. In 1893 Hargrave had perfected the box kite, an idea of such simple genius it would pave the way for powered flight within a decade. A year later, Hargrave had used four tethered kites to successfully lift himself five metres off the ground. Hargrave had his imitators and acolytes, including a Frenchman, Maillot, and a Lieutenant RG Wise of the American Army, both of whom had had success with man-lifting kites. England's kite experimenters were led by Colonel BRS Baden-Powell, brother of the famous Robert. On 27 June 1894 he had succeeded in lifting himself a few yards off the ground with a single surface kite. Elsewhere William A Eddy, a meteorologist from Bayonne, New Jersey, and Lawrence Rotch, director of the Blue Hills Observatory there, had, using advice from Hargrave, begun achieving remarkable results in lifting recording instruments into the air. In 1897 a Blue Hills meteorological kite reached a record height of 9,338 feet. Another American kite maker called Octave Chanute would adapt a Hargrave kite into the most effective glider yet devised.

With characteristic chutzpah, Cody had set out to outdo them all.

He always claimed to have gained his first experience of elementary kiting back in America, where a Chinese cook had taught him how to build and fly kites made from 'bits of stick and paper'. (Depending on which version of his life story he was telling, the Chinaman had worked on the ranch at Birdville or run the chuckwagon on one of his cattle trails.) The inspiration for building bigger and more stable kites had come 'from the big turkey buzzards I used to see in Texas', he later added. 'I was always struck by the way they used to float in the air, sometimes for ten minutes, without stirring a wing.'

At least one historian has made the intriguing suggestion that Cody may have made his first attempts to take to the air in Montana in the mid-1880s. Frank W Wiley learned about the Flying Machine Mine, a claim in the Castle Mountains, while talking to old prospectors. The old-time miners recalled the exploits of an inventive miner known simply as Sureshot Bill, who had built a vast kite or glider capable of carrying a man aloft. When his claim ran out, it seems Bill headed for another area of Montana, leaving his machine behind, unfinished and untested. 'Sureshot Bill – he built 'er. He never flew 'er,' the locals liked to recall.

According to one, the machine's body was made of 'a single, lodgepole pine about forty feet long, with a single wing and a seat for the pilot in

SURE SHOT BILL BUILT A GLIDER

PLANNED TO FLY DOWN FROM HIS MINES ON MOUNTAIN TOPS 30 YEARS AGO

And if You Care to Visit Site Where His Cabin Stood Near Ghost Camp of Castle, You Can Still See the Remains of Rude Plane that He Fashioned from Poles.

In days of old when Castle was new, great were its wonders. Montana's premier silver camp, it lay at one end of the Jaw-bone railway —that well-nigh fabled thread of steel that wound a gnarled course up Sixteen-Mile canyon from Lombard and the Northern Pacific.

Castle in 1890—its boom days— had all those wonders that could be offered for a mining camp of some 1500 or 2000 persons. Now that it has dropped to a cluster of moldering cabins, the remaining 15 inhabitants still tell tales that bear the mark of the high community ambitions that only an early mining camp—and the early mining camps' inspirational beverages— could incite.

Such a story is that of Sure Shot Bill of the Castle mountains and the airplane he built in 1890. W. B. Willey, supervisor of the Jefferson national forest, returned from a trip through the White Sulphur Springs region, tell it.

Sure Shot Bill left behind him as evidence of his early aeronautical experiments and the veracity of his remaining townspeople, the skeleton of his flier. It lies on the mountain back of Castle.

a sling underneath'. According to another it was 'a big kite, made with a framework of willows covered with cloth'.

Wiley's conclusion that Sureshot Bill and Samuel Cody must have been the same man seems to have been based on the fact that the timing of the story coincides with a period when Cody was known to have been working in Montana, that the kites described loosely accorded with designs Cody pioneered later in his life and, most spurious of all, that he too was something of an expert with a gun. Appealing as the story is, it seems little more than wishful thinking. To have built a kite of such sophistication in such circumstances would have been a remarkable achievement. It is hard to believe Cody would have abandoned all his work to turn into what one observer called 'a heap of rotten and disjointed logs', as Sureshot Bill did. It is even harder still to imagine that Cody would never have mentioned having achieved so much so early.

Cody certainly shared many of Sureshot Bill's qualities, however. Both men could have been the archetypes upon whom Frederick Jackson Turner based a passage in his seminal work, *The Frontier In American History*. In 1893 Turner summed up the fading spirit of the pioneering west thus:

> The coarseness and strength combined with acquisitiveness,
> that practical inventive mind, quick to find expedients; that
> masterful grasp of material things, lacking in the artistic,
> but powerful to attain great ends; that restless nervous
> energy; that dominant individualism, working for good and
> evil, and withal that buoyancy and exuberance which comes
> with freedom – these are the traits of the frontier.

By the dawn of the new century, displaying the combination of restless energy and dominant individualism that was to remain his hallmark, Cody was pouring more time and money into kite experiments than anyone else in England.

The dearth of details surrounding his early experiments is understandable given the ferocious competitiveness that surrounded every area of aviation at the turn of the century. According to a statement Edward Leroy later made, Cody had been flying kites since he had joined him with Lela and his brothers in 1892. This is hard to believe given there is no mention of Cody's kiting experiments during his time in Europe, nor in the early years of his return to England. The first seemingly authoritative recording of Cody's kiting comes from April 1899, when *The Klondyke Nugget* was playing Her Majesty's Theatre, Carlisle. At the invitation of the aviating Rev. Sydney Swann, Cody flew a kite of 'immense square shape' in the grounds of Houghton House, the residence of Henry Brooks Broadhurst.

It has been argued that Cody's breakthrough may have come in the wake of the St Helen's fire. The loss of all his equipment forced him to start building his kites with a fresh eye. He did later admit that a bet with one of the boys on the August Bank Holiday weekend in 1900 had first stimulated him to begin building his man-carriers. 'My son said he could make a better kite than I so we started in opposition.' Whatever the true date of his first flights, what is clear is that Cody swiftly emerged as the most innovative and successful exponent of kiting in Britain, and probably the world.

Experimenters like Hargrave, Wise and Baden-Powell had been thwarted by the instability of their kites and their inability to find a system by which they could control their ascents with them. Given his lack of formal education, Cody could do little to test the scientific theory behind their failures. Instead he relied on a combination of instinctive inventive genius, courage and sheer dogged determination to eliminate each problem as it arose. According to Edward, Cody had twelve to fifteen men helping him. His main helpers were Edward and two other men, one named Foye and another called Horst. As ever, it was Vivian, Leon and Edward who bore the brunt of their stepfather's relentless drive. Vivian later recalled how Cody was constantly trying out new adjustments to his kites. He would invariably spoil the Tuesday morning lie-ins the boys looked forward to after *The Klondyke Nugget*'s opening Monday night in a new town by barging into their bedrooms before dawn. 'He'd rouse us up. "I've got a new idea. Something we must try out. Now!" he recalled. The boys would follow him to the theatre, where they would unpack the sewing machines they were by now experts at operating, then cut out the new designs Cody had come up with. 'We'd try out a small one first, take it outside, test it on a cord in the wind, and if there was no wind just run,' recalled Vivian. 'This sort of thing went on for months and months, trial and error, test, fail, try again.'

Cody's experimentation with different shapes produced spectacular results. Soon he had added distinctive, scalloped wings to add stability. To stop the kites' tendency to 'duck' at the azimuth or height of their climb, Cody added a topsail, or 'topknot', after the bun in which he kept his long hair under control. His modifications gave the batlike kites a remarkable stability even in the most violent winds.

But undoubtedly Cody's greatest innovation was his method

N° 23,566   A.D. 1901

Date of Application, 20th Nov., 1901
Complete Specification Left, 20th Aug., 1902—Accepted, 20th Nov., 1902

PROVISIONAL SPECIFICATION.

Improvements in Kites and Apparatus for the same

I, Samuel Franklin Cody, of Theatre Royal, Stratford, E, Dramatist, do hereby declare the nature of this invention to be as follows:—

This invention relates to improvements in the construction and arrangement of kites to be used for aerial flights, the object of the invention being to provide
5   a means for enabling kites to ascend and travel with a greater weight than is possible with the ordinary method of construction, and to enable such kites to be advantageously used for military and other observation purposes in positions where my improved system of construction enables the kite to be readily collapsed, carried and re-erected for use. My invention also has reference to the improved
10   mechanical arrangements for controlling the movement of the kite and for regulating the speed of its ascent or descent by means of the improved brake or retarding device which I arrange in connection with the kite winch or mechanism for winding the cord or cable of the kite.
In carrying my invention into effect I employ a series of kites of varied and

Cody's patent application from November 1901.

for raising man-lifting kites. While Hargrave had simply attached himself directly to the lowest of a train of kites, and Wise had been hauled up by a rope passing over a pulley fastened to the main kite, Cody had come up with a much more ingenious and effective idea. It was in essence a vertical version of the cable cars he had seen in Switzerland. Using a train of lifter kites he would raise a lengthy cable into the air. The wire effectively formed a railway along which the free-flying carrier kite could move upwards and downwards with ease. By 1901 he was sufficiently happy with the device to go public. A patent application 'for Improvements in Kites and Apparatus for the Same' was submitted that November. By then he had already written to the War Office, offering them first option on 'SF Cody's Aroplaine [sic] or War-Kite: A boy's toy turned into an instrument of war.'

A.D. 1901. Nov. 20. Nº. 23,566.
CODY'S COMPLETE SPECIFICATION.

(2 SHEETS)
SHEET 2.

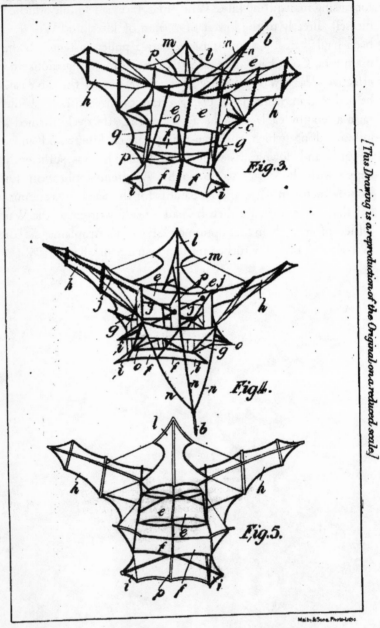

Fig.3.

Fig.4.

Fig.5.

CHAPTER FIVE

MAN-LIFTING

EXCUSE THE LIBERTY I AM TAKING IN WRITING, I BELIEVE I possess certain secrets which would be of use to the Government in the way of Kite Flying.'

From its opening sentence, the letter Cody sent the Under-Secretary of State for War in October 1901 was nothing if not intriguing.

He had put pen to paper while on tour in the Midlands with *The Klondyke Nugget*. ('This week: Star Theatre, Wolverhampton. Next week: Artillery Theatre, Woolwich', read the letter heading.)

Cody kept the letter precise and untheatrical, however, confining himself to an explanation of why he was convinced his man-lifting kite system would be 'practical and useful in times of war'. 'I can go up or down at will and my system of kites is absolutely steady in a medium wind or in a tempest without any danger to the experimenter,' he explained. 'My entire apparatus can be worked by a Company of men, five to manipulate the windlass, one officer, one signalman and one aeronaut. Communications can either be done by flag signalling, telephone or Heliograph'.

He allowed himself just the one tub-thumping moment. 'I have spent some hundreds of pounds on this and I believe I have achieved more success than any other living man — and I have kept my experiments practically a secret,' he boasted before offering the War Office a free hand to 'put them to practical tests'. 'I am, Dear Sir, Your Obedient Servant,' he signed off.

Cody knew events elsewhere in the Empire meant his approach could not be easily dismissed.

Two years into the war against the Boers in South Africa, the British Army seemed far from the invincible force that had ruled two-thirds of the nineteenth-century world. In an unforgiving and alien terrain, the resilient Afrikaaners had dragged the colonial superpower into a messy, guerrilla campaign. The losses were already far higher than expected. In all, 6,000 men would perish. The conflict, and the crisis of confidence it sparked, would mark the beginning of the Empire's slide into inertia and decline.

Of the war's few military successes, the most unexpected had come in the skies above the high veldt. In their first major conflict, the observation balloons of Her Majesty's Balloon Factory had played crucial roles in the victory at the Battle of Paardeberg in February 1900 and the action at Fourteen Streams, which led to the relief of Mafeking three months later. The introduction of the dirigibles – their envelopes made from goldbeater's skin, a resilient, absorbent and elastic compound made from cattle stomach linings, so as to absorb bullet fire – had given the British what would prove a crucial psychological as well as strategic advantage. 'The balloons were a symbol of scientific superiority on the side of the English,' the Boers' Colonel Arthur Lynch would admit when the war was lost.

Only Britain's commanders in the field knew the extent of the balloons' limitations. Inflation was a slow and frustrating process, requiring twenty tons of gas and up to ten man-hours. In even moderate winds they became next to useless. On top of all this the balloons and their equipment were so bulky that steam traction engines had been shipped out to South Africa to haul the load.

BFS Baden-Powell's trials with the most obvious alternative, man-carrying kites, had proven a frustrating failure, mainly because of his insistence on single-surface kites rather than Hargrave-style box kites. With the Scots Guards, Baden-Powell had joined his brother in South Africa, where his experiments continued. At a difficult moment in the war, Cody's letter offered a new – if unsettling – hope that a solution might be at hand.

The idea that an eccentric American cowboy and showman had solved a problem that had flummoxed one of the most distinguished names in England would have been hard to swallow. (Cody's public pronouncements on the balloon's deficiencies hardly helped. 'A man who can't invent something better than those things ought to be droving ducks for a living,' he said once.)

Though the response was slow in coming, a telegram was dispatched to Cody's hotel in Harrogate on 3 December nevertheless. It read, 'The Superintendent balloon factory will communicate with you as regards seeing experiments. War Office.'

By then an impatient Cody had already staged two official public demonstrations of his system. It was probably as well the Balloon Factory did not witness the first, at Wanstead Flats in east London, on 14 November. In missing the second, five days later at the town of Bury St Edmund's, however, the Army missed a significant – not to mention spectacular – moment in England's aviation history.

Cody had sent a second, courtesy, note to the War Office informing them of his intention to fly at Wanstead. He revealed the demonstration would mark the debut of a twenty-seven-foot-high, thirteen-foot-wide, white monster he had christened Viva, 'the largest kite in the world'. To the unruly crowd that gathered in east London, it must have seemed like the world's largest white elephant.

To the average Englishman, aviation's pioneers remained a collection of hopeless, and quite possibly insane, eccentrics. Every region of the country had its birdman legends: in Wanstead it would have been the story of George Faux, a local farmer who, in the 1860s, had kept making strange, arm-pumping jumps off the roof of his house in nearby Chigwell Row. ('I'm a really good flyer, but I cannot alight very well,' Faux kept saying each time he plummeted straight to earth. Only the threat of jail stopped his bone-breaking bird impressions.) It was little wonder most pioneers conducted their experiments far from a public that treated their efforts with scorn.

The prospect of seeing a new aviator making a public fool of himself always drew a crowd. As Cody arrived from his lodgings near the Theatre Royal, Stratford, on the morning of 14 November, the opportunity to mock a cocksure American birdman only swelled the numbers more.

Cody, it has to be said, presented the mob with an easy target. He and the boys arrived on Wanstead Flats in stetsons, garish red jerseys and coloured sashes from *The Klondyke Nugget*. As a team of helpers assembled the vast kites, they charged around on horses in an effort to keep the crowd entertained. After almost two hours of waiting, however, the mood turned surly. 'The crowd growing impatient took to "chipping" the performers, and, judging from some of the witticisms that were let fall, there seemed far more of the Wild East than the Wild West about,' wrote one witness. When Cody finally attempted to fly his Viva kite, his struggles with a lacklustre wind met with gales of laughter. 'After cutting various eccentric figures in the air, down it came at every attempt to the great merriment of the crowd,' wrote one observer. Cries of 'Koko', presumably after England's most famous clown, began ringing out. Eventually Cody announced he was cancelling flying for the day, began the long process of packing up the kites and, as one witness put it, 'surrendered himself to the heavy witticisms of the crowd'.

The episode was quickly forgotten. Five days later, on a dull yet breezy Tuesday morning, a more sober and civilised gathering of around 500 soldiers and civilians gathered in an Army barracks at Bury St Edmund's to watch Cody go through his painstaking preparations once more.

The laboriousness was inevitable. Cody's system for suspending a strong cable along which his free-flying man-carrier could ride required patience and practice in equal measure.

The operation began with the sending up of the main pilot, or King Kite, a winged box kite up to 36 feet in width attached to 500 to 1,000 feet of piano wire fed out from a winch or windlass he had designed. To this was attached a steel cable, almost an inch in circumference and with a breaking strain of two tons. Once the pilot had taken the weight of the steel line, a series of 'lifter' kites were sent up the cable, attached by leads. Cody realised the positioning of the kites was crucial for stability and had developed an innovative 'stop-cleat' device which gripped on to steel bulbs placed precisely in position on the cable. As each lifter kite locked into place, so more of the cable was paid out and more kites were added. As they did so the lifters took on the vast weight of the cable and slowly increased the tension on the line. Only when a dynamometer attached to the winch showed a pull of one ton on the cable was a final, nineteen-foot-span box kite attached to the, by now, taut and stable line. The kite was fitted with a wicker basket seat, from which Cody could operate two controls, a set of bridles which controlled the rate of ascent and descent, and a copper-jawed trolley which acted as a brake by clamping itself on to the cable.

The idea was to raise the carriers above the height where it would be susceptible to squalls. When Cody was satisfied that his anemometer showed the whole arrangement was stable enough, he would climb into the basket, issue the order for his kite to be released and, using his brake and bridle, make as fluent a climb as possible into the air.

Conditions at Bury St Edmund's were infinitely better suited to flying. In a diary of the day – written in what seems to be his own, misspelled hand – Cody recorded the crowd's sense of excitement as the King Kite was released into the stiffening, thirty-mile-an-hour breeze.

The wind seamed to increase rapidly. The flaping of convess [canvass] and the whistling of the wind amongest

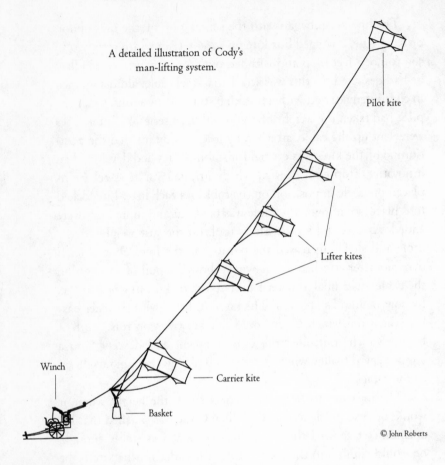

A detailed illustration of Cody's
man-lifting system.

Pilot kite

Lifter kites

Winch

Carrier kite

Basket

© John Roberts

the cross sticks and lines rezembled a sail ship in a storm.
It took eight men to hold the King Kite in this gale and
when it was released it seamed as tho nothing could stop
its progress upwords when it reached the aullued
[altitude] of 100 feet. I shall never forget my feelings when
the eger little air ship shot up like a rocket to the full
extent of the line. A slight buz of voyses came frome the
crowd of onlookers as the pilot kite soared almost direct
over head.

94

The anticipation grew as the remainder of the kites were released and Cody began preparing his man-lifter. It seems Cody had made few, if any, high-altitude ascents with the finished system before Bury St Edmund's and that some of his assistants advised him to send the man-carrier aloft with bags of sand initially. 'I was not to be perswaded. I felt determent and confident of my success,' Cody wrote. 'I then turned to warn the crowed back . . . then took my seat in the car and signeld the winless man to stand by.'

To the roars and cheers of the crowds, Cody and his kite rose effortlessly up the cable to a height of a hundred feet or so. 'My weight, which is 13stone 11lbs was added to the birdon [burden]. Even this had no efect on it. No, I was halled into the air like a streak. Loud chearing and shouting as well as a hearty round of aplaughs arose from the entire asembly,' he wrote.

An ecstatic Cody returned to the ground, then prepared for a second, higher ascent. 'I again ascended like a shot to the utmost limit of the 300 ft line,' he wrote. The first clue that something was amiss came when Cody was seen 'vigorously pulling the lines'. His attempts to right one of the kites as it was hit by a squall failed, however. Soon the train of kites was spiralling earthwards. To the crowd it all seemed to end safely, even comically. 'The kites rapidly took a downward corse, and the 500 spectators thought SFC's story of the ascent would be told in another world,' reported one eyewitness. 'But a friendly tree came to the kite-flyer's assistance, and he got off with a bit of a shake.'

Cody's own account reveals he suffered far more than a bit of a shake. The line attaching his car to the King Kite snapped, sending him falling sixty feet or so before his fall was broken by the smaller kites. As his fall continued Cody took the only action available, grabbing hold of the cable.

Upon realizing what had happened I seased the desinding line which slipped through my hands like lightning,

THE FLYING CODY.

Gets Some Way Up with his Cloud of Kites, but is Glad of a Tree to Come Down by.

S. F. Cody, of Wanstead Flats and Klondyke fame, and the one and only inventor of the "Viva" flying kite, has had a successful ascent and uncomfortable descent.

The ascent took place at Bury St. Edmunds, where the wind was blowing 18 miles an hour.

The descent took place in a tree—also at Bury.

It happened on this wise: By the help of a squall S. F. C., seated in a chair, rose gracefully from the earth, and ascended in a cloud —of kites. S. F. C., at the tremendous altitude of some 300ft., was seen vigorously pull- the lines used to prevent ducking during sudden squalls, when the supporting line from the main line snapped. The kites rapidly took a downward course, and the 500 spectators thought S. F. C.'s story of the ascent would be told in another world, but a friendly tree came to the kite-flyer's assistance, and he got off with a bit of a shake.

This narrow escape has quite decided S.F.C. to make another ascent at a future ..... with more simple arrangements.

A newspaper report on the Bury St Edmund's ascent.

breaking the bone in the third finger and burning or cuting the first and second so they were rendered usless. That is for the time being this hand which was my right one was quite 'oar des combat' [hors de combat] but as my entire weight being thrown onto the desending line with a result that the kites took a rapid downword corse this time landing me in the brances of a small tree. Then a slight crakling of branches and I again reached teare ferma [terra firma] still clinging to the basket chair.

He brushed his crash off with a shrug. 'This is not unusual to arononts [aeronauts],' he wrote, taking solace in the fact that, as he confusingly put it, 'this was the highest ascent known to man

96

with the ade of gass.' (It can safely be assumed he meant without the aid of gas!)

B Y THE TIME THE BALLOON FACTORY'S EMISSARY, A MAJOR Frank Trollope, finally caught up with the intriguing new inventor, he found not only Cody, but Vivian too in the wars. Trollope met Cody in Leeds in mid-December. At the theatre that week Vivian had accidentally set fire to a gunpowder tub, detonating a gas cylinder at the same time. 'I hope your boy is going all right and the gas explosion has not hurt his nerves,' wrote Trollope afterwards.

It fell to Leon to provide Trollope with a demonstration, at an open space at Holbeck Mow. Trollope was impressed not only by the kite but Cody's safety systems. As Leon disappeared into a steely, snow-filled sky, he remained in contact via the telephone line Cody had fitted to the main cable. 'Please send a line to the Balloon Factory Aldershot after Xmas when you would like to give a show and one of us will come down,' an impressed Trollope added in an encouraging note afterwards. When he saw Cody himself in charge of the man-carrier at Worcester in January 1902, Trollope recommended a trial for the Balloon Factory's superintendent, Colonel Templer.

In the twenty-three years since he had been given £150 to make the British Army's first balloon in 1878, Lt Col. James Lethbridge Brooke Templer had been almost single-handedly responsible for the development of Britain's airborne army. A strapping, John Bull figure with one of the most extraordinary waxed moustaches in England, Templer travelled a few weeks later to Seaham Harbour, where Cody was playing the Theatre Royal. The two men seem to have formed a modest, mutual-admiration society. Cody was so struck by Templer's moustache he frequently waxed his own from then on. Templer was so taken by Cody's kites he suggested he apply to the Army for supplies of silk to improve on the surprisingly agile contraptions. (Templer had been sure Cody would not be able to fly any of his kites in a two-mile breeze. 'However, I proved the contrary to this by sending a model silk kite aloft,' Cody wrote.)

Cody clearly felt the trials had been a success. As he duly wrote to the War Office requesting supplies of silk he wrote, 'Colonel Templer expressed his opinion that he is quite confident that it will be a very successful and useful article to use in conjunction with Balloons when reconnoitring in windy weather'. The request landed on the desk of the Assistant General of Fortifications, an H Buxton, who turned it down flat. The optimism of April slowly ebbed away as the Balloon Factory failed to take any further interest in his kites that year.

B Y THE SUMMER OF 1902, CODY'S KITING EXPERIMENTS were matching *The Klondyke Nugget* for thrills and spills. In Blackpool police were drafted in to control the crowds on the beach when Cody flew a line of seven kites close to the town's famous tower. In Glasgow, the constabulary complained that his flights from the roof of the Metropole Theatre were causing chaos on the street where the population were walking around with their heads staring skywards.

The most dramatic show of the summer came during an extended tour of the northeast of England in July. Cody had caused an immediate stir on arriving in the town of North Shields. News of his flying caused such a commotion inside a local courtroom that the magistrates adjourned proceedings. 'The Justices left the Bench, and made their way to the front entrance. Solicitors, clients, policemen, the accused, all followed, and in two minutes, the outer entrance to the steps were packed with people gazing eagerly skywards,' reported the local newspaper.

He was soon at the centre of a darker kind of drama, however. While releasing a kite from his winch in a football field,

The kite in motion. A cartoonist's impression of Cody's experiments on Newcastle town moor in 1902.

Cody alongside his windlass at Luton in 1903.

Cody was hit by a sudden squall. 'Mr Cody . . . was dragged into the air, a portion of the machine was smashed by the jerk, and the drum, turning around at great speed, jammed Mr Cody's right arm amongst the cogwheels,' recorded one observer. 'The wire then snapped, and the winch and Mr Cody fell to the ground. Upon the arm being extricated it was found that one of the bones between the wrist and the elbow was shattered in a serious manner, portions of the bone protruding from the flesh.'

That night Cody, his arm in a sling, took to the stage to apologise for his non-appearance in *The Klondyke Nugget*. Edward once more stepped into the breach.

Cody drew lessons from the accident and set about designing a new, bulkier windlass, set on a six-pounder gun carriage and capable of withstanding a strain of up to two tons anchored to the ground. He remained earthbound for the rest of the summer, fixing his attention instead on a series of spectacular meteorological experiments. Cody had been sponsored by the *Newcastle Chronicle* to fly a specially built French 'metrograph', a box containing a thermometer, hygrometer, anemometer and altimeter measuring – respectively – temperature, moisture, wind velocity and altitude. In late August and early September he sent his lightest silk kites to altitudes even he had not attempted previously. His highest ascent reached 14,000 feet, close to the Blue Hills Observatory's world altitude record of 15,080 feet. The readings obtained were easily the most detailed yet achieved in England.

Even these experiments were not without their dangers. During one mile-and-a-half-high flight on the Town Moor in Newcastle, the kite was hit by lightning, sending a huge charge flying down to the cable. Cody narrowly missed being hit by the thunderbolt and had to watch on helplessly as one of his best kites was carried away in the storm. When some schoolboys discovered it later in the day, the kite was a broken wreck.

Often after a hard day experiment when every effort
failed I have taken an evening walk. The moon as bright
as silver seemed to smile with triumph and whisper. The
question may be asked, 'Is this modern craze for aerial
flight a disease that is catching lately?' Well I don't know
really whether I am afflicted in this way, but I assure you
my air ship is never out of my deepest thought. I even
dream of all sorts of aeroplane and aerial flights among the
clouds. In fact if my dreams were to come true the moon
would be so ashamed of itself it might cease to shine.
'Strive on thou mortal being.' I shall try on, with hope some
night, to join you in a pathless stroll.
                            — From Cody's diary, November 1901

O N THE EVENING OF MONDAY, 8 SEPTEMBER 1902, dressed like a Mississippi riverboat gambler in an immaculately cut, full-length frock coat, round-collared shirt and cravat, and a huge, new, felt-lined sombrero, Cody arrived at one of England's grander restaurants, Fortt's, in the genteel spa town of Bath. To mark the rather special gathering that evening, the restaurant had been decked out according to an aviation theme: a miniature model of a balloon complete with man-carrying basket hovered above the lavishly decorated main table, even the *petit fours* had been shaped in the form of dainty dirigibles.

Ostensibly the dinner marked the 100th anniversary of the first balloon flight in England, made by the Frenchman André Jacques Garnerin, in Bath that day in 1802. In reality it offered its host a chance to confirm his position as England's most influential patron of the aviating arts.

Patrick Young Alexander's late father had been the manager of the Cammell's Steel Works in Sheffield. He had bequeathed his son a passion for science and engineering that by now embraced industrial chemistry, the manufacture of armour plate, telegraphy and meteorology. He had also left him a fortune of £60,000 with which he could indulge his obsession with the conquest of the air.

In the 1890s Alexander had been a passionate balloonist himself. In 1894 he had jumped out of the basket of one and descended with the aid of a parachute. By now restricted by illness, he had switched his attention to the manufacture of propellers and forming a friendship with every significant aviating figure. In Germany he had established relationships with the brilliant glider maker Otto Lilienthal and the airship pioneer Count Ferdinand von Zeppelin. His travels had taken him as far afield as Russia and Peking. Inevitably, he had become increasingly fascinated by Cody.

In July, through his friend, Eric Bruce, a founder of the august Aeronautical Society of Great Britain, Alexander had asked Cody to stage a demonstration of his kites for his military connections in London. Cody had reluctantly declined. 'I find it impossible to make my demonstrations this summer near London, as my theatrical enterprise keeps me pretty much in the North and Midlands,' he replied from Gateshead. The offer of joining the balloon centenary celebrations, however, had proven too good to miss.

The alumni Alexander had gathered together reflected the nature of England's embryonic aviating community. A mix of military professionals and blue-blood amateurs, they included RBS Baden-Powell back from his time with the Scots Guards in South Africa, Colonel John Capper and Major Trollope from the Balloon Factory, the Honourable Charles S Rolls, the ballooning son of a wealthy peer, and Griffith Brewer, another well-off adventurer.

Recent events gave them much to talk about over brandy and cigars at Fortt's. Alexander would, undoubtedly, have talked of his encounters with Zeppelin and the monstrous, 420-foot-long airship he had launched from Lake Constance in July 1900. Trollope and Capper could have shared a little gossip about Alberto Santos-Dumont, the wealthy Brazilian who had caused a sensation in Paris the previous October by guiding his No. VI airship around the Eiffel Tower. Bruce and Baden-Powell could have talked about the American Octave Chanute, the elderly *éminence grise* of glider flight and, most fascinating of all, Orville and Wilbur Wright, the curious bicycle-shop owners from Dayton, Ohio, of whom Chanute had talked in a letter to a member of the Aeronautical Society in March that year. Whatever the conversation, none of those present could have failed to notice Britain's backwardness in almost all areas of flight.

The first day was dominated by the dinner and a re-creation of the historic first balloon flight. At precisely the same place, day and time that Garnerin had lifted off, 6.10 p.m., the cross-Channel balloonist, Monsieur Gaudron, lifted off from Sydney's Fields in Bath on a journey to the nearby town of Chew Magna. As the second day began it was Cody's moment to take centre stage. He had not been able to bring a full man-lifting rig with him. (He may not have been fit enough to go up.) Instead he sent up a collection of novelty kites. One was fitted with an explosive device which he set off hundreds of feet in the air to the delight of the crowd. Another was attached to a giant Stars and Stripes.

Pioneers. Patrick Alexander, on Cody's left, hosts the Bath balloon
centennial, September 1902.

Afterwards, Bruce hailed the display as the '*pièce de résistance*' of the
gathering.

Alexander's party was, without doubt, the most significant
gathering in Britain's aviation history to date. Within weeks, the
new, expanded circle of friends were reaping the benefits of each
other's acquaintance. By December, through Baden-Powell and
Chanute, Alexander had been given an introduction to the Wright
brothers. On the eve of Christmas he had travelled all the way to
Dayton to listen to their ideas. ('He is certainly the strangest man
I have ever known,' Wilbur later wrote.)

For Cody too the benefits were almost instantaneous. First, in
November, his patent for a man-lifting kite, now modified to
incorporate the bulletproof goldbeater's skin used on the Boer
War balloons, was formally accepted. At around the same time he
heard that his meteorological work in Newcastle had also earned
him official recognition. By the end of the year he was heading his

notepaper, 'SF Cody, FRMS, Fellow of the Royal Meteorological Society'. But the most tangible benefit of his visit to Bath came in the New Year.

On 6 February 1903, frustrated by the Balloon Factory's inertia, Cody wrote to the Admiralty, offering his 'patented Aeroplane' to His Majesty's Navy instead. His offer was dismissed at first, largely because of the opinion of Captain George Egerton, commander of HMS Vernon, the torpedo school where Baden-Powell had met with mixed fortunes testing his system. On the eve of a demonstration Cody was planning at Woolwich in south London, Cody's new friend Baden-Powell forced a rethink. 'The kites are good,' he reassured the Assistant Director of Naval Ordnance, Reginald Tupper. At the last minute Tupper changed his mind and headed for Woolwich, where he joined Baden-Powell the next morning.

The Navy man was deeply impressed, even though Cody did not have sufficient winds to lift his man-carrier up and had to stick to a display with small, calico kites. 'This is quite the best kind of kite I have seen,' wrote Tupper in his report to the Admiralty. 'I have no hesitation in recommending a trial.'

Tupper stayed on for another demonstration the next day, as intrigued by Cody as he was by his ingenious aircraft. 'He says he has been in England for twelve years and considers himself an Englishman, and would be pleased to be naturalised if he could be employed by the Government in connection with his kites,' wrote Tupper later.

Cody's new circle of admirers within the Admiralty was soon augmented by the powerful figure of Prince Louis of Battenberg, husband of one of Queen Victoria's granddaughters, Princess Victoria, and Director of Naval Intelligence (father of Lord Mountbatten of Burma). On the strength of Tupper's reports, he recommended immediate tests. On 18 March orders were issued to the gunnery training school, HMS *Excellent*, and its sister school HMS *Vernon* at Whale Island, Portsmouth. The gunnery school would test the kite's man-lifting potential, the torpedo school its usefulness as a means of sending aerials aloft.

Cody arrived at Whale Island on 30 March in typically flamboyant style, with a small army of helpers and in full Buffalo Bill regalia. In strong, squally weather and driving rain, early tests on land, then on board the destroyer *Starfish*, were impressive enough for even the sceptical Captain Egerton to pronounce Cody's kites 'immensely superior to any kites previously tried here'.

The rivalry between the two wings of the British military was intense. Aware that the Army had

already tested Cody's kites, Prince Louis in particular was in favour of striking a swift deal. In a conversation with the Prince on 6 April, Cody once more planted the idea that he had received offers from foreign governments. (He intriguingly suggested that he had also been asked by the War Office to help with the building of an airship.) Prince Louis, taken by Cody's picturesque personality as much as his invention, it seems, wrote to the First Sea Lord recommending negotiations should immediately begin for the purchase of Cody's patents and for the employment of Cody as a kite instructor and supervisor of kite construction.

The case for Cody was only strengthened in the following week as the safety of his system again impressed the Naval observers, this time at HMS *Excellent*. One of Cody's team was sent plummeting to the ground by a sudden squall but was saved from injury by what one observer called the 'parachute like action'

of the carrier. Later that week, during trials on board the tug *Sea-horse*, another man was successfully lifted 500 feet into the air from the deck.

The captain of HMS *Excellent*, Percy Scott, joined in the praise, although he remained unconvinced about the man-lifter's abilities in bad weather. 'But as the inventor has only been working on them for two years there seems to be no reason why their efficiency should not eventually justify their use for this purpose also,' he wrote in his report.

Matters now began moving at disconcerting speed. Soon after the final trial, on 18 April, it seems Tupper asked Cody to set out the terms under which he would be willing to sell his patent and work for the Navy.

If Cody played his faro as badly as he played his commercial cards, he must have lost heavily when he took to the table of

Dodge City and Monte Carlo. His opening gambit, a letter he wrote on 21 April 1903, was disastrous. Prince Louis of Battenberg had clearly given him the clear impression that an important position within the Navy was his for the asking. 'I am led to believe by the Director of Naval Intelligence, that it is your intention to engage my services for a period of from five to 12 years,' he wrote in his introduction to his letter.

In the light of this, he went on, he was prepared to 'sell outright the entire apparatus, sole patent rights and including my services for from 5 to 12 years'. He made his price plain:

> I should be disposed to accept the sum of £25,000 as a premium for my patents, and, for my services during my tenure of office, a salary of £1,250 per annum. I to be allowed six weeks vacation in each year at a time most convenient to the Admiralty, then, at the expiration of my stipulated engagement, if my aerial apparatus, or apparatuses are still doing good service, a further premium of £25,000 to be paid on my discharge.

His letter stunned even his most ardent supporters in the Admiralty, hardly surprising since – assuming five years' service – the £56,000-plus Cody was asking for represented around two-thirds of the cost of building a large destroyer! The few printable comments that survive talk of 'wild exaggeration' and 'exorbitant demands'. It is safe to guess even choicer language was used in the corridors of the Admiralty. Even his strongest supporter, Tupper, called the claim 'excessive'. In a memo on 24 April, however, he asked his superiors to consider subjecting Cody's kites to further experiments 'if he can be induced to modify his terms to reasonable proportions'.

Cody clearly sensed he had made a massive miscalculation. Within a week he had compounded it by seemingly attempting to play the Admiralty and the War Office off against each other. On

'A sail ship in a storm.' Cody puts his apparatus to the test.

29 April, he wrote to the War Office demanding a final decision on whether or not the Army were interested in buying the patent. 'My apparatus is now perfect,' he enthused, adding – bizarrely – that he would be happy to discuss terms by which he could sell 'exclusive rights to the Army and Navy jointly'. Again he hinted at

'unsolicited' approaches from 'other Governments who are anxiously seeking information regarding my invention'. 'As my first negotiations were with the British Government, I should like a definite official answer as to their opinion based on demonstrations they have witnessed stating whether or not they are able to make use of my invention,' he concluded.

Tupper met Cody on 3 May when he seems to have asked Cody to offer a more realistic set of terms. Cody's response was to dash off a long, rambling, occasionally desperate and often angry letter the same day. 'During my interview with Captain Tupper today, statements were made which lead me to think that a wrong construction had been placed upon my letter,' he began before accusing the Admiralty of failing to understand the sacrifices he was offering to make. 'I offered to give up all enterprises and to give my entire time and study and my utmost efforts to the interests of the Government,' he claimed. And all this 'at a salary much less than my present income', he wrote, underlining the phrase for effect. Eventually Cody offered a concession whereby he would sell his patent at 'one fifth of price quoted' on the understanding he would 'put aside the idea of becoming a nationalised Englishman and enlisting in the Service'.

Time and again Cody would prove to be at his best in adversity. In positions of strength he was often at his most inept. The reasons for his disastrous rush of blood in dealing with the Admiralty is unclear. He should, surely, have learned from his ham-fisted attempt at offering his machine gun to the Army. In men like Patrick Alexander and Sir Hiram Maxim, with whom he had become friendly too, he had sagacious old heads available to him. In his defence, he had clearly been grievously misled by Prince Louis of Battenberg. His panic may have been exacerbated by a report on the validity of his patent being drawn up for the Admiralty by an engineer called James Swinburne. His grasp of the mechanics was so weak that he dismissed Cody's masterstroke, adding his batlike wings to a box kite, as a modification to which 'there can hardly be any advantage'. He had concluded, probably correctly, given the convoluted wording Cody had used, that the patent was 'invalid' in his opinion because 'there is no invention in what the patentee claims'. Whatever the cause of Cody's catastrophic tactics, the effect was predictable.

The Army's 'definite official answer' came on 9 May in a terse, ten-line reply from HC Sclater, Director General of Ordnance. The crucial paragraph read, 'I am directed by the Secretary of State for War to inform you that after very careful consideration of your invention including the recent trials by the Admiralty at Portsmouth it is not proposed to take any further action in the matter, the man lifting kite not being considered suitable for Army purposes.'

Cody's expectations of the Navy may have been raised by an order to provide a set of four man-carrying kite rigs to be tested on board the ships HMS *Majestic*, *Doris*, *Revenge* and *Good Hope*. The order, worth £635 in all, was under way by May.

Eleven days after the War Office turned him down, however, the Admiralty slammed the door shut on the outright purchase of his patents. 'I am commanded by my Lords Commissioners of the Admiralty to acquaint you that, after giving the subject careful consideration, they regret they are unable to accept your offer,' read the official letter.

Adding salt to the wound it added that 'My Lords are prepared to give you (as an act of grace) a sum of one hundred pounds in addition to the out-of-pocket expenses you have claimed.'

Cody at Calais Harbour, 6 November 1903.

CHAPTER SIX

'IT'S DOGGED
AS DOES IT'

V*ive Cody. Vive l'Amerique. Vive l'Inventeur.'*
On the moonlit evening of Friday, 6 November 1903, France once more cheered Cody to the echo.

He had arrived in Calais harbour that afternoon from Dover. At daybreak on the English coast he had discovered a strong wind blowing from France and jumped aboard the first available steamer. On the French coast he had used the last hours of daylight to prepare the flimsy, collapsible canvas-hulled boat and large, black, batwing kite he had brought with him across the Channel.

By around 7.30 p.m. a large crowd had gathered on the quayside. To applause and shouts of encouragement Cody, dressed in luminous yellow oilskins, a bulky lifebelt and a Stetson, climbed down the harbour steps, slid into the boat's covered cockpit and cast off. Until he reached open water, he remained attached to a pilot boat, manned by six local rowers. Half a mile or so out to sea, he broke loose the kite, then let it rise into the northerly winds. As he later remembered, 'Then came the words which I scarcely recognised as my own: "let go".' Back on the quay, a final cheer went up as the first attempted kite-powered crossing from Calais to Dover officially got under way.

ODY'S BELIEF IN THE SHEER FORCE OF HIS WILL WOULD never desert him. 'It's dogged as does it,' he would say. In the wake of his rejection by the military, he had switched his attention to the scientific establishment. He had sold a kite to a Scottish Antarctic expedition in 1902 and attempted to make contact with the great Norwegian, Nansen. Cody had read how one of Nansen's expeditions had come to an end when confronted by a 125-foot-high mountain of ice. 'I maintain that with my aroplaine [sic] he could surmount any such obstacles with ease even if they were twice or three times that height,' he wrote. It was with polar explorers like Nansen and Robert Falcon Scott in mind that

Cody had been developing his latest innovation, the kite boat. Trials on the River Shamrock in Ireland had gone well enough for him to announce plans to cross the Irish Sea from Belfast to Holyhead in February 1903. The crossing had to be abandoned when he failed to get the twelve-mile-an-hour winds he needed to raise the kites to the right position to pull him.

He had made his first unsuccessful attempt at crossing from Dover to Calais in October. He had arrived on the coast brimful of confidence. 'What I really want is a whole gale. Then the boat will just skim the tops of the waves and if the wind holds I calculate that I could do the passage in forty five minutes, or faster than the fastest Channel steamer,' he had boasted, to a friendly journalist, Harry Harper of the *Daily Mail*, whom he had invited to make the journey with him. After three hours being frustrated by capricious winds, Cody and Harper had abandoned the trip.

As his second attempt got under way, Cody was soon congratulating himself on the modifications he had made, in particular, his decision to use one powerful kite rather than the two smaller ones he had used in October. By now Cody had begun christening all his kiting creations. He called this one *Old Faithful*. The boat meanwhile was named *Lela*.

Cody had decided to wait for

Dover beckons.
Cody aboard his kiteboat, 1903.

115

low tide at Calais, 'when I would have wind and tide opposed to each other and I could accordingly make use of either in heading for Dover'. There was little need for the tide as, with Old Faithful once more doing him proud, he covered the first mile in fourteen minutes.

'A curious exhilaration came over me. It was a lovely moonlight night. The lights of Calais were receding in the distance and the great flash of Cape Grisnes was blinking on my left,' Cody recalled afterwards in a long conversation with Harper in the *Daily Mail*. Soon he was making even better progress. 'Then came a sudden squall. Old Faithful, whom I could clearly see in the bright moonlight, moved up higher blotting out the loftier stars and uncovering the lower ones. At the same time the pull on the line became terrific,' he recalled. 'The *Lela* was making good progress and this was really the fastest part of my voyage, six or eight miles an hour being maintained for an hour and a quarter.'

Cody's first problem came halfway across the Channel near the treacherous Goodwin Sands. As the wind dropped he began drifting backwards. 'My next glance round gave me rather a shock,' he continued. 'I was drifting fast in the direction of the South Goodwin light and behind were the terrible sands which experienced seamen had impressed upon me were so much to be dreaded.'

Then his kite began falling rapidly, forcing him to haul it into the boat. 'The boat was twelve feet long and the kite fifteen feet wide. How was I to dispose of it?' he said. 'I finally got out of my canvas cockpit and stood balancing on the gunwales. As the boat pitched and tossed in the sea, I was swung from side to side, gripping the foremast and time after time missed capsize by a fraction of an inch.'

Eventually, Cody claims, he steadied the boat by lashing the kite to the mast. Later, the boat becalmed, he climbed back inside his cockpit to settle down for the night. 'It was very cold, and I shivered violently,' he said. 'The only sounds were the knocking of

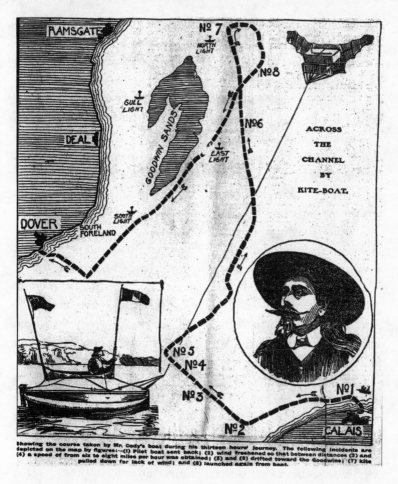

Showing the course taken by Mr. Cody's boat during his thirteen hours' journey. The following incidents are depicted on the map by figures:—(1) Pilot boat sent back; (2) wind freshened so that between distances (3) and (4) a speed of from six to eight miles per hour was obtained; (5) and (6) drifted toward the Goodwins; (7) kite pulled down for lack of wind; and (8) launched again from boat.

the lantern and the swish of a breaking wave. Ships passed at intervals and a school of porpoises began playing around me. As I saw their sharp back fins roll out of the water in the moonlight, I wondered what would be the effect if those same fins came in contact with the canvas side of my tiny vessel?'

After a restless few hours' sleep, Cody awoke to find he had drifted miles to the northeast, as far as the upper part of the Goodwin Sands, within sight of Ramsgate on the Kent coast. His troubles were far from over, however. As the tide changed the coast was suddenly receding. When a gust of wind caught the kite 'an upset seemed inevitable'. Cody hurriedly cast out the kite's line and got Old Faithful airborne. Soon he was back in control and sailing past the southern lightship on the Goodwin Sands, bound for the English coast again. Within minutes, however, he was avoiding a cargo boat, which missed him by 'a close margin of about 40 feet'. 'The force of the waves was so great that the cork fenders round the gunwale of the *Lela* were forced upside down. I cut out the broken water as quickly as possible, just as the dawn broke.'

Soon Cody was heading for Kingsdown and twice began making attempts to land there. 'However, I had told my friends I would make Dover, and Dover it would have to be.'

By 8.30 a.m., with the kite once more lashed to his mast in gentle winds, the sight of the town's famous white cliffs, the Admiralty Pier and the Lord Warden Hotel where he had been staying loomed into view. A crowd met him as he pulled his boat in. His crossing had taken thirteen hours.

Afterwards Cody told the press he had mixed feelings about the success of the trip. 'I have spent £23 on the attempt but against this must be set the 11 shillings fare from Calais to Dover saved by travelling in my own boat,' he joked before adding, 'I hope to try the seagoing qualities in a rough sea and a gale. The wind was so light that this experiment affords no proof of the great speed of which the kite boat is capable.'

In reality, he knew the trip's significance was minor. Cody would often talk of new voyages, even at one point talking of a kite-boat crossing of the Atlantic. None, as far as can be ascertained, took place. Far more valuable were the headlines with which the crossing provided him.

'His adventurous experiences in crossing the Channel . . . proves that there is nothing which the daring of man is unready to attempt,' read a leader column in the *Daily Mail*. 'He deserves and will receive our congratulations upon the pluck and persistency he has displayed in order to demonstrate that the thing can be done.'

Most encouraging of all, for him, was the wider awareness the crossing won for his kites. 'That the passage has been made with success shows that there are some possibilities in the use of kites,' wrote the *Daily Mail* again. Such was the public interest in his exploits he was signed to appear at the London Pavilion Music Hall, where he was to give 'a short lecture on kite navigation, and to relate the experiences of his night trip across the Channel'. 'He will appear with the Boat, Kite, Costume and Appliances, as used in his daring experiment,' the posters promised.

By now the banqueting hall of the Alexandra Palace had become Cody's main theatre of operations. He had taken over the space in May 1903, to cope with the Navy contract. By August, HMS *Majestic* was using its set for wireless communication. With the first, £450 instalment from the Admiralty, Cody had commissioned a splendid new letter heading for himself. Beneath a Buffalo Bill–like portrait and one of his grandest kites, he had printed, 'S.F. Cody: Inventor of the Cody War Kite, As Supplied To the British Navy'. By the end of the year the new look livery was being attached to a familiar-sounding missive.

Three days after Christmas, Cody invited a Balloon Factory representative to watch him demonstrate a new set of signal kites and man-lifters at Alexandra Palace in January. 'I have made many improvements,' he wrote. The letter seems to have gone no further than his old acquaintance, Mr Sclater. This time his reply was as condescending as it was curt. 'It is not proposed to send a representative,' Sclater replied. 'I am, however, to thank you for the trouble you have taken in bringing the matter to notice.'

Overleaf: King of kiting. Cody amidst his creations
at the Alexandra Palace, 1903.

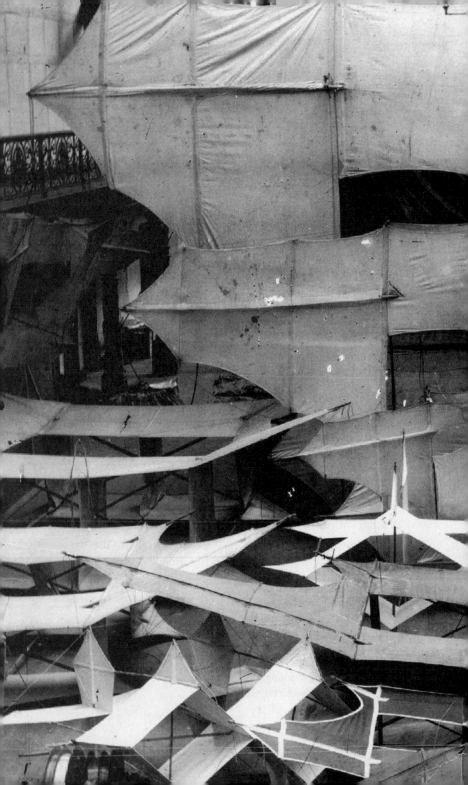

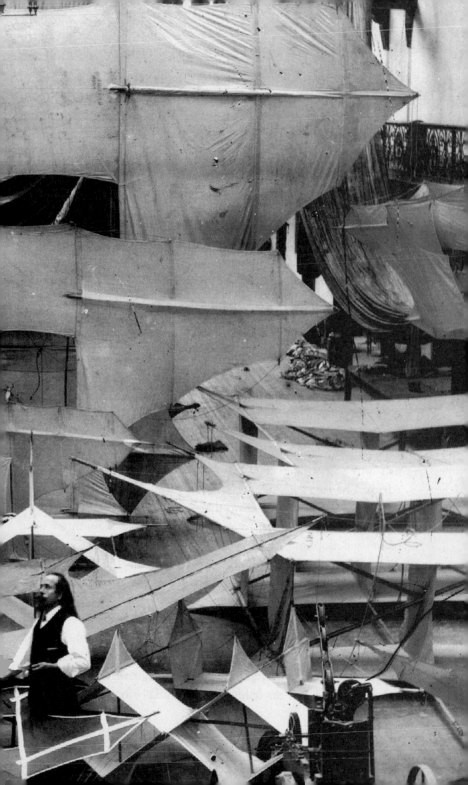

CODY WAS SOON PURSUING ANOTHER AVENUE, HOWEVER. His demonstrations at Whale Island had caught the eye of Lieutenant-General Sir William Butler, the powerful commander of the Western District of the British Army. Somehow Cody had persuaded Butler to provide him with a letter of introduction to Sir John French, commander of the British Army's main garrison, at Aldershot. French too seems to have been taken by Cody, and by the end of April 1904 had deputed one of his senior officers to pursue the possibility of testing his kites formally.

In the last week of April, it was Cody's turn to receive an intriguing letter. 'General Crabbe has shewn me your letter to Sir John French,' it began. 'I would suggest that you send a short description, one or two of the most illustrative of your photographs and a short statement of the conditions under which you are willing to give the show.'

There was even a new, friendlier tone. 'I will do all I can to assist in the matter – and am sorry that the necessary official reference will cause some delay,' it concluded. The note had been signed by a familiar name, JE Capper, Lt Col., RE.

When Cody had met John Edward Capper at Patrick Alexander's balloon centenary celebrations in 1902 the Royal Engineer had only recently returned from a successful campaign in South Africa. The two had met again on 24 June 1903, when they were both inducted as members of the Aeronautical Society. By now Capper had been appointed secretary to the new Committee on Military Ballooning set up by the Government in the wake of the dirigibles' South African successes. He was already earmarked as successor to his old mentor, Templer, as head of the Balloon Factory.

Now in his early forties, Capper had been a twenty-year-old when he had first worked at the prototype balloon establishment Templer had opened at Chatham Docks in Kent. In 1883 the two men had built the first military balloon in England, christened the Sapper. Capper had made his name in India before South Africa, first in the bloody Tirah campaign of 1898, then road and bridge building in Kashmir. During the Boer War his gift for engineering had been used to oversee the fortification of the garrisons at Bloemfontein and Pretoria. His three years had earned him a brevet colonelcy and made him a Companion of the Order of the Bath.

Within a month of sending Capper a brief description of his kites and a few photographs taken at Whale Island, Cody received another encouraging letter. 'I have pleasure in informing you that I am permitted to arrange with you to carry out experiments with your apparatus at your own expense,' he began. Capper clearly knew of Cody's reputation for loose talk. 'You must understand that any expression of views that I may personally give as to the value of your apparatus after testing . . . will be absolutely confidential and for the information solely of the War Office,' he cautioned.

A caricature of Colonel Capper, circa 1907.

Cody arrived at Aldershot at the beginning of June. In personality the moustached, monocle-wearing, cigar-smoking Capper was Cody's polar opposite. A tall, rake-thin authoritarian, he was as impeccably well mannered as he was utterly inscrutable. 'Colonel Capper, strict disciplinarian as he is, is always the acme of politeness conjoined to the smartness of the soldier whose time is valuable,' wrote one who knew him. His gift for diplomacy had provided him with 'the knack of saying a great deal without telling anyone overmuch', he added. They would form the oddest yet most effective of partnerships.

The tests got under way in the second week of June. The inevitable accidents only underlined the work Cody had done in putting his pilot's safety first. On 11 June an ascent with a Lieutenant Holwell hit trouble when the pilot kite was carried away by a sudden gust of wind. As the train of nine kites began spiralling downwards, the soldier's man-carrier began to sink slowly and was hauled 'gently to the ground'. Four days later, a Lieutenant Spaight was left stranded 1,500 feet aloft when stitching in the pilot kite gave way. The train of kites and the man-lifter began spiralling down; the man-lifter broke 100 feet in the air. 'Car and man getting a bit of a bump, but no more than when a balloon comes down rather hard,' reported Capper. Capper was even more impressed by an experiment to see what would happen if cable broke below the man-lifter. A line attached to a ballast-filled man-carrier was let go at 200 feet. 'The kite acted as a parachute and came gently to the ground with the ballast.'

The Klondyke Nugget was playing at the Surrey Theatre in southwest London. Cody was so encouraged by the tests that he announced from the stage that he had 'every confidence' they would at last be adopted by the Army. For once he was not speaking out of turn.

'I cannot speak too strongly as to the excellence of these kites as regards their design and ability to perform what Mr Cody claims for them,' Capper wrote in his report. 'The man-lifting kites will take a man into the air to practically any required height, and will keep him steady there so that he can observe. No other kites that I have read or heard of can approach them in steadiness and security combined with lifting power.'

Capper concluded by recommending that the War Office buy one set of man-lifting and one set of signalling kites. He was also convinced that the Army must sign Cody up forthwith. 'Mr Cody is perhaps the greatest living expert in the art of kite flying, certainly understanding his own kites to an extraordinary degree,' he wrote. 'I recommend that an engagement be made with Mr Cody to act as Instructor to the Balloon Section in kite flying at a salary of £50 per month.'

CAPPER'S VIEW OF CODY WAS PROBABLY NOT SHARED BY the 17,000 people who attended the Bradford Exhibition in Yorkshire that August.

Cody had travelled north to give a man-carrying display at the show. Grounded by a lack of winds during the first few days, he had been persuaded to train a young, local man called Baker to make an ascent. On the day of his flight, however, the winds were gusting up to fifty miles an hour. No sooner had the man-carrying kite been released than the boy was flying upwards at what one eyewitness called 'a terrible rate'. Cody's frantic shouts for him to 'pull the black rope' went unheeded. 'A human being never flew up into the atmosphere so far and so quickly as did this Bradford youth, the whirr and the diminishing size of this human atom alike striking those tens of thousands of onlookers with wondering awe,' wrote the correspondent from the *Leeds Mercury*.

Soon the panic-stricken boy had reached the maximum height. Six hundred feet above them the huge crowds saw the 'kite swooping and diving, and he swinging in huge and eccentric orbits'.

A large group of men charged the windlass and began hauling down the kites manually, badly buckling the main cable in the process. Baker remained in a state of blind panic. When his kite finally dropped to the height of the rooftops he grabbed hold of a chimney stack and jumped to safety.

Tempers remained high for the rest of the afternoon, a furious Cody blaming the boy for ignoring all his earlier instruction. He cancelled his plans for further demonstrations and headed back to London the next morning. Cody swore never to allow an

untrained civilian to take joyrides with him again. As it turned out, he would not need to.

Capper returned from a two-month trip to Chicago and the World's Fair at St Louis, to press harder for Cody's employment by the Army.

Cody had by now submitted the terms under which he was prepared to join up. They were less demanding than those of 1903. He asked that he be paid £500 for supplying a complete man-lifting system and offered two alternatives for the purchase of all patent rights: a one-off payment of £8,000 for all rights or a smaller fee of £5,000 if the government agreed to employ him for twelve years at £600 a year. This time, at least, the authorities were willing to negotiate, albeit at their usual snail's pace. In the interim Cody accepted an initial three-month contract at £55 a month.

Cody had, at last, fulfilled the ambition he had been driving towards for the past four years. As 1905 began, he broke the news to Lela and the children that he intended closing down *The Klondyke Nugget*. He also intended moving the kite works at Alexandra Palace to a new workshop at Sydenham near the Crystal Palace, where they took on a spacious town house nearby.

Leon and Vivian remained his most talented kite makers and were happy to follow him. For Edward, however, it marked the parting of the ways. Instead he remained with his great love, the stage, where he was, by now, performing with his wife Blanche. His flair for melodrama kept him in regular employment for years to come.

C ODY REPORTED FOR DUTY ON 1 FEBRUARY 1905, ARMED with a completed set of man-lifting equipment ready for Capper's inspection. 'I am exceedingly satisfied with the way in which this contract has been carried out,' Capper was soon writing to his superiors. 'I trust you will arrange for early payment to be made.'

His satisfaction grew as the hand-picked corps of men from the Balloon Sections of the Royal Engineers proved willing students of Cody's man-lifting science. There were the mandatory mishaps, of course. In February the seemingly luckless Lieutenant Holwell suffered concussion when the inexperienced sappers lost control of the rig in uneven winds, leaving him to fall heavily from the basket. By April, however, a Sapper Moreton had become such a master of Cody's machine he beat even his instructor's altitude record with a climb of 2,600 feet. 'I do not think anyone connected with the kite is in anyway shy of going up,' Capper wrote.

As negotiations dragged on, Cody's initial three-month contract was extended in May and again in August. In October, Capper pushed for Cody to be given a permanent position. In a memo he wrote,

> I was wrong in thinking, as I originally did, that the use
> of these kites could very quickly be learnt, and that an
> examination of their construction in the air would enable
> any intelligent person to fly them properly. I have had

officers and men under instruction for varying periods from a fortnight to six weeks and there is not one of them who at present is competent to put a flight of these kites in the air with certainty, nor to whom I would trust the responsibility of supervising when men are being lifted from the ground.

Cody was eventually given an extension on his contract for five months, pending the opening of the new Balloon School at a site on nearby Farnborough Common on 1 April the following year. He agreed to postpone discussion of the sale of his patent rights until the Army had a better idea of the kites' true benefit in warfare.

Astride his beloved Bergamo and dressed in Stetson, thigh-high leather boots and Mexican spurs, Cody immediately established himself as a hugely popular personality with the lower ranks. He would perform impromptu displays of horse riding and trickshooting and coach willing volunteers in both.

Inevitably his maverick manner clashed with the rigour of the Royal Engineers' officer class. It was soon clear he was at Aldershot to stay, nevertheless. In August 1905, Capper circulated a memo: 'confidential to all officers of Balloon Companies and Mr Cody'.

The seven-point directive invested Cody with absolute authority in all matters relating to kiting. 'No officer will issue orders whilst Kiting that conflict with those issued by Mr Cody, and no officer will try any new experiment without the previous concurrence of Mr Cody,' he declared. As far as Capper was concerned, the officers' mess would have to learn to live with its new recruit. 'It is expected that all officers of the Balloon Cos. and Mr Cody will endeavour to co-operate cordially,' he wrote.

CHAPTER SEVEN

SECOND TO NONE

IN THE AUTUMN OF 1906, CODY TRAVELLED UP TO LONDON to take collection of his first car, a gleaming Simms-Welbeck open tourer he had spotted in the window of a showroom on the Edgware Road. To the horror of the sales staff, he accepted the keys, then jumped into the driver's seat and rolled straight out into the morning traffic. A friend had bet him £5 that he could not drive the twenty-five miles or so back to Aldershot 'without preliminary practice at the steering wheel'. 'I'm going to do it,' Cody promised his passengers as they bucked and weaved their way home.

'All the way we were grazing carts and brick walls by hair-breadths, but Colonel Cody never turned a hair,' said one, recalling the 'most hazardous and exciting' journey years later. 'He was laughing and joking as he gripped the steering wheel and experimented with the various switches and levers. He had all the light-hearted, boisterous enthusiasm of a child with a new toy who was finding out "how it worked". We did reach Aldershot safely – I don't know how.'

For the next three years the sight and sound of Cody, dressed in a long white dustcoat and flat cap, klaxon blowing, scarf trailing behind him as he tore along the Hampshire country lanes, epitomised the Balloon Factory's frontier spirit. The first private vehicle on camp, the Simms-Welbeck – like its owner – seemed a colourful and clamorous symbol of the Army's march into a new, mechanical age.

'A new toy'. Cody at the wheel of his Simms-Welbeck, 1906.

Cody had John Capper to thank for this new and conspicu-ous affluence. No sooner had he officially succeeded Templer as superintendent of the Balloon Factory, and commandant of the newly formed Balloon School, on 1 April that year, than Capper had confirmed Cody's new, two-year contract as Chief Kite Instructor to both Balloon Sections. Predictably, the contract had been the subject of intense argument between Cody and the War Office. Both sides had dug in: Whitehall refusing to discuss the patent rights, Cody insisting he wanted either £8,000 outright, or £5,000 plus a twelve-year contract at £600 a year. Eventually a clause in his new contract offered negotiations on compensation once he – and his kites – had been in full-time service for a year. As compensation, Cody was given a generous new salary of £1,000 per annum plus 'free forage for a horse' and elevated to the rank of honorary officer. 'Mr Cody's status is that of an officer of his Majesty's Army, though he has no command,' Capper wrote in a memo in September. Cody's travel and expenses allowances were later fixed at the level of a lieutenant.

His new salary allowed Cody to move the family to the village of Mytchett, within a short drive of the new headquarters of the Balloon Sections, at Farnborough. Patrick Alexander had been renting a large house, Pinehurst, from a prominent local family and had agreed to vacate it so that Lela and Cody had a suitable base for their children instead. (Alexander's generosity was based on his certainty that he would be dead by the age of fifty. His inevitable appointment with the bankruptcy courts arrived a few years later when he began pouring cash into his new passion: levitation. 'No record has been left of any success he may have achieved in this field,' wrote a puzzled friend after his death.)

After their years of nomadic wanderings, the oak-panelled house and its large, rambling garden provided Cody, Lela, Leon, Vivian and young Frank with a permanent base, at last. When Lela's eldest daughter Lizzy, or Liese, lost her husband Arthur Whittall in August 1906, she and her four children, Leon, Viva, Leonie and Joyce, joined them there too.

For all its complex origins, Cody and Lela's relationship conformed to the simple values of the Victorian age. Lela's belief in Cody was, if anything, more absolute – and unquestioning – than ever. 'Make your husband your king and your home your world,' she advised young girls in years to come. He returned her support with unfailing devotion and a benign dictatorship.

Beneath the brash, occasionally bullying exterior, Cody seems to have been an avuncular and genuinely loved father and grandfather. Film footage remains of him arriving home to be assailed by his grandchildren. The affection Lela and her children felt towards him was encapsulated in a poem Edward scribbled on the back of an envelope to mark one of his birthdays around this time.

To Frank:

A big rough diamond, whom many scorn,
Who's rough exterior contains a heart so warm,

May you see many a happy year,
Replete with joy, undimmed by tear.
Teddieboy.

Cody quickly ensured that Leon, now twenty-six, and Vivian, twenty-three, were part of the new Farnborough setup. In June, Capper agreed to engage both at a wage of £2 10s. (£2.50) a week. (One can almost hear Cody's voice warning, 'What if the Germans made the boys an offer to build kites for them?') The boys' expertise at the sewing machine quickly proved invaluable as Cody's experiments branched out into challenging new areas that summer.

Capper's ambitious aviation programme was by now divided into three sections, balloons, man-carrying kites and aeroplanes. Cody was set to work in each of them. In early 1906 he began working on a 'motor kite', an adaptation of his bat-winged kites powered by a three-cylinder, twelve-horsepower Buchet engine. The unmanned machine was intended as a stepping stone towards a bigger craft. It was not the first free-flying construction Cody had built. He had brought a 'glider kite' he had constructed at Crystal Palace to be tested at Jubilee Hill near Aldershot the previous summer, 1905. In appearance, at least, the glider was reminiscent of Sureshot Bill and The Flying Machine Mine in Montana. It had a wide wingspan and carried a man in a sling under the main spar. Unlike Bill, Cody built 'er and flew 'er too, achieving glides of up to 240 feet himself. It had been Vivian who had completed the longest glides, however, steering the craft for more than 700 feet. He had come to grief on a turbulent day and fallen from a height of fifty feet or so, badly injuring his back and effectively destroying the glider in the process.

Doubtless with this in mind, Capper had insisted Cody test the passenger-less 'motor kite' by flying it along a wire attached to two posts 200 feet apart. There were successes but Cody found the experiment frustrating. 'It was supposed to be let loose, but the authorities were afraid I might do some damage by letting it go up in the sky,' he confessed two years later.

Cody's ultimate ambitions had been obvious now for more than two years. 'I do not wish to assert that I have produced a flying machine in the full sense of the term but I must confess that I have ambitions in that direction,' he wrote in a sales pamphlet for his 'War Kite' in 1904. 'And I hope at no very distant date to play an important part in the complete conquest of the air.' Persistence may have put him in the right place to achieve his aim. It is doubtful whether he understood the powerful political obstacles that stood in his way.

Capper's rise to what was now the most powerful position within British aviation had been a masterpiece of subtle Machiavellianism. No one had provided more useful leverage than Orville and Wilbur Wright, whom Capper had come to know well in the wake of his visit to the St Louis World's Fair and then Dayton in the autumn of 1904. Like the rest of the world, Capper had been sceptical of the reports of the Wrights' successful flights with a powered flying machine at Kitty Hawk in South Carolina in December 1903. (The news had barely made more than a paragraph or two in the English newspapers.) He left Dayton convinced they had solved the greatest scientific mystery of the age. In the three years since, the pathologically untrusting brothers had come to regard Capper as if he were an endearing English uncle. They called him Jack; his wife Edith exchanged pot plants with their sister Katherine; they seem to have been sure he would deliver them a deal with the British Government, to whom they had turned in the face of their own authorities' coolness towards their work. Unknown to the brothers, however, their trusted friend had by now become the most influential advocate against their cause. Like Cody's, the Wrights' genius seems not to have extended to doing business. Their first quote to the British proposed a formula by which the cost of the plane would depend on the number of miles travelled in a test trial. They had also refused to let an American-based officer, a Colonel Foster, see the plane flying in advance of any contract being struck. 'I am inclined to think that the sum asked will be too great for acceptance and that we must do our utmost to build successful machines ourselves and learn their use,' Capper had concluded in his submission to his overlords at the War Office.

A second attempt at negotiating a sale had got under way that autumn, with the Wrights' price now fixed at £20,000. By now, however, Capper was even more set against doing business with Orville and Wilbur. Asked for his opinion, he said their price was 'entirely out of all proportion to the benefits to be gained'.

His motives were a mix of the patriotic, the professional and, it seems safe to guess, the intensely personal. As a patriot Capper was more determined than anyone that Britain should lead the way in the conquest of the air. 'It seems to me it is rather bad for us to allow the Americans to lead us in that direction,' he told the Aeronautical Association of Great Britain in December 1904. As a professional soldier in the most cost-conscious of armies, he also knew his superiors would not thank him for spending a fortune on technology that could easily be equalled and overtaken at any time. On a personal level, there is reason to believe Capper sensed some glory for himself. By the summer of 1906 he had built his hopes around the Englishman he was convinced would lead Britain into the air age.

Unlike Cody and the Wrights, John William Dunne was one of Capper's kind. The son of the distinguished General Sir John Hart Dunne, he had been invalided home from South Africa suffering from a combination of malaria and heart problems. An intense and enigmatic young man, Dunne had turned to building gliders. His experiments had been helped by influential family friends like the writer HG Wells, whose garden he used for tests. On a recommendation from a senior member of the Royal Engineers, Colonel John Winn, Capper had installed him at the Balloon Factory in June 1906, within a few weeks of taking over as superintendent.

No one at Farnborough could have been in any doubt whom Capper wished to see in the air first. The Royal Engineers, to whom the Balloon School was still attached, had granted £600 for experimental gliders in June 1906. While Cody seems to have been confined to his tethered gliders, Dunne was set free to work on the construction of his prototype aeroplane, the D.1. As he continued to advise against doing business with the Wrights, Capper banged the drum for Dunne's design. 'I have little doubt that we shall be able, thanks partially to the scientific attainments and ability of Lieutenant Dunne, to turn out within reasonable time a Flying Machine on much the same lines as that of the Wright Brothers, but we hope superior to it in several essentials, at an infinite fraction of the cost demanded by them,' he wrote in September 1906.

In December 1906, Capper ordered Cody to travel to Paris. He was to attend the Paris Motor Show, where he was authorised to spend up to £550 on 'a really good engine which if practicable you will bring back with you'. When Cody arrived back at Aldershot with a new, four-cylinder Antoinette engine, the purchase proved less of a bargain than it appeared, mainly because it was almost impossible to start. Cody modified the engine by fitting a spoked wheel for starting. He seems to have been the only man capable of generating enough force to turn the wheel sharply enough to fire the magneto. 'Mr Cody was one of the strongest men I have ever seen,' recalled the Balloon Factory workshop's long-serving superintendent, PE Crosson, years later. 'He was the only man who could turn the heavy engine over at a sufficient speed to get a spark.' When it came to controlling the direction of his work, however, Cody was powerless.

Cody had almost certainly believed the engine was to be used for the purposes of the powered aeroplane he was already planning. Instead the engine was soon being requisitioned for a different purpose: the completion of Britain's first powered airship.

Colonel Templer's earliest efforts to construct a rigid airship had floundered for a variety of political and financial reasons, not least the prohibitive cost of the goldbeater's skin he would have needed for the airship's envelope. (One of Cody's workers calculated that to cover the 15,000 square feet balloon required the stomach linings of 200,000 cattle.)

By early 1907, however, news had reached Aldershot that a new German airship, the Zeppelin LZIII, was nearing completion in Friedrichshafen. The French were also making progress with their own giant dirigible, *La Patrie*. Capper was ordered to begin an immediate response. Cody, despite his belief that balloons offered a road down an aviating cul-de-sac, was enlisted to act as his chief engineer.

In common with every other project at Farnborough, his work on the airship was shrouded in a veil of secrecy. During the first nine months of 1907, Cody maintained the monastic silence Capper demanded of him. His contribution to the ship, by now named the *Nulli Secundus*, (or 'Second to None' in Latin), was crucial. Using all his expertise, he integrated the Antoinette into a propeller-based propulsion system, then designed its complicated configurations of wings and ailerons.

In the grip of a great idea, Cody became a difficult man to live with. He would frequently sleep in his workshop. In the middle of dinner at Pinehurst, he would push his plate to one side, then start scribbling drawings on napkins, tablecloths or whatever scraps of paper he could find.

As the summer of 1907 wore on Cody became a distant figure once more, spending long nights at the airship shed, handcrafting each component on his lathe, then fixing them in place on the vast, 15,000-cubic-foot airship taking shape there.

By the morning of 9 September, as the front page of the *Observer* revealed, he and Capper were ready to unveil the results of

'An officer of his Majesty's army.' Balloon Factory officers assist
Cody with his 'motor kite', 1907.

his hard work. The headline read: 'WAR BALLOON – ALL IN READI-
NESS AT ALDERSHOT – PROBABLE TRIAL THIS MORNING'.

As the huge metal doors of the airship hangar were opened,
the vast shape of what was officially known as the British Army
Dirigible No. 1 emerged with Capper, Cody and Farnborough's
chief balloon instructor Captain King in its passenger basket, or
nacelle. With Capper at the controls and Cody overseeing the
engine, the ship floated up to 800 feet and performed two circles
of Farnborough Common, covering three miles in twenty minutes. The trip came to a premature end when one of the engine's
leather belts snapped. Yet the *Nulli Secundus*'s first outing was
acclaimed an immediate triumph. 'Undoubtedly the airship is at
least the equal to any of its competitors,' thundered *The Times*
patriotically, if misleadingly.

Free at last to talk to the press, Cody pronounced the flight 'a
big success'. 'To bring an airship right out of the workshop and
successfully navigate it through the air is certainly no small
accomplishment,' he said before adding, 'We do not pretend, however, to be perfect yet. We shall go right on improving this branch
of the service until the British Army will be in the first rank so far
as military airships are concerned.'

Typically he made no secret of his contribution. 'The entire power-production section of the airship is of my design, and a great deal of it was made at the forge, lathe and bench with my own hands,' he explained. 'I designed all the aeroplanes or wings by which the ship was steered.'

I N THE MESS ROOMS AND PUBS OF ALDERSHOT, THE SAPPERS rarely referred to the great airship in the Latin. They preferred the more Anglo-Saxon 'Saveloy The First'. Soon even they were forced to pay it a little respect.

For all the patriotic fervour that had greeted their first trip, Capper and Cody were all too aware that the *Nulli Secundus* was far from the equal of its competitors. In July *La Patrie* had made a circular journey of forty miles from the French aviation establishment at Chalais-Maudon, averaging an impressive speed of twenty-two miles per hour. In the first week of October news arrived from Germany of an even more spectacular flight, in which Count Zeppelin had taken his airship on a nine-and-a-quarter-hour, 200-mile circuit of Lake Constance. In a moment of uncharacteristic impulse, Capper decided to respond.

At 10.30 on the morning of 10 October 1907, the *Nulli Secundus* was eased out from its hangar once more, this time with only Capper and Cody on board. On a breezy morning they were soon aloft and making progress northeast at a rate of twenty-five miles per hour. Capper was in his uniform, Cody in his white dustcoat. At around 10.50 a.m., as they passed over Pinehurst, Cody sounded the klaxon he had brought with him. 'I'll be home in time for supper,' he shouted as Lela and the children waved to him from the garden below.

The sight of Cody sailing overhead had a profound effect on Lela's young grandchildren in particular. From then on they would refer to the setting sun as 'Grandpa's red balloon'.

A squad of seven sappers followed underneath in Cody's car. Capper's plans became clear when, approaching Brentford on the

THE SPHERE

AN ILLUSTRATED NEWSPAPER FOR THE HOME

Volume XXXI. No. 403. {REGISTERED AT THE GENERAL POST OFFICE AS A NEWSPAPER} London, October 12, 1907. {WITH SUPPLEMENT} Price Sixpence.

THE BRITISH MILITARY AIRSHIP, "NULLI SECUNDUS," ROUNDING ST. PAUL'S

DRAWN BY CHARLES WYLLIE

western fringes of London, he let a message streamer drop in the car's path. 'We shall enter London and attempt to circle St Paul's. Keep close, in case of emergency,' the note read.

The driver's job became even more difficult as the noise of the airship drew thousands upon thousands of Londoners out into the streets. On the green at Shepherd's Bush, three children were crushed as a multitude fought for the best views.

During a royal visit to the Balloon Factory, Capper had promised King Edward that he would end the airship's first voyage to London with a landing in the gardens of Buckingham Palace. As it hovered over the house at the end of the Mall, the cheering crowds assumed the dipping of the *Nulli Secundus's* nose was an act of deference on the part of the pilots. In reality it signalled the final lurch of their unsuccessful attempt at landing in the King's courtyard. Instead Capper and Cody pressed on towards St Paul's.

As they cruised over Whitehall several members of the Army Council – including the notably anti-aviation Chief of General Staff, General Sir William Nicholson – climbed on to the rooftops to wave white handkerchiefs in a salute. While Capper stood ramrod straight, Cody simply smiled, waved his hat and carried on blaring his klaxon.

The climax of the trip came as the *Nulli Secundus* reached St Paul's Cathedral at around 12.20 p.m. As the ship circled the great basilica of London's tallest building, then turned homeward, however, it ran into a strong easterly headwind. Realising they would be able to make little progress back towards Aldershot, Capper and Cody headed first for an overcrowded Clapham Common and then the less congested – and to Cody, at least, familiar – space of Crystal Palace. Shortly after 2 p.m., the *Nulli Secundus* eased itself down on to the park's cycle track, where its pilots were met by the sappers in Cody's car. It had been in the air for three hours and twenty minutes and had travelled a total distance of around fifty miles. Every British aviation record was theirs.

'We have got a decent, slow-speed airship, which we can navigate if the wind is not too strong,' a modest Capper told the scramble of reporters at the Crystal Palace afterwards, a cigar on the go. The British public could not share his restraint, however. The flight of the *Nulli Secundus* marked a turning point in the public perception of aviation in Britain.

Second to None.

TO THE CREW OF THE "NULLI SECUNDUS."

(With apologies to Mr. Rudyard Kipling.)

We sent our Liners over the sea,
    And our railways o'er the plain ;
And then on our laurels rested we,
    But you dreamed of a new domain.
Who bounds his quest by north, east, west,
    Has left the task undone ;
Oh, if grit is the price of Admiralty,
    You shall be second to none !

Ye are the sons of a roving race,
    And the air is your last new love.
North, south, east, west, we crowd all space,
    But there's room "at the top of above" !
So you built a ship for a trial trip,
    Whilst the fatuous world made fun,
And if toil is the price of Admiralty,
    You shall be second to none.

To make the ruler of the wave
    Of air the suzerain,
To patient toil your minds you gave,
    You tried and tried again.
On luck deferred your hope you spurred—
    Success was failure's son,
And if pluck is the price of Admiralty,
    You shall be second to none !

              DENIS DUVAL.

'Sons of a roving race'.
Cody and Capper in the gondola
of the Nulli Secundis at Crystal
Palace, October 1907.

Over the following days front pages were devoted to photographs and artists' impressions of the historic moment when the ship circled around St Paul's. Editorials eulogised the dawning of a new aerial age. 'There were crowds in every street gazing wide-eyed and open-mouthed up into the sky,' read the one in the *Daily Mirror*. 'It only needed a little imagination to suppose that sausage-shaped marvel the advanced guard of a Martian invasion. Here was the dream of Jules Verne and of Tennyson come true. Fact has gone one better than Fiction.'

Capper found himself thrust into an unfamiliar light. 'Some men climb slowly into greatness; others leap into it,' began one of the many profiles on the so-called First Admiral of the Blue that were soon filling newspapers and magazines. 'Colonel JE Capper, C.B. . . . leapt into fame at the rate of a thousand feet per second.' Cody too was lionised, this time for keeping his mouth closed for once.

'Colonel Capper and his assistants must be warmly congratulated on having (as the Americans say) "shot no hot air" in advance,' said the *Daily Mirror* in an editorial to accompany its front-page story. 'In these days of babble and brag their self-control deserves the highest commendation. They have followed the traditional British plan of letting deeds speak for themselves.'

Their moment of triumph proved short-lived, however. Capper had allowed the *Nulli Secundus* to remain inflated and tethered to the grounds at Crystal Palace, watched over only by a team of six sappers. Clearly intending to make a return trip to Aldershot, he ordered new supplies of hydrogen to be ferried over from the Balloon Factory. Over the next three days, however, the balloon was hit by almost constant wind and rain. Cody got the engines going on the Wednesday but, by now, the balloon's envelope was too saturated with water to float properly. Rather than deflating and dismantling the airship, Capper insisted on trying again the following day. Early the next morning, with the sappers at breakfast, a severe wind hit the nose of the *Nulli Secundus*, ripping the airship free from almost all of its moorings. By the time the soldiers arrived the ship was flailing around in the winds and on the verge of breaking loose completely. Only the quick thinking of a Corporal Ramsay prevented the ship from floating away. He slit the balloon open with a knife attached to a long pole.

While Ramsay was apparently promoted to sergeant the next day for his initiative, Capper was left to explain why he had left the pride of the nation exposed to the elements in such appalling weather conditions. Despite an effective campaign to persuade the public the damage was minimal, the *Nulli Secundus* would never fly again.

Capper's rapid fall from grace was compounded within days. The success of the *Nulli Secundus* had provided a convenient smokescreen for Dunne's aeroplane. In July, the D.1 had been quietly dismantled, packed on to a train and sent 500 miles to a remote piece of land on the estate of an old aristocratic friend of Capper's, the Marquess of Tullibardine, the eldest son of the Duke of Atholl.

Such was the veil of secrecy in which Capper shrouded Dunne's activities that little record remains of the work. It is probably just as well, given the farcical picture that emerges from the skimpy remaining evidence.

Intellectually Dunne was comfortably Cody's superior. He would go on to write a series of semi-mystical books on subjects as diverse as time and fly-fishing. (HG Wells would base some of his later, fictional heroes on his dreamy young friend.) As a pioneer aviator, however, he could not hold a candle to his resilient and inventive rival. 'If he had been a character in one of the books of that great Victorian writer H Rider Haggard, he would almost certainly have been named "He-who-drops-nuts-in-the-long-grass,"' wrote one leading aviation historian, Percy Walker. When Dunne first put his two Buchet engines together he did so with them back to back, and pulling in opposite directions. At one stage he admitted that he often got confused about which direction was east and which was west!

His greatest handicap was his health, however. In the wilds of Scotland he was frequently laid low with fever. With Dunne unfit to fly himself, every available body was enlisted – even Capper's friend the Marquess of Tullibardine, who at one stage agreed to hurl himself off a 2,000-foot cliff in Dunne's gliders. As he got ready to leap, however, the aristocrat spotted a white patch in the distance. When he saw it was his doctor, gravely spreading out a groundsheet and an array of medical instruments, he thought better of the offer.

Capper, it seems, was the most willing pilot. (The suspicion that he had designs on being the first to fly in Britain is irresistible.) He was certainly at the controls when the D.1 was unveiled before a high-level contingent who had travelled to Scotland as the autumn drew on. The party included the Duke of Atholl himself as well as the War Office's powerful Director of Fortifications and Works, Colonel RM Ruck and the Master General of the Ordnance, Colonel CF Hadden. By far the most significant visitor, however, was the Secretary of State for War, the intellectual Richard Burdon Haldane, who had become increasingly intrigued by the work going on at Farnborough and Blair Atholl in particular.

Capper, wrapped in a round, fencing-mask-like helmet, took the glider's controls for the official test. Dunne's launching technique was to mount the V-winged craft on to a trolley, which then ran along a track. As Capper slid down the runway, the glider duly lifted into the air, where it hovered for about eight seconds. Suddenly, however, it started dropping earthwards and clattered into a wall. The sight of the head of the Army's aviation programme emerging from the wreckage, covered in blood and being mollified by his wife, would have profound repercussions for the entire aviation establishment.

It seems another test was carried out with the Buchet engines in place. The result was no better, the plane ending up on its nose in a field. Soon the D.1 was so badly damaged it was not possible to attempt any more flying before the snows came. As with the loss of the *Nulli Secundus*, Capper tried to put a positive spin on matters. 'The result, though to an unskilled eye disastrous, in effect showed that Lieutenant Dunne's calculations were entirely correct, the machine being poised for eight seconds,' he wrote in his official report on 2 November. It was enough to win the project a reprieve, within the War Office, at least.

Dunne's loss was Cody's gain. In the wake of the disasters of the autumn of 1907, it seems that Capper sensed Cody must be given a chance to restore the Balloon School's severely dented reputation. As the year drew to a close, he began working full time on an aeroplane at last.

Dunne aside, Cody's most serious rival was the determined young Englishman Alliott Verdon Roe. At the Brooklands motor-racing circuit in nearby Surrey, Roe was working on a large-scale version of a prizewinning model aeroplane he had constructed two years before. Roe was intensely envious of Cody's facilities, and with good cause. In truth, Cody was in a position that was second to none.

At the Balloon Factory he had access to all the material he needed to build a plane – silk and linen for the wings, bamboo for the struts and framework and wire for the control systems. In Vivian, in particular, he could draw on a growing expertise in fabrics. His friend Patrick Alexander was willing to provide him with the propellers he had by now begun manufacturing. Not only was Cody free to use the huge airship shed that had housed the *Nulli Secundus*, odds and ends from the ill-fated airship were his too.

On top of all this his years of experience with man-lifters provided him with a practical experience none of his rivals could match. If kiting had taught him anything it was that the conquest of the air would be a matter of persistence and experimentation. As he set about constructing a plane in the late months of 1907, Cody sketched out a machine that would allow him to feel his way into the skies.

No one realised it yet, but Cody's design drew heavily on Capper's inside knowledge of Orville and Wilbur Wright's plane, the Wright Flyer. (Intriguingly Capper later asked Dunne to return photographs he had taken of the Wrights' machine. 'They are my personal property,' he wrote.)

The basic configuration was essentially the same as the Wright plane, consisting of forty-foot biplane wings, fitted with a tightening or 'warping' mechanism, a forward elevator to control pitching, a single rear rudder and an engine, driving – through chains – two propellers in counter-rotation to each other.

Cody had, inevitably, added his own touches, making as many elements as possible movable for experimentation purposes. His machine also reflected the unique set of circumstances under which he was working. Capper's specification had demanded a much larger plane than the single-seater the Wrights had built. Cody was instructed to build a plane that could carry two, 170-pound men, maintain a cruising speed of twenty-five miles per hour for an hour and climb to a height of 2,000 feet with a full fuel load. The unforgiving conditions of Farnborough Common played their part in the design too. While the Wrights experimented on the cushioning sands of Kitty Hawk, and the leading

French flyers, Farman and Delagrange, hurled their planes unencumbered around huge *champs de manoeuvre*, Cody had to trundle around on the pitted, tree-lined surface of Farnborough Common. Powerful steel compression springs were attached to the supporting struts. Cody also included bicycle wheels on the wing tips and a unique buffer wheel, a single wheel placed in front of the plane above the ground. The wheel was intended to stop the plane from tipping on its nose on landing and take off and to act as a shock absorber in the event of a collision with earthbound objects. It would prove useful in the months ahead.

As the plane took shape, Cody once more adhered to another of his favourite mottos: 'Work will do it.' He exercised absolute rule in his workshop, did not suffer fools and expected others to work with the same obsessional energy as he did. His blend of bravura, energy and sheer charm usually won his workers over. Such was the devotion he engendered, he seems never to have been short of willing helpers.

As the plane, codenamed British Army Aeroplane No. 1 by Capper, took shape in the early months of 1908, a number of Farnborough wives were recruited to the cause. Their seamstress skills helped produce the vast forty-foot wings of the biplane. (It is unclear whether it was one of the new recruits who discovered the extra strength added by coating the wings in tapioca!)

By the early months of 1908, Cody had produced a machine that he believed was capable of flying. There were still political as well as engineering hurdles to overcome, however.

Cody had been fighting a long and dispiriting battle over his kite patent. His superiors at Aldershot were in no doubt he deserved a reward for an invention that had revolutionised the Balloon Sections. The garrison's command said as much in a letter in the autumn of 1907 recommending a 'gratuity . . . in view of the valuable services he had rendered to the country'. The ultimate seal of approval had come in the autumn of 1907, at the annual meeting of the all-powerful Army Council, where it was decided to include Cody kites 'in the normal equipment of a Balloon company'. In January 1908, Capper had backed this up with a long eulogy in which he praised Cody's kites for 'putting us, in respect to observation, on an equality with, if not in a state of superiority to, other nations'. Apart from anything else, Cody had saved the Army thousands. If the Balloon Sections were called to fight another war, its three companies could travel with two sets of kites each as opposed to the six balloons they had taken into battle in South Africa. With eighteen balloons costing around £5,000 and six sets of kites £1,000, the conclusion was obvious. 'The actual cash saving on the first campaign in which a Balloon company would take part . . . will, I think, prove considerable,' argued Capper. Capper had concluded that Cody 'could not consider himself any way wronged by an immediate cash payment of £3,000 in satisfaction of all his claims, direct and indirect on the Government'. A further, more detailed study by the MP, FD Acland, the Ordnance Council's Finance Member, came up with the same figure. (Acland worked out that, in addition to saving £4,000 in equipment and 'nearly doubling the efficiency of our Balloon equipment', Cody was saving the Balloon Sections £900 in gas and wear and tear each year. He also recommended a payment of £1,105 as compensation for the cost of developing and making his kites.)

By now, however, the War Office were more concerned with making sure Cody was not about to lodge an exorbitant claim for his aeroplane too. He was soon issued with an ultimatum.

Capper wrote to him at the beginning of the month asking that he 'place in writing your notification that you understand that the experiments, if successful, will give you no further claim to reward than would be the case with an officer of the Regular Army'. When Cody deliberately stalled, pressing instead for an answer of compensation for his kite first, Capper spelled out the position in the clearest terms possible. 'I have the honour to point out to you officially, that I am not authorised to allow this machine to be completed except under the terms stated,' he wrote on 8 April. He had no choice but to write back to Capper agreeing to the terms.

Cody soon had cause to curse the Army hierarchy again. By now ready to begin installing an engine, Cody had expected to be able to use the Antoinette from the *Nulli Secundus*. Unfortunately, Capper's dream of a great airship had been reborn and work on a *Nulli Secundus* Mark II was suddenly given top priority at the Balloon Factory. In May 1908, within weeks of being ready to start trials with his aeroplane, Cody was forced to move from the old airship shed to another, less well equipped, shed.

Cody's mood changed as he took delivery of a new Antoinette engine from France in late July. At the end of the month he told newspapermen that he had 'perfected' his aeroplane. 'Mr Cody is not only a skilled mechanician but a superbly daring aeronaut. His friends are seeking to lay money that the Cody will fly this month, and to a greater distance and a far higher altitude than has ever before been attempted,' one newspaper was soon reporting. His optimism proved fleeting once more. On the morning of 9 August 1908, Cody – like every other aspirant airman in Europe – came crashing back to reality.

At around 6.30 the previous evening, at the Les Hunaudieres racetrack at Le Mans, in France, the lean, sober-suited figure of Wilbur Wright had climbed into the cockpit of the 'Wright Flyer', set off on a short, powered run and eased his plane into the air. At first it appeared the flight would be a disaster. The aristocratic French crowd had let out screams of panic as the plane headed straight for a line of trees at the end of the arena. Their shouts had turned into roars of approval as Wilbur effortlessly banked his plane sharply in a turn, then straightened out and swept down the other side of the oval racetrack. As relaxed as if he were out on a Sunday morning bicycle ride, he had continued in the same vein for a minute and three quarters before, with the most immaculate timing of all, flopping his machine gently back on the ground.

France had grown used to the sight of its great pioneers – first the Brazilian Santos-Dumont, then the homegrown Delagrange, Bleriot and Farman – stuttering and staggering their way into the skies in their cumbersome machines. Turns of any kind were achieved in open country and over a distance of hundreds of yards. In comparison, Wright's performance was a miracle.

In the five years since reports of their first flights at Kitty Hawk, the brothers had been called charlatans, hoaxers, even 'clever acrobats'. That evening France's aerial fraternity took back every withering word. '*Nous sommes battus,*' the great Delagrange told *Le Matin*. ('We are beaten.')

The news flew across the Channel. 'The scoffer and the sceptic are confounded. Mr Wilbur Wright last evening made the most marvellous aeroplane flight ever witnessed on this side of the Atlantic,' reported Lord Northcliffe's *Daily Mail* on 10 August. 'A bird could not have shown more complete mastery of flight.' 'Mr Wilbur Wright is the hero of the hour,' the *Daily Telegraph* proclaimed. 'The superiority of his machine over other aeroplanes becomes more and more apparent. Anyone who has seen M Delagrange, Mr Farman, M Santos Dumont, M Bleriot, and others practise with their machines . . . will at once see the immense superiority of the Wright method . . . It is no wonder . . . that such experts as M Delagrange . . . admit they have been beaten by the Wrights.'

Cody had no time for such defeatism, however. 'Show me the pictures,' he boomed as he ran into the newsroom of the *Daily Mirror* in London the following Monday morning. He was soon scouring every print for hints on how to improve his own fledgling flyer.

CHAPTER EIGHT

ACROSS THE GREENSWARD

NOT EVERYONE IN ENGLAND APPRECIATED THE BEAUTY of Wilbur Wright's timing. Only a fortnight before the flight at Les Hunaudieres, Britain's War Office had imperiously dismissed the dangers of a new air age. 'The military authorities have had experts employed in watching the flights of the various airships and aeroplanes and the impression is that for a long time to come there is nothing to be feared from them,' declared Sir William Nicholson in an official communiqué.

Within ten weeks, Nicholson was taking his place alongside an assortment of military leaders and Cabinet Ministers at the first meeting of a special Imperial Defence Committee on Aerial Navigation hastily convened by Prime Minister Asquith. 'Can they set towns on fire?' the Liberal leader, David Lloyd George, asked, terrified, like everyone else in Britain, by French talk of dropping petrol bombs from nimble fleets of Wright-style aeroplanes. He, Nicholson and the committee looked ashen as an expert witness nodded: 'Yes.'

The Wright Flyer's sensational performance came, if anything, at an even less opportune moment for Colonel Capper. Only the previous month he had stymied the Wrights' hopes of selling the plane to the British for a third time by contriving a near impossible list of 'requirements' the plane would need to meet. 'They ask only that an applicant should jump over the moon! through a hoop!! six times!!!' fumed the brothers' father, Bishop Wright, in a letter. As Wilbur continued to thrill French crowds, questions were already being asked about why Britain had made no attempt to purchase the Wright machine.

Cody was left ruing the sequence of events more than anyone, however. The aviation-obsessed Lord Northcliffe had, as usual, caught the public mood best in his newspaper, the *Daily Mail*. 'The one note of regret in all this advance and activity is that so little is being done in England,' wrote RP Hearne, regurgitating the views of his proprietor. 'So far not a single successful aeroplane has been flown in the United Kingdom. We are painfully backward in every branch of aerial navigation; and yet for naval and military reasons it is most essential that we should lead the world in the new science.' As he scanned the newspaper pictures and reports of the Wright flight, Cody knew he and his machine were within touching distance of providing the response the British public now demanded. To his frustration, events had conspired to ensure he would spend the first months after Le Mans everywhere but in his aeroplane shed.

Cody spent the rest of the week of 10 October helping Capper with the troubled *Nulli Secundus II*. Teething problems had set in after the airship's maiden voyage on 24 July. Cody joined Capper in the nacelle for brief flights twice, on Friday, 14 September, and again on Saturday the 15th, but could do little to change the ship's luck. The first trip lasted fifteen minutes before a fuel pipe burst, spewing petrol all over the crew. The second lasted little longer. This time, with the squally winds tossing the ship around like a toy, it was the turn of a water pipe to break. A propeller and two rudders were damaged on the descent when the ship was hit by a sudden blast of wind. Within a week or so Capper had ordered the balloon envelope deflated and the *Nulli Secundus II* was quietly consigned to history.

By then, however, Cody was involved in an even more distracting duty. On 17 August, the Monday morning after the final flight of the *Nulli Secundus II*, he jumped in his car and headed down the A3 to Portsmouth and Whale Island. Five years after he had first demonstrated his kites, a new, more rigorous set of tests had been requested by the Admiralty. Still the Army's official Kite Instructor, Cody had been ordered by Capper and Aldershot command to spend the best part of a month at the Admiralty's beck and call. The Navy's renewed interest had been sparked by the 1904–5 war between Russia and Japan and the lethal success of both sides' mine-laying submarines. While the kites would also be tested for their suitability for general observation, spotting gunfire, signalling and photography, the Navy's main interest lay in knowing whether Cody could spot submerged objects from the air. After a relatively uneventful – and inconclusive – first fortnight, disaster struck on Monday, 31 August. Around 800 feet in the air, a freakish wind set Cody and his man-carrier in a vicious downward spiral. The official observer of the tests, a Lieutenant Usborne, described how Cody hit the water at potentially lethal speed. 'The carrier kite struck the water at about the speed a man acquires when diving from a height of 20–30 feet. The car turned over when it struck the water and Mr Cody dived out and then held on to the car which supported him,' he recorded. Usborne's claim that Cody was 'none the worse for wear' is hardly borne out by the fact that Cody insisted on heading home to Lela that night rather than spending the night in Portsmouth. (In its understanding way, the Navy later deducted fifteen shillings (75 pence) for a night's subsistence from his expenses.) Cody completed the first phase of the tests on Friday, 5 September, and headed straight back to Farnborough and Army Aeroplane No. 1.

I N THE THREE-WEEK HIATUS IN THE ADMIRALTY TESTS, FINAL work had begun on improving the Antoinette engine and the crude, V-shaped cooling radiators Cody had had built earlier in the summer.

Cody knew the pressure was now on. Despite managing a short 'hop' of between seventy-five and a hundred yards at Brooklands in June, AV Roe was struggling against a lack of resources. The race to be the first man to fly in Britain had developed in a straight shoot-out between Cody and Dunne.

Ten months after his disastrous last outing, Capper's favoured candidate had returned to the Highlands and Blair Atholl with two new machines, his V-winged Dunne D.3 glider and the powered version, the Dunne D.4. The first phase of his testing in the Highlands would involve the glider. The powered plane would take precedence when work on the engine and the undercarriage was completed at Farnborough. At Blair Atholl, Dunne had many advantages, not least secrecy and the ability to concentrate totally on his plane. Cody's almost demonic drive remained the supreme asset, however.

A note written by the ethereal Dunne in his diary on Saturday, 19 September 1908, summed up the difference. 'Could have had her out today but on arrival I found that the runners had collapsed. Worked till 4.30 pm strengthening them. The wind had died away altogether by this time so I knocked off work,' he wrote. While Dunne enjoyed the civilised surroundings of Blair Atholl Castle, three hundred miles away, his rival worked on into the evening. Shortly before the sun faded that evening, the results of Cody's round-the-clock endeavour were being wheeled as quietly as possible out into the early autumn air.

Drawn by a team of horses and accompanied by a small detachment of sappers, Cody and the boys led Army Aeroplane No. 1 to a clearing called Jersey Brow. Cody was at this stage interested only in testing the engine and its ability to propel the plane along the ground. The huge, throaty roar the machine generated as the engine was started up drew pockets of locals on to the common nevertheless. If the Wright Flyer was aviation's perfect first-born child, Army Aeroplane No. 1 was its bigger, clumsier, ugly-duckling sister. With its unfeasibly wide wingspan and convoluted engine arrangement, it made an ungainly sight as it bumped and bounced its way across the uneven Farnborough ground. As its engines were started up and Leon, Vivian and the sappers helped push Cody off, however, its qualities shone through. Cody guided the plane about a quarter of a mile before bringing it to a halt. He pronounced the test a success, returned the plane to the sheds for the night, then spent the Sunday making further adjustments.

Cody returned to the controls of the plane again on Monday, when it was taken on to Farnborough Common. Cody's main interest this time was in testing the plane's balance at speed. Gathering up to thirty miles per hour, Cody later claimed, he lifted the wheels momentarily off the ground. The main discovery of the test was that the machine was 'nose heavy', with too much weight loaded on to the front. As he headed back towards the Balloon Factory, however, he received his first setback. Within sight of the shed, Cody misjudged the width of his wing, the right-hand aileron hit a post, and the plane swung suddenly around, hitting a mounted policeman as it did so. Neither the plane nor the policeman was damaged by the experience. The press jumped on the mishap nevertheless.

Newspapermen had been positioning themselves around the vast open spaces of Farnborough Common for days. Even the brief reports on the first trial had been presented as a failure by some papers. 'A secret trial of a mechanically propelled aeroplane built at the war balloon factory at Farnborough was made recently, and proved a failure, the machine failing to rise from the ground,' wrote the *Yorkshire Post* after Cody's first outing on the Saturday.

The same paper seized on the second trial with even more glee. 'It now appears that a further trial was made with disastrous results,' the *Post* reported in a long and overblown account of what was in reality the most minor of setbacks. Elsewhere there were jibes at Britain's 'grasshopper airman' and his 'mowing machine'.

This time the press's animosity was directed at Capper as much as Cody.

Two days before Cody had made his first trial run, Capper had written a circular to all the country's leading newspapers and agencies asking that they 'refrain from publishing anything' on the forthcoming trials. 'No attempt will be made to fly in the initial experiments but if the press should publish information that the experiments are taking place, or are about to take place, the experiments will inevitably be greatly interfered with by the crowd, and there will be constant fear of damage to someone.'

His request was as unreasonable as it was unrealistic. While his protégé Dunne was able to conduct his tests far from the public gaze, Cody's trials were taking place on common land that was open to the public at all times. With Dunne approaching the stage where he would test his own engine-powered craft, the suspicion that there were more sinister forces at work is hard to ignore.

While most newspapers grudgingly went along with Capper, many took his heavy-handedness as their cue to redouble their efforts to follow events at Farnborough. Even the venerable Thunderer of Fleet Street, *The Times*, was by now intrigued by the unfolding events and had a man permanently posted at Farnborough. Three days after the accident, its correspondent saw Cody guide the plane out for a third trial, this time on Laffan's Plain, a large stretch of open land, a mile and a half or so from the Balloon Factory buildings. Despite the severe bumpiness of the ground, Cody succeeded in making three runs of between a half and three-quarters of a mile each in the morning and afternoon. 'No attempt was made to rise from the ground,' *The Times* man wrote in his daily dispatch that evening. He thought the trials 'were made at a very fair pace' even so.

In reality, Cody was still feeling his way into the air. For the next set of trials on Monday, 28 September, he tried the plane with a much smaller version of the triangular-shaped 'fantail' he had added at the rear. The modification proved an instant success. As he made his final run before returning to Whale Island, the plane left the ground for the first time.

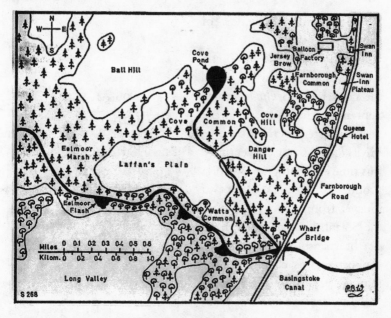

Farnborough Common, 1908-1909.

After a series of runs of between a quarter and half a mile, witnesses described how during the final run back towards the factory 'the wheels of the machine lifted clear of the ground'. Cody himself seems to have been unaware of what exactly had happened. 'Mr Cody declared that during his last trip for something like a hundred yards there was an entire absence of vibration, and he surmised, therefore, that the aeroplane must have lifted,' the *Times* team reported the next day. When Cody and his helpers returned to the scene they discovered a gap in the tyre tracks of seventy-eight yards. Cody presented a philosophical face to the press afterwards. 'Mr Cody, however, attached no importance to the circumstances, which he said was, after all, only a jump.' Cody knew a powered jump was all AV Roe had achieved in his tests in June. To those who did not understand what was going on, however, the distinction was lost. One newspaper talked of the 'futility of placing untried aeroplanes in the hands of beginners'.

Cody returned to Portsmouth to set to sea on board the cruiser HMS *Grafton* on 30 September. Later in the week he transferred to the destroyer HMS *Recruit*. Cody concentrated this time on photographic work, producing a remarkable set of images from 1,000 feet above the Solent. Unfortunately, none of the snapshots offered much support for his claims that the man-carriers would allow the Navy to detect underwater objects like submarines and mines from the air.

He returned to Farnborough on 7 October to inspect

Triangular fantail

Rear rudder

Single tail wheel

British Army Aeroplane No.1
© John Roberts

the extensive modifications under way. By now Cody knew the first bona fide flight in Britain was within his sights. His optimism would have been increased by the snippets of news he would undoubtedly have gleaned from Blair Atholl.

Dunne had made good progress with his glider. As early as 20 September, his pilot, a Royal Artillery lieutenant, Launcelot Gibbs, pulled off twenty 'short, soaring glides'. 'She was very stable,' Dunne wrote of his machine in his diary. His REP engine, however, remained at Farnborough, where it had proven unreliable and incapable of generating much thrust. 'We have had a good deal of trouble with it, and it certainly will not last long,' Capper wrote to Dunne on the day after Cody's reappearance, 8 October.

Cody's technical problems were, in comparison, minor. His biggest cause for concern had been the fact that his bulky, V-

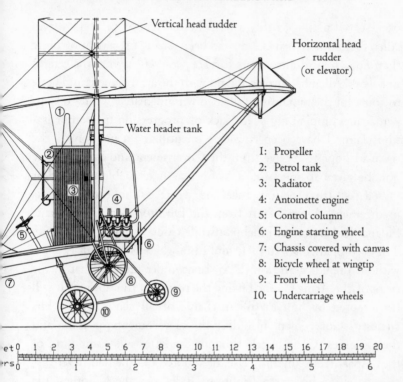

Vertical head rudder

Horizontal head
rudder
(or elevator)

Water header tank

1: Propeller
2: Petrol tank
3: Radiator
4: Antoinette engine
5: Control column
6: Engine starting wheel
7: Chassis covered with canvas
8: Bicycle wheel at wingtip
9: Front wheel
10: Undercarriage wheels

shaped engine-cooling radiators had badly obstructed his view during the September trials. By now they had been shifted from their original position in front of him on to the outboards of the wings. He had also asked that the wing-tip ailerons he had installed be removed. He had decided that his 'top rudder' would be his sole means of controlling the plane's roll. The troubles clouding his life away from the aeroplane shed only added to his motivation.

To Cody's irritation, Capper had issued orders that he should not attempt a full flight until the military hierarchy had been notified. The edict only added insult to the injury heaped on him in recent days.

On 21 September, before returning to Portsmouth, Cody had

been served with a writ by a Manchester firm of printers, David Allen & Sons. For years Cody had been paying off a debt of more than £900 for colour posters for *The Klondyke Nugget* at the rate of £1 a week. Allen had grown fed up with the arrangement and gone to court for the remaining £580. Cody immediately wrote to Capper, again complaining at the lack of progress on his compensation claim. 'I have been counting on utilizing a portion of the reward I hope to receive from the Government and I trust I may now be given so much of it at once as may enable me to clear myself of this encumbrance,' he wrote as he explained his predicament. A £500 draft from the Director General of Army Finance had arrived at Pinehurst while Cody was at Whale Island. The accompanying letter left him fuming. 'This payment is made without prejudice and on the distinct understanding that in the event of the Army Council fixing the reward at this amount it will be accepted by him in full discharge of all claim against His Majesty's Government including the Governments of India and the Colonies.' Cody clearly thought the letter was some kind of trap. Apart from anything else, he pointed out, he had never discussed selling his patent rights to India and the Colonies! He wrote back immediately demanding a personal appointment at the War Office. 'The question of this reward is of such importance to me, that I would ask, in justice to myself, to be allowed to place my claim direct before the high officials who deal with these matters,' he concluded in his letter of 10 October. He enclosed the £500 draft in the envelope with it.

CODY RESUMED TESTING ON THE MORNING OF 14 OCTOBER with a series of successful if unspectacular runs with his modified machine. Cody was, by now, placing more and more emphasis on the curvature of his wings. It is unlikely he understood the science as well as the Wright Brothers, by now the world's leading authorities on wing-warping and its crucial place in flight theory. As a prototype test pilot, however, Cody possessed a combination of instinct, experience and sheer courage that made him Orville and Wilbur's equal.

Cody now understood that by increasing the curvature of the wings the nose of the plane tended to be forced downwards and vice versa. By the afternoon he had guessed that by reducing the convexity by one-third, from four and a half to three inches, he could achieve huge improvements in the lifting ability.

Sure enough the third trial of the day saw the plane lift into the air once more. 'The aeroplane suddenly sprang into the air, and soared a distance of about sixty yards well above the heads of the spectators, nine or ten feet from the ground,' wrote one observer. 'The machine maintained its equilibrium perfectly and took the ground again without any perceptible jolt.'

Cody still regarded these as 'only jumps' and spent the next day Thursday, 15 October, back in the airship shed overhauling the plane and paying special attention to what he now called the 'curves'. The day proved significant for other reasons. That morning the *Daily Mirror* published the first fuzzy images of the Army's new secret weapon. 'Above appears the first photograph that has ever been published of the first British Military Aeroplane,' read the caption above a huge photograph of Cody and his plane.

A furious Capper issued a telegram to all news organisations withdrawing his restrictions. 'Owing to unauthorized photographs Cody's aeroplane published today we cannot ask Press to refrain longer,' he wrote. No one by now believed him as he added, almost desperately, 'But still uninteresting. Not attempting flight.'

Capper was away from the Balloon Factory the following morning, 16 October. With pressmen now positioned all over Farnborough Common, Cody began, in his by now customary way, making two or three circular runs. With the plane warmed up he headed up a hill towards the Swan Inn Plateau.

The more observant pressmen had noticed that Cody had

fixed a small Union Jack to one of the struts at the rear centre of his wing. The flag's significance quickly became apparent.

As he headed up the hill Cody opened his throttle, rose into the air and flew for seventy yards or so up on to the plateau above him. Encouraged by this Cody took the plane to the perimeter of the open fields and the brow of a hill. Once more he opened the throttle and built up his speed. Within a few yards the plane was rising to thirty feet or so. This time it remained there.

Soon it was flying towards Cove Common, Cody guiding the plane on what one witness called 'its beautiful smooth flight'. 'In less than 100 yards he had reached an altitude of between 30ft and 40ft so that the spectators on the southern boundary of the common saw the aeroplane flying above the roof of the balloon shed,' reported the *Times* correspondent. 'Shaping a course that led to Cove Common, Mr Cody kept the aeroplane about thirty feet from the ground, and he travelled across the greensward for a quarter of a mile.'

Twenty seconds or so after realising his triumph, however, Cody was once more faced with its twin impostor. He had seemingly underestimated the strength of the wind and suddenly found himself heading towards the clump of birch trees he had been keen to avoid when he first set off.

Somehow he clambered his way up and over the trees. As he did so, however, a severe air disturbance flipped his right wing up. As it did so the left wing-tip wheel hit the ground hard. As he steadied the plane again he was now facing a new direction and yet more trees. At this point the plane suddenly wheeled even more violently around to the left and hit its left wing on a clump of bushes. The following seconds were described by the man from *The Times* thus:

> This evolution was fatal to further progress for the left wing dipped, the aeroplane itself lowered and the small cycle wheel on the left extremity of the cross spar struck

the ground with such force that the timber snapped. Deprived of its counter-balance, the right wing swung around as if on a pivot, and then that too struck the earth, and the whole fabric toppled forward to the ground.

As he emerged unblemished from the wreckage, Cody saw that the end section of the left wing had collapsed completely. In addition he could see that the right wing had been partially damaged, the engine flywheel had been broken and his wheels had buckled. He was soon surrounded by a small posse of sappers and young boys. With their help he quickly organised returning the plane to its shed, then headed back to the main buildings. As repair work began on his machine, he set about salvaging his relationship with Capper.

Capper returned to the Balloon Factory early in the afternoon, furious at Cody's insubordination and the fact that he had been compromised in the eyes of Fleet Street and Whitehall. Somehow, however, Cody seems to have succeeded in persuading him that the morning's excitement had been little more than an accident. His story formed the basis for a hasty dispatch to the War Office, effectively apologising for the damage Cody had caused.

'Mr Cody has been running the machine about on a good many occasions in order to get its balance, but he was instructed to attempt nothing sensational or any long flights,' Capper began in his report on the morning's proceedings. He continued,

As soon as he was sure he could really fly he was to let me know with a view to our having a proper trial.

This morning Mr Cody took the machine out as usual, and ran up a slight slope on to a plateau, near the Farnborough Road; to his surprise it lifted off the ground for about fifty yards when going up this hill but he did not attach much importance to this. He ran along the plateau and down the slope when, to his astonishment the machine went to a considerable height in the air.

The rest of the letter amounted to a long and detailed accident report. 'The damage done to the machine is: left wing, good deal broken up, silk somewhat torn, head rudder stay is damaged, right wing, slightly damaged, wheels buckled, engine fly-wheel broken,' wrote Capper. Only towards the end did he include the statistic that acknowledged Cody's achievement. 'The total distance of flight as far as can be measured by corresponding path of travel was 1,390 feet,' he wrote before concluding, 'I do not propose to abandon trials of this machine. It appears that it is probably somewhat better than the Farman Delagrange type.'

Capper's anger at Cody eased slightly as the day wore on, it seems. He sent two more notes to his superiors that day, the first floating the question of whether Cody should be retained to fly the plane once it had been rebuilt, the second launching an appeal for the use of a more suitable airfield. 'Mr Cody has constructed an aeroplane which shows considerable promise. Also he is the only man who has been in it,' Capper wrote beginning the first letter. 'The aeroplane is now damaged, and it will take some little time to reconstruct, also some money. When it is reconstructed it will probably be exceedingly useful to train Mr Cody in flying. It is a question whether at present the Government wishes to train Mr Cody in flying?'

Cody wisely kept his comments to a minimum afterwards. For once, he could comfortably leave his actions to speak for themselves. He reassured the press that the damage to the £1,000 plane would cost 'about £30' to repair. 'I am sorry that the accident occurred,' he said simply in a conversation with the man from *The Times*. 'But I have accomplished what I aimed at: I have constructed a machine which can fly.'

DISASTER TO BRITISH ARMY AEROPLANE AT ITS FIRST ATTEMPT TO FLY.

The *Daily Mirror*'s report on Cody's ill-fated flight.

H IS FLIGHT HAD LASTED TWENTY-SEVEN SECONDS AND taken him over a distance of about a quarter of a mile. Yet the story of Britain's first flight, and its sensational conclusion, made the front page of almost every newspaper the following day. In the days and weeks that followed, magazines and technical journals analysed the achievement, postcards of him and his crumpled plane sold in their thousands and newspapers from around the world beat a path to his plane shed.

'For what was practically a first flight I think the new aeroplane achieved wonders. In six weeks I shall have it ready for work again,' he told a visitor from *The Times of India*. 'Then I guarantee that I will fly for an hour on one day, and for three hours on the next. So far as I am concerned the secret of flight – that is, of maintaining one's equilibrium in the air – is solved.'

There were still those who questioned his fitness to be leading the Army's air experiments, but there were few now who could dare question either his commitment or his courage. 'He has been unlucky with his airships but he has been so fortunate in himself escaping hurt that he is bound, with a continuance of such favour, to do big things,' read a leader column in the *Daily Sketch*. 'A man who backs his theories with his life as he does deserves all sympathy and encouragement when tantalising trifles bar him from the success which we all feel he merits.'

Even among those who thought the plane a monstrosity, there was widespread admiration for what Cody had achieved in far from ideal conditions. 'Cumbersomeness is perhaps the word which best expresses the general defects of the new machine,' read an editorial in *The Car*, which criticised Army Aeroplane No. 1 for 'lacking the grand simplicity of the Wright aeroplane'. It too predicted great things – provided Cody was given better flying facilities.

We must expect hard knocks in the aeroplane school until our beginners have acquired some of the skill and experience of the Wrights. It might be pointed out that Mr Cody is much handicapped by not having such splendid manoeuvring ground as that available for the French aviators, as trees apart from presenting natural obstacles lead to many subtle wind disturbances, which are very trying to the novice in the air. If some vast, treeless expanse, fairly level, and not too difficult for wheels to run over, could be found in these islands, much more rapid progress could be made.

As he was fêted around the country, however, Cody offered no excuses. On 8 December, his colleagues at the Aeronautical Society in London gave him a hero's welcome. 'I have done very little to shout loud about, but still, I have accomplished one thing that I hoped for very much, that is, to be the first man to fly in Great Britain, the country I am living in, at the time mechanical flight became popular,' he said, opening an illustrated talk on the events of 16 October. His most defiant language was reserved for those who had already compared his plane to the Wright Flyer. 'You will notice the similarity of the Wright machine and mine; not only that, but the curves and the system of constructing the curves are precisely alike,' he admitted. Yet he was adamant his plane was the work of Samuel Cody rather than Orville and Wilbur Wright. 'The Wright machine was not public property when I built mine. My machine was finished over three months before the Wright machine came out,' he said.

Cody's analysis of his flight added little to a story that had, by now, been dissected in minute detail for weeks. He admitted that his accident had been caused by his pulling the rudder too sharply when confronted by the second set of trees. 'I turned the rudder and turned it rather sharp,' he explained, pointing at a photograph of the left wing of his broken plane. 'That side of the machine struck, and it crumpled up like so much tissue paper.'

If there was a surprise, it came as Cody explained the motivation behind his flight. No one who knew him could seriously have believed that the inaugural flight had been an accident. By now Cody could not resist sharing the truth. 'I was accused of doing nothing but jumping with my machine,' he said, a playful smile of protest, no doubt forming on his face. 'So I got a bit agitated and went to fly . . .'

CHAPTER NINE

A CLEVER EMPIRICIST

EQUILIBRIUM COULD BE AS ELUSIVE ON THE ROAD as it was in the air. At the wheel of his car a few weeks before Christmas 1908, Cody was hit by a horse and cart that swerved into his path on the streets of Aldershot. Yet again, he emerged from his battered machine unscathed, but Lela was not so lucky. 'Unfortunately one of the shafts of the cart ran into Mrs Cody's side, fracturing her ribs internally,' Cody wrote to a friend in early December. 'Our doctor is quite satisfied with her progress and assures me she is quite out of danger. Naturally she will be confined to her room for some weeks.' The latest mishap to befall Britain's accident-prone aviator seems to have proven manna from heaven for the newspapers. 'As usual the newspapers have tried to make a sensational article,' grumbled Cody in his letter.

The indestructible public persona masked an occasionally thin-skinned temperament. In the wake of 16 October, Cody felt cheated of the respect his maiden flight should have earned him, and angry at the sneering to which he was still subjected. 'I wish some of the anonymous letter writers knew more about my services under the British Government,' he complained in another letter around this time, to RP Hearne, editor of *The Car Illustrated*. 'I think they would find that if the nation were to trust their Aeroplane experiments to my abilities that they had displayed good judgement.'

Of course, each slight only served to stoke the fire of his determination. Yet, as he revealed in the same letter, the fatalist in him was already resigned to a posthumous place in history. 'I can certainly point out and prove that there are scientific points in the structure of the Cody Army Aeroplane that none of the other biplanes can boast of. These points are recorded in the secret books of the War Office and they may become public property some day, possibly when I am gone,' Cody wrote to Hearne. 'But as the War Office will record my name in connection with them, therefore I hope the nagging press will allow this nation to give my name the credit it deserves.'

His sense of injustice only deepened as the year drew to a close. With their usual, impeccable timing, the War Office and the Admiralty delivered the latest double blow on Christmas Eve. Amid the euphoria of 16 October, Cody had put his Admiralty trials to the back of his mind. Admiral Fanshawe, superintendent of the Navy at Portsmouth, had raised his hopes by strongly recommending their adoption. On 24 December, however, Fanshawe was informed that 'in view of the difficulties and risks at present attaching to the use of kites . . . it is premature to supply them to sea-going ships'. Cody was left in no doubt that this marked the end of the road with the Navy. On the very same day, the Army Council wrote, setting out its offer in settlement for its adoption of the man-carrying kite. Cody's case had been becalmed by bureaucracy for months. As early as the summer the all-powerful Ordnance Council were recommended to grant Cody 'a moderate award, as an act of grace'. The decision reflected the fact that he had introduced 'an invention of some military value' and had saved the Balloon Companies several thousands of pounds in the process. It did not, however, accept that it owed Cody anything for his patent. Six months on, the Army Council offered Cody 'a reward of £1,000 in discharge of all claims against the Government, including the Governments of India and the Colonies for his invention'. Cody regarded the offer as yet another insult and wrote back almost immediately. 'I certainly cannot see my way to accept as an adequate and just remuneration the £1,000 offered,' he replied early in the New Year.

CODY HAD RETURNED TO THE BALLOON FACTORY IN THE first week of 1909. On the afternoon of 6 January, a new, bigger and bulkier version of Army Aeroplane No. 1 emerged from the airship shed on to Farnborough Common. The most obvious physical difference was the plane's extended length and the disappearance of the distinctive fantail. Students of the subtleties of aviation would have noticed new, double-surfaced wings. To the unsubtle eyes of the press, however, the new plane's appearance, like its performance, seemed all too familiar.

Cody had to ease his machine through the trial process once more. An initial test on 9 January proved the plane was 'top heavy' and that the radiators needed repositioning. By now Cody's regular reassurances that he was 'perfectly satisfied' with his plane's progress was regarded as a standing joke by many. As the familiar, emollient noises emanated from his shed, the arch satirists at *Punch* poked fun. In an acidic piece called 'Flights of Fancy, A Peep Into The Future', the magazine ridiculed Cody by running a speculative diary of the 'progress' his experiments would make in the next few years. In October 1909, he would be 'as usual, well satisfied' with a run of 100 yards along the ground. By November 1911, he would be ready to test the new tyre he had fitted. 'He expects there is no reason why he should not remain in the air for quite a quarter of an hour,' ran the piece before adding scabrously, 'Two first class Brazilian Aerocruisers passed over the Plain at an altitude of 400 feet during the trial.'

The jibes once more left Cody 'agitated'. It is probably no coincidence that on the same day *Punch* appeared, 20 January, he succeeded in raising his new plane into the air for the first time. This time Cody covered 1,200 yards in the more open environment at Laffan's Plain. Once more, however, the flight ended prematurely as Cody attempted a sharp turn. Vivian later recalled how he heard a 'sharp crack of bamboo', then saw the elevators at the front fold back over the top. 'The plane seemed to stop dead, just as though some giant hand had grabbed it, then it went down, nose first into the ground.' Cody later admitted he had been worried that he would fly into a fence and had applied the head rudder 'too violently'. 'Personally I think it lucky that this mishap took place so close to the ground and that there is so little damage done,' he added.

In contrast to the October flight, Capper was present to witness the events from a viewpoint on a nearby plateau. The distance that now existed between the two men was apparent in the reports Cody's mentor submitted afterwards. 'Mr Cody is, I am glad to say, uninjured,' Capper wrote before adopting an exasperated tone. 'I shall advise Mr Cody to put in a smaller front rudder, but as the design is entirely his own, though I make suggestions at times, it rests entirely with him whether he follows them or not,' he wrote.

Capper even went so far as to suggest that Wilbur Wright should be handed the controls of the Army aeroplane. 'I am of the opinion that this manipulation must be very difficult to learn and that if we can induce Mr Wright to go up in the machine, after studying the controls, with the practice he has had he might safely work it, but that we shall have a good many smashes before Mr Cody has learned to manipulate the controls,' he opined.

The next frustrating month of trials would have done little to dissuade Capper of his opinion. On 18 February Cody lost balance during a short hop and burst a tyre on landing. Four days later the plane, as he put it, 'seemed to stand still' in midair and dropped straight to the ground. On Tuesday, 23 February, he put the plane through a rigorous run-out, 'turning from right to left, jumping from the ground at will and landing at will'. He ended the day with 'one fairly straight flight really to convince the press representatives present that my reckless manoeuvring was intentional and that the machine was completely under control'. His report on the day's flying was the most upbeat since October. Cody claimed he had 'mastered' the art of 'side balance' and was on his way to understanding the art of 'banking'. 'When I have mastered this difficulty I shall have no trouble in flying from the Factory to the Long Valley and possibly to Portsmouth or Salisbury,' he wrote.

In reality, only Cody was able to fully grasp the progress he was making. The Army hierarchy was now past caring.

The next day, 24 February 1908, was one of the unhappiest in Cody's life. He was called in to be shown a letter from RH Brade, Assistant Secretary to the War Office, which had arrived at the Aldershot Command office that morning. There is no evidence of who broke the news to Cody but the communication itself survives. The gist of Brade's letter read, 'I am commanded by the Army Council to inform you that, in view of changes which are contemplated in connection with balloons and flying machines, it has been decided to terminate the engagements of Lieutenant Dunne and Mr SF Cody.'

SECRETARY OF WAR HALDANE'S PERFORMANCE IN THE heat of the Aerial Navigation Committee had been a masterclass in political manoeuvring.

The Blair Atholl debacle of the previous year had persuaded the stern Scots intellectual that Capper and his programme were an acute embarrassment. In the face of the work being done elsewhere in Europe, and in particular in Germany, where the Privy Councillor Rudolf Martin was boasting of a fleet of 10,000 Zeppelins, each of which could carry twenty soldiers 'which should land and capture the sleeping Britons before they could realise what was taking place', he had grown convinced a new, more scientific response was needed.

'We were at a profound disadvantage compared with the Germans, who were building up the structure of the Air Service on a foundation of science,' he later wrote. Haldane bracketed Capper, Cody and Dunne with Orville and Wilbur Wright, whom he had met during a visit to London. He did not doubt that each of them was a brave and inventive pioneer. As scientists, however, they were nothing more than amateurs, or 'clever empiricists', as he preferred to put it.

Haldane had astutely limited the Balloon Factory's opportunities to offer an alternative view. Dunne's second season at Blair Atholl had ended in anticlimax once more, his powered D.4 managing little more than forty-yard hops. 'I have had long talks with him, and I do not think you will get any more from him,' Haldane said testily when it was suggested the English flyer appear before the committee. (When Dunne communicated his plans to sell his plane to the entrepreneur Sir Howard de Walden for £2,000 via his influential father, no one seemed interested either way.) Capper too was given short shrift, and performed poorly during his one visit to Westminster to give evidence.

Given the uninspiring précis of his work presented to the committee, it is hardly surprising no one seems to have considered asking Cody to give evidence. Capper's oblique correspondence on the flight of 16 October had clearly formed the basis for the report presented. 'An aeroplane has been tried. It promised to be at least as successful as the Delagrange or Farman machines, though possibly inferior to the Wright,' read the relevant submission. 'An accident in turning has, however, stopped further experiment at present. Another aeroplane of new design has been constructed, and will, it is understood, be tried shortly.' Nowhere was it mentioned that Cody rather than Dunne was the man responsible for taking the programme this far. Capper's only real reference to Cody gave the impression that his aeroplane was little more than a hobby. He worked on the machine, Capper told the committee, 'when he is not engaged in instructing or making kites'.

At the prompting of Haldane and the equally anti-aeroplane chairman of the committee, Lord Esher, a decision came in mid-February. The final report concluded that while the Navy and Army should receive £35,000 and £10,000 respectively for the development of airships, work on aeroplanes 'should be discontinued'. (At this stage the committee's main recommendation on aeroplanes seems to have been that foreign powers should be allowed to develop machines and that Britain should then copy their designs!)

While Dunne's removal barely merited a mention in the press, Cody's demise divided the nation. His most virulent critics seized on the sacking with a delight that left a sour taste in many mouths. 'Cody's Farewell. God Save The Taxpayer. We could not love you, Sir, so much, loved we not money more!' ran an article in one, accompanying a photograph of Haldane visiting Cody at Farnborough shortly after the announcement was made. 'The War Office has parted with Mr Cody, and we publish above the photograph of his pathetic if somewhat undignified exit. It will be hoped that the authorities will now finance an ENGLISH-MAN'S experiments,' read one particularly nasty account.

His supporters mounted a fierce defence, papers like the influential *Westminster Gazette* decrying the decision as little more than snobbery:

> It has evidently perturbed the minds of many people that an ex-cowboy should have broken down all the social barriers in this country by securing an appointment in His Majesty's Army. Nor do they seem to have forgotten that the intrepid aviator was once a showman . . . they seem to imagine that he had bluffed the War Office into giving him an appointment in which he could enjoy all the sweets and emoluments of a 'soft' job and live voluptuously at the expense of the taxpayer.
>
> It is quite an easy thing to sit in one's armchair and ask

why Mr Cody has done this, that and the other thing, but those who talk most can usually do the least. Mr Cody has done quite as much, and a good deal more, with his aeroplane than the majority of Continental aviators.

For Cody, the news was a shattering blow. Yet once more the crisis saw him at his best. Unlike Dunne, whose contract could be terminated immediately, Cody technically still had a job. Under the terms of his contract as Chief Kite Instructor, he had to be served with six months' notice. He knew from experience that War Office bureaucracy would find it hard to remove him more quickly. Almost immediately he set about campaigning to salvage his operation.

On 1 March he wrote to the War Office expressing his 'great regret and disappointment' at the decision. In a long and digni- fied letter he went on to 'earnestly request that the machine be handed over to me in order that I may continue experimenting at my own expense, it being understood that I do not in any way neglect my duties as Chief Kite Instructor in order to do so'.

There were those who wanted Cody out of Aldershot and Farnborough immediately. 'Of course if it is found that we can get rid of Cody earlier so much the better,' wrote one unidentified officer during the protracted negotiations that accompanied his sacking. For a while, it seems no one was keener for Cody to leave Farnborough than Colonel Capper. Despite having initially backed Cody's request, Capper tried to block it, astonishingly arguing 'on the grounds that colour will be lent to the suggestion that we are still favouring Mr Cody'.

Determined to hold on to his plane and his access to Farn- borough Common for six months at least, Cody lobbied everyone he could at Aldershot. 'Mr Cody came to me in great despair and asked to be allowed to remain on and use government grounds for his experiments,' recalled one of Aldershot's senior commanders, Sir Horace Smith-Dorrien later. 'This I readily agreed.'

A hero abroad if not at home.
A French postcard of Cody on Laffan's Plain, early 1908.

Other senior figures at the garrison proved equally sympathetic. On 7 April Cody was granted ownership of his plane, the 'loan' of the Antoinette engine and permission to base his portable plane shed out at Laffan's Plain, until 30 September. The only condition was that he report the results of his experiments to the War Office. 'I have to express my thanks ... for this most generous treatment,' Cody wrote two days later, seemingly straight-faced.

THE REALITY OF CODY'S SITUATION WAS SUMMED UP within days of his dismissal notice. On the snowy morning of 3 March he had been forced to recruit a local coal merchant and his horse to pull the plane out on to Laffan's Plain. The newspapers enjoyed the fall from grace. 'MR CODY'S AEROPLANE TOWED BY A COAL CART', ran one headline. For now, however, Cody was determined to take maximum advantage of his stay of execution and was willing to accept help from wherever it came. There was no shortage of willing helpers, among them a gardener who had been working at Pinehurst, Charlie Phillips, an old stagehand from *Klondyke Nugget* days, Sam Wackett, and George Broomfield, a local railway clerk. (Broomfield's devotion to Cody was almost evangelical. 'When he was "sacked" by the War Office,' he later wrote, 'I made up my youthful mind that I would never desert him and that every spare moment of my life should be devoted to his service.')

In theory Cody remained answerable to Aldershot command. In practice, he was already reverting to his old, spontaneous showman ways. On the morning of 13 May, the visit of the Prince of Wales to army manoeuvres at the nearby Caesar's Camp at Aldershot provided him with an unmissable chance. Capper had been showing off his new dirigible, a lemon-shaped, miniature version of the *Nulli Secundus*, appropriately christened *Baby*. Cody started up his engine and took to the air, heading in their direction. As he roared overhead, the troops interrupted their manoeuvres to wave and cheer. Cody repaid the compliment by making a second swoop and leaning out to wave with one arm. When Cody eventually landed on the aptly named Danger Hill he realised he had flown farther than ever before, a full mile. News of a new British record distance for a straight-line flight quickly spread and by the end of the afternoon the Prince and Princess of Wales had joined the flow of people popping in to pass on their congratulations. Cody staged an impromptu royal command performance flying 600 yards across the plain. 'No smash or accident occurred while the Prince was present,' he recorded proudly in his report to the War Office later.

As the summer began, Cody worked hard to ensure every report ended that way. Day in, day out, he practised flying at differing altitudes, speeds and in as many weather conditions as possible. The winds were his greatest enemy, in particular the 'punty' gusts that swirled around Laffan's Plain. 'The most difficult thing in aerial flight is the negotiating of the numerous eddies,' he mused later. 'They are as treacherous to the aviator as the crosscurrents near a rocky coast are to a sailor.'

Steadily, however, he was emerging as one of aviation's master mariners. Each evening and weekend, vast crowds would pour on to Laffan's Plain to watch his progress. The area's young boys would spend their entire holidays camped around Cody's shed. One visitor, Sir Theodore Cook, editor of the society magazine *The Field*, was 'aghast at the liberty permitted' to the huge weekend gatherings. 'They swarmed round the doors of the shed; they stood in serried ranks round the machine itself; they came in motor cars, in gigs, in landaus, and their bicycles were as thick as grasshoppers,' he wrote. 'With any less skilful aviator than Cody, there would undoubtedly have been a serious accident.'

Cook was as thrilled as any seven-year-old by his first thrilling glimpse of the American in action. 'The most breathless moment was the start. The clang of the motors was drowned by the whirl of the propellers as full power was turned on and the aeroplane began to run on her bicycle wheels over the grass,' he wrote. 'The instant when she rose . . . all sense of laboured effort left the spectator. When her gathering speed swung her lightly upwards, she seemed flying of her own volition; effortless and free, she purred away towards the far end of Laffan's Plain, keeping very low and skimming like a swallow.'

Cody's new-found mastery of the air impressed Cook more than anything. 'The most remarkable feature of these flights was the astonishing ease with which Cody made a sharp turn,' said Cook. 'Cody made straight for his mark, and no sooner was he seen to reach it than he seemed to be on his way back again.'

——————

By 7 August, Cody was ready to take the next significant step forward. 'I am quite ready to carry my first passenger,' he wrote in his report that day. A week later, on Saturday, 14 August, he rewarded the biggest crowd yet with a historic evening's flying. After starting the engine and taking the controls, Cody signalled for Colonel Capper to take his position in the plough seat he had fixed behind him at shoulder height in the plane. Relations between the two had remained strained over the previous months. Still technically obliged to the Balloon Factory's superintendent, however, Cody almost certainly had little option but to offer his old mentor the opportunity to become the first passenger to fly in his plane. He ensured Capper did not forget his flight in a hurry.

The plane coped with the additional load without any visible signs of stress. 'I accelerated and left the ground about 150 to 200 yards from the shed,' Cody wrote later in his official report. 'The machine seemed to ride and balance in every way equal to previous occasions.'

On the way back to the Balloon Factory, Cody decided to inject a little drama into Capper's evening. 'I took both hands off the steering column and allowed the machine to practically take her own course,' he recounted later. The pilotless plane was soon veering towards Capper's old airship shed. 'On approaching the shed I was obliged to take hold of the steering column as a turning movement was necessary,' Cody recorded matter-of-factly in his report. Capper's reaction to his hair-raising ride into the sky was not recorded. It was some time before he climbed back into the passenger seat again, however.

No sooner had he deposited on terra firma the first passenger to fly in Great Britain safely than Cody was being approached by the second. While Capper had been in the air, Lela had had her hair wrapped in a heavy scarf and the lower half of her dress bound tightly with tape. It seems she had volunteered for the trip herself and had braced herself for a bumpy ride. 'Though I was not afraid, for I should never be afraid to trust my husband's skill, I was a little apprehensive of bumping at the start,' she explained. She was surprised at the smoothness of the experience. 'Mr Cody asked me if I was ready and I said "Yes". Then apparently nothing happened for a minute or more, and I asked, "Aren't you going to start?" "We have started," he replied quietly, and then I saw the ground was skimming away from under us, several yards below.'

Cody spared Lela the aerial trickery, but her trip was not without its incident. As he turned at the end of Laffan's Plain, the plane lost lift and struck the ground. A hundred yards later, however, it was back in the air. Back on the ground Lela was surrounded by spectators eager to greet the nation's first aviatrix. A 'glorious sense of exhilaration' was how she described the experience to reporters. It had also cured her of a particularly painful case of neuralgia, she added.

The fact was that Cody's

The first aviatrix.
Lela prepares for her maiden flight,
14 August 1908.

passengers were taking their life in their hands. A week later, when
Frank and Vivian became the next to join him on board, a piece
of steel tubing broke free and cut a long hole in the petrol tank.
'The petrol poured out on the motor but did not catch fire,' Cody
recorded coolly.

No one seemed bothered by the risks, however. No more than
a few dozen people in the world had experienced the sheer sen-
sory thrill of flying. The queues to join Cody in the air became
never-ending. 'The world's first aerial omnibus', he was soon calling his service.

On Wednesday, 8 September, with three weeks to go before the end of his Army contract, Cody took off over Laffan's Plain and headed over the surrounding villages of Rushmoor, Tweseldown and Fleet. At this stage the longest flight he had made was a cross-country trip of eight miles in nine and a half minutes, on 28 August. On a clear morning, with the plane performing faultlessly, he lost all sense of time as he circled the Hampshire countryside. It was only when he heard the engine spluttering to a stop that he realised he had used up all his petrol. Fortunately he was on his way back to Laffan's Plain and could see his normal landing strip ahead of him. 'I knew there was nothing for it but a long glide to earth,' he said later.

Vivian and Leon had been watching the entire flight. 'He's going to smash,' they shouted as he made a rapid descent. Instead Cody brought the plane sliding smoothly to a halt. As the boys and a crowd of onlookers rushed towards the plane he climbed out. 'What's the matter with Cody's aeroplane now?' he beamed. The stopwatches and maps revealed that he had been airborne for sixty-three minutes and covered more than forty miles. The previous world record for a cross-country flight had been set by Louis Bleriot in travelling the twenty-five miles from Etampes to Orleans. News of the new world record was splashed all over the newspapers that night and the following morning.

The publicity drew an even bigger crowd of visitors the following Saturday, among them the exiled Empress Eugenie, the eighty-three-year-old widow of Emperor Napoleon III of France. Cody ensured the photographers were on hand to record the moment. ('THE EMPRESS AND THE HERO OF THE RECORD FLIGHT' dominated the front page of Monday's *Daily Graphic*.) Cody then made two special flights in her honour. As he prepared to end the second, in which he performed a particularly impressive midair turn above Danger Hill, Cody looked down to see his landing area overrun with spectators. 'Consequently I made a very bad landing to avoid the trees and people,' he recorded afterwards. 'I buckled one of my main wheels and the buffer wheel.'

He discovered the real cost of the mishap the following Monday evening. While the main wheel had been replaced by a spare, the buffer wheel had not been so easily replaced. As he landed his plane in a hollow near his shed, the main springs compressed so far that the forks holding the wheel hit the rising ground, burying themselves in the earth and bringing the plane to what Cody called 'a violent stand-still'. Cody's momentum sent him flying on to the broken outriggers, where he suffered his worst injuries yet, 'a severe cut near the left eye'. While

'The Empress and the hero'.
Cody entertains Eugenie of France.

his staff dragged his stricken plane back to the shed, a heavily bleeding Cody was taken to a doctor in a cab. 'Though my wound was rather alarming I felt no pain whatever,' he said with his customary stoicism in his report.

The extent of his wound was all too apparent at the House of Commons the next day. Cody had been invited to Westminster for a lunch in honour of Louis Bleriot. The reception was the latest in a long line of events in recognition of the Frenchman's sensational flight across the English Channel to win Lord North-cliffe's £500 in July.

Around the table, were Cody's old friends CS Rolls and RBS Baden-Powell and his adversary AV Roe. Among the politicians present were the host Sir Benjamin Stone and David Lloyd George. Bleriot gave a gracious speech. Cody in his turn paid his tribute to the Frenchmen. 'I should have come even if I died this night,' he said in a brief speech in which he could not resist voicing his unhappiness at the War Office's behaviour in stalling on the War Kite.

With Cody's departure from the Army now a matter of days away, it was left to others to attack the shabby treatment meted out to their American colleague. (The injustice was made all the more hurtful by the way Haldane and the Aerial Navigation Committee's chairman Lord Esher were already performing a volte-face. Bleriot's proof that England was as one politician put it 'no longer an island' had forced Esher to accept the aeroplane's 'incontestable superiority' over airships. 'It is evidently desirable that thirty or forty of these machines should be purchased without delay for the use of the Army,' he was soon recommending, paving the way for the formation of the Royal Flying Corps.)

Another aviator, Captain WG Wyndham, addressed his comments directly at Lloyd George and his fellow politicians. 'In France any man who did anything in the cause of aviation was welcomed by the whole country, but it was different over here,' he said, to the accompaniment of sterling-silver cutlery being tapped on the dining table. 'Mr Cody has conquered the air in spite of the Army.'

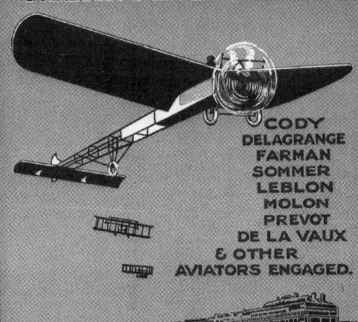

FIRST AVIATION
MEETING IN ENGLAND.

CODY
DELAGRANGE
FARMAN
SOMMER
LEBLON
MOLON
PREVOT
DE LA VAUX
& OTHER
AVIATORS ENGAGED.

DONCASTER
15TH TO 23RD OCTOBER
1909.

CHAPTER TEN

THE FLYING CATHEDRAL

I MAY SAY THAT I HAVE ACHIEVED SOME SUCCESS AS A
result of my scientific studies. The limit of my success, however, is bound by the limit of my capital.' Cody's comment to
a reporter from the Paris edition of the *New York Herald* in the
autumn of 1909 put a rather elegant gloss on the grim reality of
his return to civilian life. At the end of four years' service, he left
the Army all but broke.

Even his irresistible force had failed to shake the immovable
object that was the War Office. It had stonewalled all Cody's
requests for an increase on the offer of £1,000 that summer. The
knowledge that, only a mile or so from his shed, Japanese, French
and Swedish army officers were being trained to operate his man-
lifters made their niggardliness all the more galling. 'Foreign Governments are now in a position to construct and use these kites
for themselves, without dealing with me in the matter, so that the
monetary value of my invention abroad has been very adversely
affected,' Cody wrote in a querulous letter that summer. 'I cannot
rest constant with the decision conveyed to me.' An alternative
approach came from Capper, with whom Cody had resumed cordial, if cool, relations since his first passenger flight. He suggested
an appeal to the government's senior financiers at the Treasury. 'I
am advised that it is the correct course to take,' he wrote to Cody.

All this only served to underline the fact that his biplane now represented Cody's only real means of making a living and supporting his family. In his more gung-ho moments he was confident it was capable of taking on and beating the leading aviators by now competing for the lucrative air prizes being awarded around Europe. 'I'll beat them all at the game,' he said in September. In his heart, however, he must have already suspected the life of the freelance flyer would not be that simple. Just how treacherous the route to airborne riches would be became apparent soon enough.

There had been no shortage of invitations. Cody had, for instance, been asked to fly from Aldershot to Paris in October. In the wake of the first great air-race meeting at Rheims, in August, a second 'festival of flying' was to be held at Juvisy. The prospect of a risky and expensive flight across the Channel was quickly dismissed. 'I certainly should not attempt such a flight unless an adequate prize was offered for accomplishing the journey,' Cody said in September.

At first it seemed his likeliest lifeline was that offered by the *Daily Mail*. Lord Northcliffe's genius had allowed him to sell newspapers and support his passion for aviation at the same time. Coverage of Bleriot's triumph in his £500 cross-Channel challenge had proven a huge circulation booster. It had been during his time in the Army that Cody had first talked up his prospects of winning the £10,000 prize Northcliffe had offered for the first flight from London to Manchester. Bleriot too had expressed an interest in going for the prize. 'I hope to lick him all ends up,' Cody had said with characteristic gusto. Cody had even set about planning a route and a means by which to navigate the 170-mile journey. He talked of laying out huge, 150-foot-long, white sheets cut in the shape of arrows to point him in the right direction. With the help of the famous firework makers, Brock's, he had even come up with a second scheme — to have sky rockets filled with coloured smoke mapping out his path through the clouds.

As he began life as a self-financed flyer, however, the doubts quickly crept in. 'As a matter of fact I should much prefer attempting some less ambitious flight were there prizes to win,' he confessed when asked about the challenge shortly before leaving the Army.

Within days his plans to fly to Manchester had – rather conveniently – self-destructed. Cody's public pronouncements had left him with no option but to make an attempt at the £10,000 prize. In perfect flying conditions, a large crowd gathered to see him off from Laffan's Plain on Saturday, 9 October.

After a couple of failed attempts at take-off Cody and his plane limped back to the shed. After a quick inspection of his engine, he announced to the gathered pressmen that an assistant had somehow forgotten to switch off the tap between the oil tank and the sump the previous night and his motor was now flooded. According to one description of the day, Cody subjected the man responsible to 'some of the gems of the profanity he had known as a cowboy'. By mid-morning Cody had announced that, with regret, he would have to abandon the trip. The reaction of the crowd was predictably mixed. 'Many of the public were angry at being deprived of the sensation promised,' wrote the *Aldershot News* correspondent, 'but others took the matter philosophically observing they had scarcely hoped for more considering the bad luck which seems to have attended so many of Mr Cody's attempts.'

Even Cody's most supportive local newspaper voiced its suspicions at the 'strange mishap'. 'The ordinary precautions which any inventor anxious for the success of a serious enterprise would take, one would think, would easily prevent careless bungling of the nature of the accidents mentioned,' wondered the *Aldershot News* reporter.

His scepticism seems to have been well founded. That afternoon Cody began dismantling his plane and packing it into a large lorry. The following Monday morning, when he should have been completing his flight into Manchester, he drove north to Doncaster instead.

If Cody was being cautious, it was perfectly understandable given the size of the prize on offer on the other side of the Pennines in Britain's inaugural air meeting. The race to stage the nation's first air show had become intense. Britain's overseers of sporting aviation, the Piccadilly-based Aero Club, had signed the Frenchmen Fournier, Paulhan, Leblanc, Rougier and Farnham, as well as the dashing Englishman Hubert Latham, to fly at their maiden meeting at Blackpool towards the end of October. A consortium of Doncaster businessmen had undermined the event by stumping up £20,000 in prize money for a rival meeting beginning days earlier on 15 October. Frenetic negotiations with the Doncaster committee had ended with Cody being guaranteed £2,000, simply for turning up.

Cody was to share top billing with the great Leon Delagrange of France. Among the others invited were LeBlon, Sommer, Schreck and Molon.

Cody, Sommer, Schreck and four others arrived at the Danum Hotel in Doncaster early in the week to find letters from the Aero Club waiting in their pigeonholes. Each of them ignored the threat that they would be disqualified from future competitions if they flew at Doncaster. (So many injunctions would arrive at the meeting, the aviators began ripping them up in view of each other with the words 'Blackpool again'. Cody, in particular, refused to be dictated to by a club which had — until his world-record flight — refused him membership.)

Cody's status as the top-of-the-bill performer had produced a fuller mailbag than most. As ever he had divided opinion. A letter from a local woman asked that he pay her £300 to accompany him in a flight. 'You can spare it as you will have made £20,000 before Christmas,' she wrote, indignant at the large fee reported in the newspapers already. One of his many female admirers gave him a mother-of-pearl pig, which Cody immediately placed on the chain of his watch for good luck, 'with Madame Cody's permission', of course. ('The pig will fly,' he doubtless told her.)

By the Wednesday before the meeting's Friday start, Cody had joined nine of his rivals on the airfield. Cody seemed uninterested in the other flyers. 'He never, so far as I could see, cast a glance in their direction,' recalled one observer later. They, on the other hand, were fascinated and faintly amused by the show's supposed star turn.

In his more realistic moments, Cody had admitted the reality of the situation. 'Up to the present, with experiments etc., I have not yet spent £2,000, a mere bagatelle compared with what M Bleriot and others have laid out,' he explained in an interview in September. In the same interview he had admitted that his plane was far from ready to go on sale along with the Voisins, Farmans and Wrights. Cody's original brief from the Army had taken him down a path that no other European plane maker had followed as yet. He had constructed a dreadnought, capable of lifting at least two heavy men into the skies. 'My biplane is nearly twice the size of most others,' he explained that autumn. 'It is also very heavy, as when laden with a passenger it weighs over a ton.' In contrast, the machines assembled around him had been built simply for lightness and speed.

Cody and the bearded J LeBlon seem to have irritated each other from the outset. When the Frenchman challenged him to a £10,000 race around a lap of the circuit Cody politely declined. The dilettante Delagrange and Cody, on the other hand, seemed to form a cautious camaraderie immediately.

A newspaper interviewer recorded Delagrange's thoughts at the time. 'I had noticed Delagrange . . . gazing on several occasions at Cody's machine, which when compared with the graceful French Bleriots, Antoinettes and Farmans, bore the same resemblance as would a Grimsby fishing smack to his Majesty's racing yacht *Britannia*,' he wrote later. 'I asked him his opinion of this weird contrivance and, to my surprise, he replied gravely: "This aeroplane is the best yet made. Monsieur Cody is right and we are wrong. His machine is a flying machine, all ours are toys. I take my hat off, as you say in England, to Mr Cody."'

It was Delagrange and his fellow French flyers who provided Cody's plane with its new nickname. The sheer scale of the machine and the vast, special shed in which it was housed reminded them of Rheims and its famous landmark. Looking over Cody's plane they learned that one of his many distinctive features was the 'kinked' shape of his biplane wings. In the mechanical argot of the aviators the configuration was known as a 'katahedral'.

By the first day of the Doncaster meeting, the monolith's new moniker was being seized on by press and public alike. Cody and the Flying Cathedral would remain inseparable in the public mind from then on.

T HERE IS NO EXPECTATION OF DANGER, BUT EVERYONE entering the aerodrome does so at his own risk.' At times during Britain's first 'aviation week', the notices that dotted Doncaster's racecourse might have been aimed at the aviators as much as their audience.

Tens of thousands poured on to the city's famous racecourse, home to the annual St Leger classic. For much of the week, however, they stood huddled in the stands and beer tents watching the rain driven across the course by strong, cold northerly winds.

Their patience quickly snapped. 'Sport? More like robbery with violence,' complained one beer-filled Yorkshireman, aggrieved at having forked out for his place in the 'sixpenny stand'.

Under pressure from Charles Theobald, the blustering chairman of the organising committee, the aviators took it in turns to start up their engines and trundle up and down before the grandstand every now and again. At one point Count Vanderburgh and Sommer challenged Saunier and Kenet to a piggy-back race along the St Leger course. Cody placed Schreck in a wheelbarrow and ran him along the course too.

With the first day threatening to be a complete washout, it was – inevitably – Cody who made the only real attempt at a flight in the conditions. He could not resist an offer of £100 if he could get his plane up and provide a local businessman with a passenger ride, and so took to the course in the fading light of the late afternoon. To the cheers of the crowd he sent the Cathedral along the course 'with a tremendous whizz'. The headwind was far too strong even for him to get the plane airborne, however, and he drew up short of the railings at the end of the racecourse. As the plane was pulled back to its shed, Cody ran back along the racecourse, chased by gangs of children. Grateful for its first glimpse of a plane in motion, the crowd in the stands applauded him all the way.

Even his entertaining heroics could not please everyone. Back at the Danum Hotel that night he picked up a postcard. 'What price Yankee Doodle?' its author had scrawled. 'When are you going to start and earn that £2,000????'

With the weather improved, Cody wasted no time in taking to the course the following morning. The Cathedral made a perfect take-off and he began the first circuit of the track. Before completing his lap, however, he was forced down. As he flopped on to the racecourse and began his run back towards the sheds, he was forced to cross a sand-filled ditch. Cody and his fellow flyers had insisted the organisers fill in the obstacle but the job had been done poorly. The Cathedral's wheels sank into it, the machine pitchforked into the earth and tipped upright.

The accident caused panic back at the grandstands and workshops. France had already lost one of its aerial heroes, Captain Ferber, in eerily similar circumstances when his plane had flipped forward. Delagrange jumped into his monoplane and flew across the racecourse to investigate. He found Cody pinned underneath and officials and members of the crowd pulling him

'Wild West methods successful: the Cody machine being righted after having been lassoed.' The report from Doncaster in the *Illustrated London News*.

free. He emerged covered in cuts but generally intact. 'Wal, how did I survive that?' he said.

The sight of Cody in one piece was, according to the *Times* correspondent, 'hailed with almost delirious enthusiasm' by the packed stands. Cody was more concerned with righting the Cathedral and rescuing his reputation. With a cameraman on hand to record the event, he uncoiled a rope, then lassoed the tail of his machine so that a group of policemen and helpers could haul it into place once more. The picture was seized on by the press and became one of the most popular postcards of the event.

Cody was forced to leave Doncaster for London and replacement parts. He returned to Yorkshire to find tempers fraying once more. Saturday's flying had rescued the organisers from a lynch mob, with both Delagrange and Le Blon providing breathtaking displays around the circuit. Given the disappointments of the Friday, all the flyers had agreed to stay on for an extra two days at the end of the week. (The aldermen of Doncaster had declared the entire week a public holiday so as to allow the population to enjoy the additional entertainment.)

As the second week of the meeting began where it had left off, the situation descended into acrimony. The cantankerous Theobald had spent most of the weekend suppressing the suspicion that he had been taken for a ride. 'We have been fooled long enough. We will shut the show up if there is not flying at once,' he finally snapped on the Monday as the aviators once more remained in their sheds.

In full glare of the press, Theobald accused Cody of failing to fulfil his contract. Cody shouted back that he had been the first to volunteer to fly for an extra two days at no extra cost. 'And this is how you thank me,' he said. Cody blamed the organisers' failure to prepare the airfield properly for the lack of his own activity. 'I cannot help it if the people come and burn the place down,' he said.

The meeting continued with mixed success for the rest of the week. By the Thursday, with the weather once more against flying, Cody had managed little more than a few circuits. His most memorable contribution to the chaotic climax of the air show came on the ground.

Halfway through Thursday morning, with the crowds growing surly once more, Cody strode out from his shed alongside the bowler-hatted figure of Doncaster's town clerk, Mr Tovey. As the band of the Yorkshire Dragoons formed into a half-circle, reporters, photographers and some of the aviators formed another crescent. The crowd's mood lifted as the announcer explained that Cody was to take an oath of allegiance to the King and become a British citizen.

Cody knew his American status disqualified him from many of the events the patriotic Northcliffe in particular was organising. He had set the wheels in motion at the end of August by submitting an official application to the Home Secretary via his solicitors, Amery-Parkes, Macklin and Co. of Fleet Street. He had made the application, his papers stated, 'because he has for very many years enjoyed the protection of the English Laws and desires to be able to owe allegiance to His Majesty in return there-

Oath of Allegiance.

I, *Samuel Franklin Cody*

do swear that I will be faithful and bear true allegiance to His Majesty King Edward, His Heirs and Successors, according to law.

So help me GOD.

(Signature of Alien) *Samuel Franklin Cody*

Sworn and subscribed this *21st* day of *October* 19*05*, before me

(Signature) *H. A. H. Tovey*

~~Justice of the Peace for~~

A Commissioner for Oaths

Address { *Doncaster*
          Yorkshire

Cody's naturalisation papers.

for'. The details were as unreliable as ever: he gave his date of birth as 7 March 1862, his birthplace as Birdville in Wize (sic) County, Texas, and named Samuel Franklin Cody and Phoebe Jane Cody as his parents. His statement that he was married was, technically at least, accurate. Cody would have known that his application would be investigated by the police and had lined up a reliable selection of witnesses: Colonel Capper and several friends, including Harry Underwood, a local 'Hay and Straw Dealer', and Alfred Wright, a Civil Engineer. Each described Cody as 'a respectable man', the Metropolitan Police's investigating officer, an Inspector Riley, reported. It seems no checks were made with the American Embassy. Cody must have wondered quite how far the enquiries would extend. Fortunately he received notice that he was 'naturalized as a British Subject' that week. All he now needed to do was take an oath of allegiance before a legal commissioner for oaths.

Cody stood sentry-still in the middle of the Doncaster race-course, raised his right arm upward and declared, 'I, Samuel Franklin Cody, do swear that I will be faithful and bear true allegiance to His Majesty King Edward, his Heirs and Successors according to law. So help me God.' He then signed the form on the back of Mr Tovey's overcoat.

As the band struck a version of 'God Save the King', Cody offered a military salute. On the roof of his portable shed, a Union Jack was raised alongside the Stars and Stripes. 'It was beautiful, beautiful,' wrote an observer. 'Nothing better has ever been seen on the Drury Lane stage.' It was certainly the best Cody could manage at Doncaster. He left the meeting the following day having failed abjectly to fly more than a few full circuits, let alone win any of the prizes on offer.

Matters continued much in the same vein for the rest of the winter. Within an hour of taking his oath of allegiance, Cody had wired the *Daily Mail*, informing them of his intention to compete for a £1,000 prize for the first 'all-British' one-mile circuit.

He had spent a sizable chunk of his Doncaster money on an order for a new, fifty-horsepower Green engine that would help him finally meet the 'all-British' requirement. To his annoyance, he soon learned that the wealthy young Charles Moore-Brabazon had put an order in ahead of him. Cody could do little as Moore-Brabazon collected his Green engine, fitted it to a copy of the Wright Flyer built by the English company Short Brothers and qualified for the £1,000 prize at the end of October.

In the immediate aftermath of Doncaster, Cody had set his sights on another £1,000 prize, this time offered by the business-man Sir John Hartley for the first flight from Liverpool to Man-chester. As he overcame the problems that had blighted Doncaster, Cody based himself at Liverpool's Aintree racecourse.

He once more found himself up against terrible weather and had to wait until the end of December to make an attempt at the thirty-six-mile trip. A dozen miles into the journey he accidentally hit a telegraph wire and had to make an emergency landing in which the plane was badly damaged once more.

As 1910 began, the financial drain his aeroplane work was now placing on him was immense. Desperate for money, he had taken up Capper's advice and opened a new battlefront, this time with the Treasury. He had written asking for £3,000 in lieu of the expenses he claimed he had run up in developing the man-carrying kite for Army use. It was no longer a time for preserving pride. 'If I am not remunerated at least to the full amount of these expenses, which just exceed £3,000,' he wrote on 8 March, 'it will be impossible for me to carry on in my present business, and I shall have left the Government service practically destitute.'

In the meantime the Army Council had set a deadline of 31 March for accepting its offer of £1,000. Cody, by now, had no choice but to accept. On 30 March, the day before the offer expired, he wrote a curt note. 'I beg to inform you that I accept the offer of £1,000 mentioned,' he wrote.

If the War Office had hoped this was the end of the matter, however, they were mistaken. In his acceptance letter, Cody made it clear that he also intended an appeal to the Treasury under the Patent and Design Act, claiming compensation for his invention. The monumental disdain with which the Army's hierarchy now regarded their fractious former employee was summed up in a confidential memo dispatched by a senior officer called Harris, when a copy of Cody's claim duly arrived at the War Office a few weeks later.

Cody had, it seems, failed to make his claim on the correct legal form. 'We have duly warned Cody as to the necessity for legal forms and so on in his claim,' wrote Harris. 'But he seems to be a thick headed and ignorant person and has apparently misunderstood or forgotten what he has been told.'

VIVIAN'S FIANCÉE EVA COPELAND HAD BEEN SHOCKED BY the reaction when she had arrived at Pinehurst to meet her prospective parents-in-law. 'Go home quickly and change into something else before the Colonel sees you,' Lela had told her, brushing her back through the front door. Eva's mistake had been to turn up in a pretty dress of bright, green brocade. Cody's demand that no one wear the colour in his presence was only one of a series of superstitions he had adopted.

At the shed he refused to start work on a new project on a Friday. He always used the number 12a rather than 13 when labelling parts. He had pinned a horseshoe over the front door and kept a lucky black cat at hand at all times. It formed part of the deliberately eccentric image he knew his public loved. (Cody often talked in gobbledegook: electricity was 'electrickery', magnetos were 'magnuisances'.) Yet his rituals reflected too the very real awareness he now had of the risks he was taking.

Since Orville and Wilbur Wright's assistant, Lieutenant TE Selfridge, became the first casualty of the aeroplane age in 1908, flying had begun to claim a depressingly large toll. In the months following Doncaster, Cody was shocked and saddened by the loss of Delagrange at an air show in France.

Cody treated death with a blend of bad comedy and morbid philosophy. By now he had begun building a new, Mark II, Cathedral fitted with an English ENV engine. 'I can give you my epitaph right here,' he quipped: 'CODY. ENV. RIP.'

On another occasion he told Harry Harper, 'When my time comes, I hope my death will also be swift and sudden, death from one of my own aeroplanes.' The concept of quitting while he was ahead was beyond him, it seems. Cody had apparently smiled blankly when an eavesdropping mechanic heard his comment to Harper and suggested his boss devote himself to design and construction 'and let younger men do the piloting'.

Cody had 'retired' his original Cathedral in the wake of Aintree and begun working on a new, equally gargantuan biplane, this time with two front elevators, two rudders and a single propeller, powered by the ENV engine. On the morning of 23 June after a successful flight the previous day, Cody took to the Hampshire skies once more. He was on his third circuit of Laffan's Plain when he was hit by a powerful gust and the plane fell crashing, nose first, to the ground. Edward Leroy and Vivian were among the small group who saw Cody thrown violently forward from his seat. (The idea of a seat belt was anathema to him.) When they reached the plane they found it wrecked. 'Cody himself was entangled with the plane and apparently stunned or unconscious,' reported one newspaperman who attended the scene. 'His face was covered with blood and it trickled through his beard. His workmen asked if he was hurt badly, and receiving no reply set to work to extricate him.'

Vivian and Edward rushed Cody back to Pinehurst, where a distraught Lela feared he was dead. By the evening, however, she was telegraphing the *Daily Mail* offices in London. Cody was 'progressing favourably but was still delirious', she told the paper's news desk.

At the age of forty-three, Cody was rapidly losing the physical condition of his youth. He had always had, by all accounts, an enormous appetite. (Photographs of him polishing off a three-course meal became popular postcards at the time.) As a young man he had burned off the calories with ease. His fading powers of recovery were not helped by the excess weight he was now carrying. For the rest of the summer he was unable to do more than give lectures and collect 'attendance fees' at various air meetings up and down the country.

Cody's sagging spirits were not helped when he travelled to make a small contribution to the Bournemouth meeting in July. Along with a crowd of several thousand, he watched on in horror as his old friend CS Rolls fell to his death when the rear elevator

became detached from his Wright Flyer during a sweep across the arena's grandstands.

Cody was one of the first to reach Rolls's lifeless body and had burst into tears. His friend's death must have thrown Cody's own situation into chilling relief. Rolls's fortune had been assured by his collaboration with Henry Royce and the formation of their automobile company in 1906. Rolls had passionately believed that aeroplane manufacture provided as great an opportunity and had joined the growing band of entrepreneurs now eyeing a place in the embryonic aviation industry.

The previous October, Bleriot had been given a seat on the board of a new company formed with the sale of £100,000 in ordinary shares to sell the British rights to his planes. A handful of companies, Alliott Verdon Roe's Avro, Bristol, Frederick Handley-Page's eponymous operation and Short Brothers were soon forging ahead with their businesses. The new 'aerodromes' which had opened that year at Eastchurch, Brooklands, Larkhill and, most successfully, at Hendon in north London, where the dashing Claude Grahame-White had opened a factory and an aviation school, symbolised the explosion of interest in flying. In comparison, Cody remained isolated at Laffan's Plain, a one-man band, perennially strapped for 'capital'.

Rolls's death seemed to act as a catalyst. Around this time he began negotiations with a businessman, Ebenezer Davis, to launch British National Aeroplanes Ltd. The company and its articles of association were drawn up but the deal was never signed. Cody made an attempt at selling his own plane at £1,200. He also placed adverts in the aeronautical press for Cody's Flying School, Laffan's Plain. ('The perfection of British Workmanship', the advert promised.) The response was underwhelming.

As he recovered from his accident, Cody's only option was to continue on the competition circuit. His Mk II Cathedral, fitted for the first time with two Green engines, proved an abject failure when he took it to a meeting at Lanark in Scotland. Back at Laffan's Plain he reverted to a single Green engine, with much better results.

By the late autumn, he was confident enough in his new plane's capabilities to enter the prestigious British Empire Michelin Cup, which offered a £500 cash prize and a £500 trophy for the 'all-British' flyer who could register the longest distance within a closed circuit before the end of the year. The previous year's prize had been won by Moore-Brabazon with an aggregate of just nineteen miles. As the 1910 contest got under way in earnest in the late autumn, it was clear Cody would need to travel at least ten times that distance to win the prize.

The race developed into a three-way contest between Cody and two young pilots, Thomas Sopwith, flying out of Brooklands, and Alec Ogilvie, whose base was on the south coast of England, at Camber Sands, near Rye. The writer Graham Wallace summed up the events of that winter best. 'Their struggle to remain airborne the longest was as exciting as an episode in Cody's *Klondyke Nugget*.'

A series of flagstaffs now marked out a compact, two-and-a-

THE
"CODY FLYER"
30 - 35 h.p.   **50 - 60 h.p.**

The Perfection of British Workmanship.

Early delivery can be obtained of
——— either models. ———

Aeroplanes built to client's own designs.
Flying taught.   Pupils taken.
Propellers built.

Apply—

Cody Flying School, Laffan's Plain, Farnborough.

Remember, one hour's flight is guaranteed with each " Cody Flyer."

half-mile circuit around Laffan's Plain. Cody set the standard for his young rivals with a ninety-two-mile flight in the autumn. Sopwith soon improved on this in November with a distance of 107 miles. It was in December, however, that the race really hotted up. On 16 December Cody stayed aloft for just under three hours for a flight of 115 miles. As the winter weather deteriorated badly over the next fortnight, he had spent Christmas wondering whether that would be enough to win him the prize. It was soon clear it wasn't. On 28 December, Alec Ogilvie went up from Shellbeach to record a sensational 139 miles in three hours and fifty-five minutes. Cody went up that day too but was forced down after a mere fifty miles with engine trouble. He barely slept over the next two nights as the weather in Aldershot remained poor. At 4 a.m. on New Year's Eve, Lela had drawn back the bedroom curtains at Pinehurst to find him pacing the gardens, looking anxiously at the skies. By daybreak it was clear the weather had picked up. At just before 8.30 on a frosty morning he lifted the new-look Cathedral into the air. He had loaded twenty-five gallons of petrol on board, enough for five hours of flying. By 11.30 a large crowd had gathered to cheer the news that he had officially beaten Ogilvie's mark. Their joy gave way to apprehension as news came through from Brooklands that Sopwith had taken to the air at 9.40 that morning and was also still in the air. Attempts to relay the message to Cody failed miserably. (Cody later said he had spent the journey certain his rivals were in the air too.) Soon after noon Cody dropped his flying altitude to 100 feet to avoid the turbulence he had begun experiencing at his normal height of 250 feet. By 1 p.m. and his seventieth circuit the crowds could hear his engine missing badly, a sure indication that he was on his last drop of petrol. Midway through his seventy-eighth lap, at 1.14 p.m., he dropped down and made a safe landing. (Even then he claimed his descent was an accident, caused by his elbow flicking the wrong switch on his dashboard.)

According to one version of the day's events, Cody emerged from the plane with his beard and moustache white with frost. The newspapers the next day described how he was mobbed by a crowd who began singing a popular Army song, 'The Conquering Hero'. Soon the official marker, a Lieutenant Fox, announced that Cody had spent four hours and forty-six minutes in the air and had covered 189.2 miles, a new British record. For the next, tense, hour or so, however, Cody had to wait to discover whether it was enough. A series of frantic telephone calls were made to Brooklands and Rye from where rumours had arrived of a last-ditch attempt by Ogilvie that afternoon. Soon it emerged that Sopwith had come down at 1 p.m., having covered almost exactly 150 miles. Ogilvie's flight had come to a premature end when his engine broke down after only fifty miles. By late afternoon the Royal Aero Club had confirmed that Cody had won his first major trophy and the £500 first prize.

THE NEW YEAR'S NEWSPAPERS CONFIRMED THE SHIFT IN his fortunes. 'It is a peculiar pleasure to congratulate Mr Cody on his success,' admitted the *Manchester Guardian* in its report on the Michelin win. 'The prize is a reward not only for a particularly fine flight but for two years of persistent effort, patiently sustained in the face of many difficulties and much criticism, not always kept within fair limits.' His huge popularity among the ordinary public was underlined by the commissioning of a wax likeness of him at Madame Tussaud's. (The model bore an uncanny resemblance to Lenin rather than Cody.)

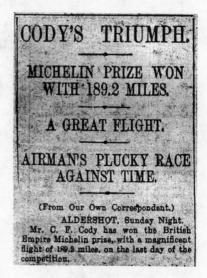

CODY'S TRIUMPH.

MICHELIN PRIZE WON WITH 189.2 MILES.

A GREAT FLIGHT.

AIRMAN'S PLUCKY RACE AGAINST TIME.

(From Our Own Correspondent.)
ALDERSHOT, Sunday Night.
Mr. C. F. Cody has won the British Empire Michelin prize, with a magnificent flight of 189.2 miles, on the last day of the competition.

Cody collected his Michelin Trophy at a glittering dinner at Prince's Restaurant in London on 31 January 1911. A few weeks later, he met his old acquaintance the former Prince of Wales, now installed as the new King George V, at the second annual Aero Show at Olympia. Cody had been amused at the way the King now kept referring to him as Colonel Cody. 'If the King of England is pleased to call me Colonel then Colonel I will be in future,' he smiled afterwards. George joined in the congratulations, then asked, only half jokingly, about a trip in the Cathedral. Within weeks George visited the shed at Laffan's Plain but, it seems on the advice of his officials, decided against a flight.

Cody put on a command performance nevertheless, bringing the Cathedral to a halt only a few feet from the King's party. The next morning's newspapers were horrified that Cody could have put the monarch's life at such risk. 'As if I would endanger a hair of the King's head,' he fumed.

CHAPTER ELEVEN

SHOWMAN OF FLIGHT

A monster comes next, rolling in the breeze, and gliding down over us with a shining steel propeller slowly turning. It is a weapon to make an executioner's mouth water. So deadly a thing has no right, we feel, so near us.

'Cody in his Cathedral,' cries a voice, and there is a scamper of photographers. The monster comes smoothly to earth and Mr Cody, whose physique matches that of his machine, dismounts.

—*Daily Mail* report on Cody's arrival at Hendon for the £10,000 Circuit of Britain Air Race, 22 July 1911

'VAST BEYOND RECKONING,' ONE WITNESS CALLED THE half-million-strong crowd that camped out at Hendon for the start of the inaugural Circuit of Britain Challenge. 'The scene was one of incomparable brilliance and fascination. It seemed as though some great and sudden impulse had awakened London this day for the first time to the spell of flying.'

The mania had made its way over from the Continent, where enormous, excitable crowds had cheered the Paris-to-Madrid and Paris-to-Rome challenges of that summer. The winners of both had been lured to England by Lord Northcliffe's £10,000 prize, for the first man to fly the 1,010-mile round trip from Brooklands

to London, Edinburgh, Manchester, Bristol, Exeter and back. The dash and daring of the Paris–Madrid champion, Vedrines, and the bearded French Naval officer, Lieutenant Conneau, nicknamed 'Beaumont', would captivate millions. Neither would quite threaten Cody's status as the race's entertainer-in-chief.

Even at the helm of a new, slightly smaller, speedier 'Mark III' Cathedral he had built specifically for the race, Cody knew he had no real hope of beating the lightweight, eighty-mile-an-hour monoplanes of Vedrines and 'Beaumont'. 'If the race is to the tortoise, then Cody will win,' he joked with the *Daily Mail*'s air correspondent, his old friend Harry Harper, in the run-up to the race.

The Cathedral's limitations were obvious at Brooklands on Saturday, 22 July, at the start of the curtain-raising hop to Hendon twenty miles to the northeast. 'Beaumont', contestant No. 1, led off in his Bleriot monoplane at 4 p.m., followed at five-minute intervals by the hundred-mile-an-hour Birdling monoplane flown by HJD Astley, then the Briton C Compton-Paterson in Graham-White's 'Baby' biplane, Vedrines in a Morane-Borel monoplane and the Englishman 'Jimmy' Valentine in his Deperdussin monoplane. Cody, No. 20 in the race, set off half an hour or so later at

The tortoise takes off. Cody leaves Brooklands to begin
the Circuit of Britain Challenge.

an altogether more sedate pace. One witness described how he
'floated away in the distance with his huge propeller lazily wan-
dering around'.

What it lacked in speed, however, the Cathedral more than
made up in endurance and reliability. The news that he had made
the trip in the fifth best time of the day only added to the euphoria at Hendon on the Saturday evening.

Cody spent Saturday and Sunday night preparing the Cathedral – and himself – for the real test ahead, the 383-mile first leg of the main race, from Hendon to Edinburgh at dawn on the Monday morning. The trip would be broken up into three legs, a 182-mile flight to Harrogate, in Yorkshire, then a sixty-eight-mile trip due north to Newcastle and a final ninety-three-mile flight to the northwest into Scotland and the Firth of Forth. For Cody, like every other competitor, the flight north represented a journey into the unknown.

Beneath the romantic veneer, air racing was the most perilous sport twentieth-century man had yet devised. Fatalities were commonplace, mainly because navigation remained a crude, at times desperate business for the long-distance aviators. All manner of ideas had been tried to help guide them safely. In Paris, for instance, huge, reflecting glass balls had been laid out to spell giant letters visible to racers from 2,000 feet. Elsewhere large arrows had been painted on the ground, captive balloons and kites had been positioned in their flight paths, railway lines had been painted white and damp straw fires had been lit to mark the route, all to little avail. The recent invention of rubber-lined, gimbal mountings had at last improved the airman's chance of getting a sensible reading from his compass. (In the early days, the vibration of the plane was so violent the compass needle spent most of the flight dancing around unintelligibly.) Even that had not removed the risk that, in poor visibility, airmen faced the real risk of flying into mountainsides.

The prospect of flying around the British Isles brought its own terrors. Cody and his rivals marked their maps with every landmark possible, from roads and railways to masses of woodland and water. As a student of wind variations, Cody paid particular attention to hills and mountain ranges where he might expect sudden shifts and squalls.

Just before four o'clock on the Monday morning, he gave his map one final scan and climbed aboard the Cathedral once more. At just after 4.05 a.m. he set off, five minutes behind the early

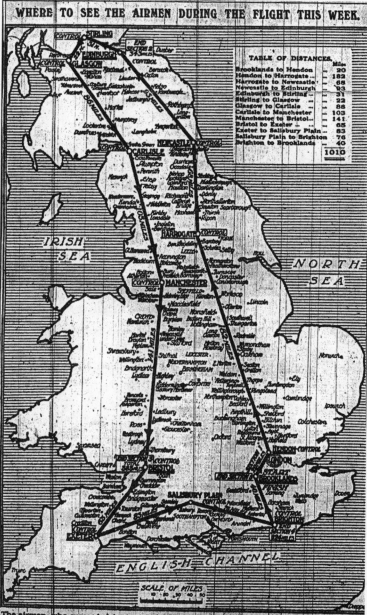

WHERE TO SEE THE AIRMEN DURING THE FLIGHT THIS WEEK.

TABLE OF DISTANCES.	
	Miles
Brooklands to Hendon	20
Hendon to Harrogate	182
Harrogate to Newcastle	66
Newcastle to Edinburgh	93
Edinburgh to Stirling	31
Stirling to Glasgow	22
Glasgow to Carlisle	88
Carlisle to Manchester	103
Manchester to Bristol	141
Bristol to Exeter	65
Exeter to Salisbury Plain	83
Salisbury Plain to Brighton	76
Brighton to Brooklands	40
	1010

The airmen who succeeded in completing Section I. (Brooklands to Hendon) on Saturday start early this morning on the more serious part of the 1,010 miles flight. The map shows the route and the principal places the competitors may be expected to pass over. A descent must be made in every control.

leader, Vedrines, Beaumont, Valentine and the fourth-placed flyer, the Englishman Gustav Hamel.

True to his promise, the tortoise set off at a stately fifty to sixty miles an hour. His No. 20 was cheered by crowds over Nottingham, at around 5 a.m. Three hours into the flight, however, his radiator sprang a leak, sending boiling water spraying into his face. He was forced to make an emergency landing at the small village of Tinsley Wood in South Yorkshire, but – the leak mended and the radiator refilled – was on his way again within half an hour.

By around 11 a.m. the crowds at Harrogate had seen the two clear leaders land and take off again. Vedrines had arrived just after 7 a.m., Beaumont, hot on his heels, a few minutes later. Both men had refuelled and resumed their journey by 7.45 a.m. A few minutes before that, around 7.40 a.m., the popular Jimmy Valentine had touched down to collect a prize of silver tableware for the first British competitor.

As the fourth arrival loomed into view the crowds were amazed to see the vast silhouette of the Cathedral. 'What, Cody? Never!' Harry Harper heard one incredulous member of the 150,000-strong crowd say.

The acrid fumes emanating from his engine only added to the sense of amazement. A petrol tank had ruptured during the flight over Leeds and Cody had made the descent into Harrogate in the knowledge his plane could explode at any moment. 'I reckon I know how to nurse little things of that sort,' Cody assured the concerned crowd. He had become accustomed, he revealed later, to using one hand to hold ruptured petrol tanks in position while flying with the other.

Resourcefulness was one thing, resources another. Cody was not in a financial position to compete with the drilled professionalism of the Frenchmen. 'Instantly Beaumont or Vedrines or Hamel alighted in the evening, their machines were surrounded by their teams, who worked right through the night, going over every part of the plane and its motor, so as to have it in perfect trim next morning,' Harry Harper reported during the race. Cody in comparison was a one-man band. As the *Times*'s air correspondent put it, 'He carried all his tools in his pocket, and when his machine required repair, he came down and tinkered it himself with such material as he carried, or that could be procured from the local blacksmith.'

Cody was faced with long hours of work on the plane and spent the night in Harrogate. He left at 5 a.m. the following day, to even more rousing cheers than the previous day.

The events of the first day had opened the Harrogate crowd's eyes to the frightening physical and psychological strain the aviators faced. Gustav Hamel had arrived literally paralysed with fear after a terrifying journey through the turbulent winds of the Midlands and South Yorkshire. His face was, according to one witness, 'ashen grey, streaked with blood and rigid as marble'. Officials had been able to unclench his hands from his steering gear only by forcing brandy between his lips.

Even for Cody, who had spent more hours being battered by winds than any man alive, the race offered a fearful new experience. Heading north for Newcastle he found himself enmeshed in heavy fog and lost his bearings. Disoriented, he made another emergency landing, this time near Brandon Hill colliery outside Durham, just seventeen miles short of his destination. A group of miners helped point him in the right direction but his choice of landing field had been disastrous. As he tried to take off again the Cathedral struggled to build up speed in the boggy conditions. His undercarriage caught some barbed wire and he ran into a brick wall, denting the rib of the right wing. He immediately realised the extent of the damage and cabled ahead to the Newcastle control point.

LANDED NEAR DURHAM. DAMAGED WING.
HOPE TO ARRIVE WEDNESDAY.

For thousands of ordinary Britons, manned flight remained the stuff of HG Wells novels and fanciful Jules Verne adventures. The prospect of a first-hand encounter with the magnificent men and their flying machines was remote. As news of Cody's downing spread, so many people climbed up on to Brandon Hill from the surrounding towns that the police had to be called in to fence the Cathedral off. After a few hours sleep at the nearby colliery, Cody faced another day's work to get his plane fit for the air again. (He had by now been joined by his small support team – Leon and Vivian in the car!) By the time he eventually left Durham and completed the twenty-five-minute trip to Newcastle early on the Wednesday evening he had lost two days. In that time the whole complexion of the race had changed.

The Circuit had gone to form and settled into a head-to-head contest between Vedrines and Beaumont. Vedrines' early lead had slipped on the southward leg of the course. Beaumont had pressed home his advantage and arrived at Brooklands at just after two o'clock that afternoon, five days after the start of the race. His total flying time of twenty-one hours and forty-eight minutes was a clear hour and thirteen minutes faster than Vedrines'.

The Royal Aero Club officials informed Cody he was one of a group of eight still on the course. Only two lay ahead of him. Valentine remained in clear third place and had reached Glasgow. To the astonishment of those who had seen him in Harrogate, Hamel had also made it to Scotland. Behind him, back in Harrogate, were Lt Col. HRP Reynolds of the Royal Engineers in a Howard Wright biplane, Astley in his Birdling and the Frenchman Olivier de Montalent flying a biplane for the Breuguet company. Trailing the field were CP Pizey in a Bristol biplane back at Melton Mowbray in Leicestershire and BC Hucks in a Blackburn monoplane was at Luton, barely twenty miles from Hendon.

Cody spent the following day in Newcastle seemingly uncertain what to do. By the end of the day, however, the Royal Aero Club officials had confirmed that Pizey, Astley, Reynolds and

Hucks had now retired. With Montalent ordered to withdraw by his French sponsors, no other planes remained on the southern half of the course. Even more encouraging for Cody was the news that both Hamel and Valentine were experiencing trouble with their planes and were still on the northern leg of the race in Scotland.

Cody now realised he could finish third but more importantly be the first Briton and the first biplane pilot to complete the circuit. The officials learned of his intentions when they heard a loud banging on the door of their hotel at around 3.30 a.m. on the Friday. Forty minutes later he was in the air en route to Edinburgh. His greatest enemy now was the clock. The Royal Aero Club had set a deadline of 7.30 p.m. on Saturday, 6 August, for the completion of the race. Cody had taken just over a week to complete the first quarter of the course. He had another seven days to complete the remaining 740 miles.

He IS ALMOST THE FATHER OF FLYING,' ONE OFFICIAL WAS heard to say as Cody disappeared into the distance at Newcastle. 'He knows as much as anyone about it.' Even Cody had not known conditions like those he faced that morning. 'The worst I have ever had in my life,' he later called the experience. 'In such weather as I experienced a monoplane would have turned turtle.'

His troubles began at the Scottish border where a 'terrific gale' pushed him and the Cathedral out to sea. 'Try as I would, no headway could I make, and all the time I was being carried farther and farther out to sea,' he said later. 'I was now flying at a height of 3,800 feet and it looked as though my next landing place would be Holland – if indeed, I ever saw land again.'

Conditions got so bad, Cody began making plans to ditch in the North Sea. 'I looked down and there below I saw a ship passing. I determined to dive down to pitch into the sea and get them to take me aboard: for this seemed to be my only chance in the circumstances,' he explained afterwards. 'So down I came to a height of 1,500 feet, when, to my surprise and delight, I found myself in comparatively smooth air, and quite able to continue my flight towards the land.'

Cody eventually landed next to a cluster of tents he had spotted. It turned out to be Edinburgh's Boys' Brigade, who pointed him in the right direction. Even then his flight to the landing point was not uneventful. Once more he found himself in thick fog. 'I almost ran into Edinburgh Castle without seeing it,' he said making light of it all later.

Cody arrived at the most northerly point of the circuit at around 8 a.m. and with his decision to fly on vindicated. He learned that Hamel was stuck in a small town called Carronbridge in an even worse physical and mental state than earlier. His father had joined the growing band of friends and advisers begging him to give up before he killed himself. Valentine's smooth progress had slowed down, too. Across the English border he had been forced to return to Carlisle with engine trouble.

Cody's hopes of seizing the initiative were dashed by more heavy winds. By 7.30 p.m., however they had died down and he pressed on for Stirling, making the trip in forty minutes. As huge crowds fanned around him he ran into some ropes. This time the damage was no more than a broken strut. He was ready again the next morning and made the trip to Paisley near Glasgow where he, like his rivals, would be required to rest over the Sunday night.

The Cathedral was, by now, the worse for wear, guzzling petrol at a ferocious rate and, more worryingly, 'coked up' by heavy carbon deposits in the engine itself.

Cody began the second week of the circuit with a burst of demonic energy. By now he knew Hamel had finally given in to his father's pleas and retired. Determined to set after Valentine, he left Paisley at just after 4 a.m. and within fifty minutes had arrived at Lanark. While his staff began fixing the extra petrol tank he had ordered there, Cody jumped in a cab to the train station.

At around 1 p.m. Cody arrived in Carlisle across the English border. He was soon climbing out of another taxi and marching into the Royal Aero Club's control point. No one was more shocked to see Cody than Valentine, who remained in Carlisle while repair work went ahead on his Deperdussin. He immediately headed off on the next leg of the race to Manchester.

Content the officials would keep the control point open for the rest of the day, Cody headed back in the opposite direction across the Scottish border. He was back in Carlisle by evening at the helm of the Cathedral.

News of Cody's feverish activity drew a large crowd. As he clambered out at 7.25 p.m., he apologised for his lateness, then promised, for a small admission fee, of course, a full account of his journey so far at Her Majesty's Theatre that night at 10 p.m. The money was soon in the pocket of James Winskill, a mechanic from the Beacon Motoring Works at nearby Penrith, who was called in to work on the engine through the night.

Cody understood and was better equipped to deal with his fame, and the expectations that came with it, than any other early aviator. The first celebrities of the air age, Orville and Wilbur Wright, were painfully shy to the point of social ineptitude. ('I know of only one bird – the parrot – that talks; and it can't fly very high,' Wilbur used to say when refusing to make speeches.) The military men and aristocrats of the Anglo-French flying classes liked to think themselves above their admiring fans in more ways than one. In contrast, Cody was a showman through and through. He accepted every hand proffered to him, scrawled (albeit slowly, in his vast, childlike writing) every autograph asked of him, engineered every photo opportunity that presented itself – and the people loved him for it.

'Twelve years ago I told an audience in this theatre that I hoped to fly. "Oh, it's mad, Cody," they said. Now I tell you I hope to fly faster than a Bleriot monoplane,' he told the thrilled audience in Carlisle that night. His speech was a blend of bluster, *Boy's Own* adventure and bulldog patriotism. He played on the fact that he was the sole 'all-British' competitor on the circuit. His plane, he told the crowds, had 'not a stitch or screw' designed by anyone other than him. With luck and God's grace, he concluded, he would be 'spending Saturday evening with Madame Cody at Aldershot'. The cheering apparently went on for five minutes.

By the morning Winskill had boiled the engine in caustic soda so as to remove all the carbon deposits. By the late afternoon the engine had been refitted and Cody was on his way to Manchester. The crossing over Morecambe Bay proved difficult and, with progress slow, Cody was forced, for the first time, to fly in darkness. Unable to see his map, compass or even the moon and stars in cloudy conditions, he thought better of it and landed a few miles short of Manchester at Hutton, near Preston, shortly after 10 p.m. He was away again at 4 a.m. on the Wednesday, this time headed via Worcester to Bristol.

By now Cody's procession around the country had caught the imagination of the entire British public. The next morning, when an engineer working at the top of a forty-foot telegraph pole spotted him in the far distance, heading towards the small, hilltop community of Woore in Cheshire, his shouts emptied every bed in the village. 'The news spread like wild-fire and men, women and children turned out of their houses pell-mell, and had ample time to fix themselves in position for the best possible view,' reported one local newspaper. Cody spotted the crowds and obliged by slowing down and dropping to within a few yards of Woore's new church tower. 'A wag in the village called out to him "stop and have a refresher" and it is reported that Cody replied that he should like to only that he was flying against time,' the newspaper added.

Cody arrived at the Filton aerodrome outside Bristol shortly before noon. As a large crowd swirled around him he received mixed news. Valentine had left the aerodrome at 5.30 that morning for Exeter, the southwestern extremity of the course. Despite dreadful foggy conditions he had arrived there at 8.25 a.m. and was

CODY IN WESTON.

Graceful Descent on the Sands Opposite the Grand Atlantic Hotel.

GREAT EXCITEMENT IN THE TOWN.

Friday Morning's Memorable Scene Illustrated.

VIEW OF THE AEROPLANE.

Cody Interviewed by a "Gazette" Representative.

preparing to strike on for the next control point at Salisbury the next morning. The better news was that he, Valentine and Vedrines would share a £250 prize awarded by the head of the Bristol plane company, Sir George White, for getting this far. Once more Cody was frustrated by the weather. He was kept at Bristol that night and the next day. It was only after 7 p.m. that he was able to head off for Exeter. With the winds whipping up into a storm, he was forced to make another unscheduled stop at the holiday resort of Weston-super-Mare, where he landed at 8.30 p.m.

Once more the sight and sound of Cody and his deafening dreadnought emptied every house in the town. Once more Cody capitalised on the situation by charging a small fee for a talk on the pier at 9.30 that night. Most of the crowd of 4,000 were unable to sleep and were there waiting for him when he re-emerged at three o'clock the following morning. As he roared along the brazier-lined beach, then disappeared into the distance, the crowds stood transfixed. 'Long after there was any chance of catching another glimpse of the airman or his machine, thousands continued to gaze as if spellbound in the direction in which he had vanished,' wrote one eyewitness. 'The sands and the sea front were black with people as they at last reluctantly moved away, tired perhaps, and heavy-eyed and sleepy, but thankful withal to Col. Cody for having given them an opportunity of witnessing the latest wonder of the world.'

Cody arrived in Exeter at 5.10 on the Friday morning. He was away again towards Salisbury by 6.40 a.m., but, his bearings lost again, ended up heading to Bristol. By the time he arrived at Salisbury it was too late to go on any farther. He spent the Friday night making preparations for the following day, the last of the race. By now, however, he knew the honour of being the first Briton home would not be his.

Valentine had left Exeter on the Thursday morning. He had reached Salisbury by 11 a.m. and gone on to Brighton and the gold cup for the first British pilot to complete the circuit at 7.30 that evening. He had almost come to grief on his run home to Brooklands that Friday. He had broken a stay over Horsham and had taken almost nine hours to complete the trip. He had arrived there just before seven o'clock on the penultimate night of the race nevertheless.

Encouraged by the ever-present crowds, Cody was determined to be the final man home. He was in the air by four o'clock on the Saturday morning. By 6.15 a.m. he had made it to the Brighton control point at the Shoreham aerodrome. By 8.25 a.m. Cody was away again in the direction of Brooklands.

The last leg of the trip proved the least troublesome of all. Riding a forty-mile-an-hour following wind, Cody and the Cathedral covered the forty miles in a little over half an hour. His spectacular morning's work caught Brooklands by complete surprise.

With the race due to close officially that evening, the Royal Aero Club staff had expected Cody in the late afternoon. Cody touched down at 9 a.m. to find the aerodrome deserted. 'No crowd waited to herald with cheers the descent of the breezy, jovial aviator. His arrival was so unexpected,' reported one news-paper, 'not even an official timekeeper was present.'

In fact the warmest welcome seems to have come from Valen-tine, who was preparing his plane to leave. At the end of their journey, Beaumont and Vedrines had been treated to a champagne reception at the Savoy by Lord Northcliffe. Cody and Valentine paid for their own pot of tea and a plate of potted-shrimp sand-wiches at Brooklands' Blue Bird café .

CODY'S WINNINGS HAD BARELY COVERED THE CIRCUIT'S £100 entry fee. Yet his epic feat was greeted as the outstand-ing triumph of the fortnight. 'It may be stated without fear of contradiction that Cody's is the finest performance in the race,' wrote CG Grey, the editor of *The Aeroplane*, in his report on the great air race. 'And one can say this without any disparagement of Valentine's very plucky show. Cody built his machine himself, without any financial assistance, and against odds which would have beaten any ordinary man years ago.' The fact that, at the age of forty-four, 'Papa' Cody was a 'grandfather' – Leon's wife Flor-ence had given birth to a daughter, Leonie, in November 1909 – and twice the age of many of his young rivals only endeared him to the public more.

His heroics in the following weeks only underlined his status as a national treasure. In September and October Cody won both the Michelin trophies on offer that year in England. The first 'Series II' Michelin race was open to the pilot who could cover a 125-mile cross-country circuit in the fastest time. Cody took three attempts to even manage the course, setting a poor target of just over three hours on 11 September. To his amazement, however, no one beat it and he collected the £400 first prize. The £500 'Series I' race, which he had won the previous year, required a minimum flight of 250 miles, to be registered by 31 October. Two days before the deadline, 29 October, he took to the skies above Laffan's Plain once more. He spent the first four hours cruising comfortably at 1,200 feet averaging fifty-one miles per hour. Around noon, however, the plane was buffeted by heavy winds. For the next hour the biplane was, as one observer put it, 'tossed around like a bird in a storm'. Cody struggled on until 1.20 p.m. then landed, having covered just over 255 miles, a new British record for a single long-distance flight. He was surrounded by what *Motor* magazine called 'an enthusiastic concourse of thousands'. 'With what applause he, always the favourite of the public . . . was carried shoulder high.' Once again his young rivals could not match him. The £500 and the Pegasus-like Michelin Trophy were his again.

Prophet of flight S.F. Cody has been, conqueror he has lived to be. It is said that his aerial prophecies have been unduly warm. But it is no use being silent under neglect. And it is surely permissible to gossip to newspaper reporters when you know you can make good. None of his prophecies concerning flight have failed. He built the first man-lifting kite, which belongs to the British Army; it is still unpaid for. He built the first British aeroplane that actually flew . . . and the original record of forty miles. Since then he has flown to win three Michelin Cups and 1,000 miles round England for honour, and the admiration of his adopted countrymen, which is exceeding great. With his dramatic entrances and exits on his great biplanes, he is the British public's chief and best-loved showman of flight.

—*Vanity Fair*, 'Men of the Day', November 1911

His huge public popularity only added to Cody's frustration at the commercial shortcomings of his operation. 'Why do people always buy Bleriots and Farmans?' he would complain. 'Why don't they buy Cody instead?' Here, at least, he was far from a voice in the wilderness.

Britain's fledgling aviation industry had become increasingly angry at its lack of support from the government. The depth of feeling had intensified after the major reorganisation of the old Balloon Factory, in April that year, 1911. The era of the balloon and the man-carrying kite was officially consigned to history as the old Balloon Companies were replaced by the Air Battalion of the Royal Engineers. (Colonel Capper returned to the regular Army where he fought gallantly in World War One.) The premises at Farnborough became home to the Army Aircraft Factory and the Airship Company, while the open spaces of Larkhill on Salisbury Plain became the far more suitable home for the Aeroplane Company. Yet the change had reduced rather than increased the opportunities for Britain's private plane makers. A brilliant young designer, Geoffrey de Havilland, had been engaged to build planes in-house at Farnborough. In the interim, early orders for training craft had been given to French companies. The new Under-Secretary of State for War, Colonel FE Seely, had fanned the flames further by accusing British planes of lacking 'efficiency and safety'. 'There are at least ten machines in the possession of the Air Battalion, most of them built in France, which are in every respect inferior to the Avro and the Cody,' protested the *Daily Telegraph*'s air correspondent, Major CC Turner, on their behalf.

As the storm of protest grew, Whitehall finally bowed to the pressure. That autumn the War Office announced trials, to be held the following August at Larkhill. The tests would determine the best type of aeroplane for equipping the Royal Flying Corps, the new aeroplane reconnaissance unit to be formed the following May. The RFC would buy the winning plane off its owner and undertake to commission a second replica plane in addition.

Even this did not entirely pacify the British plane makers, who objected to the fact the contest was open to foreign manufacturers. Cody made an impassioned speech at a Royal Aero Club meeting that autumn. The War Office bowed once more, offering two cash prizes: an international prize for the best plane, of £4,000, and an award solely for the best British manufacturer, of £1,000.

The offer galvanised the entire British aviation business. Immediately the leading companies, Bristol, Avro, Short, Sopwith and Marty-Handasyde, began work on machines to compete in the contest. For Cody too it was the opportunity he had been waiting for. Once more it was a time to gamble everything.

In November he and the family moved from Pinehurst and Mytchett to a cheaper house, Ash Croft, in the neighbouring village of Ash Vale. Cody began supplementing his income by charging two guineas (£2.10) for flights and, in return for their grant of £75, training new pilots pursuing their Royal Aero Club licences. Every resource he had was poured into preparing the Circuit Cathedral for a tilt at the trials. To add to the financial drain he also began designing a second plane, his first monoplane.

All winter he scribbled out drawings for a sleeker, speedier, single-wing craft that would be the antithesis of the blunderbuss Cathedral. With its high wing, enclosed cockpit and a tail unit of twin rudders the plane that was soon taking shape was, comfortably, the most advanced and elegant machine he had yet built.

With money tighter than ever, the inevitable setbacks were more hurtful than ever too. Cody's most promising trainee pilot, a young naval lieutenant, Wilfred Parke, had become the first man to be allowed to fly the Cathedral solo. In cross-country flights from Hendon to Brooklands and in a duration contest for Army and Navy officers, the Mortimer Singer trophy, he had proven as adept and reliable a flyer as Cody himself. On 7 December, however, preparing for another long-distance race at Laffan's Plain, the young pilot turned too sharply into a strong wind, hit a ridge and crashed. Parke emerged unscathed but the plane that had survived all the Circuit of Britain could throw at it was almost destroyed.

For a while the accident looked like a blessing in disguise. Since being retired in 1911, Cody's old Cathedral – minus its now useless engine – had been kept mothballed at Laffan's Plain. Cody was in no position to buy it a new engine and instead acquired the impressive, 120-horsepower, Austro-Daimler engine he had seen flown by an Austrian pilot at a competition that summer. The engine was by far the most powerful he had ever used. Fitted to the older plane it quickly proved the best too.

By the late spring of 1912, Cody had cause for quiet optimism. He knew the Army trials would require above all else a blend of brute strength and durability. With the Austro-Daimler engine in place, the Cathedral was carrying as many as four passengers. To Cody's delight it had also beaten the first product of de Havilland's reign as the Army Aircraft Factory's designer, a much-vaunted 'silent' biplane powered by a British-made Wolseley engine. Cody and de Havilland had wheeled their machines out on to Farnborough Common with a passenger each, in Cody's case Frank. They had taken off together before heading round a circuit of the area. Cody had won by twelve seconds, clocking up speeds of almost seventy miles per hour.

With his monoplane reaching speeds in excess of eighty in its trials, his optimism was restored. Even the Mk III Circuit Cathedral had been painstakingly restored in the wake of December's crash and was ready to return to the air. It could not last this way, of course.

In the wake of the Parke crash, Cody had been ultracautious about entrusting any of his planes to students. 'Cody, who also had no money, was loath to let me fly unless accompanied, and up to the very last evening before the test, sat immediately behind me, keeping a watchful, too watchful, as it proved eye upon me,' recalled one of his pupils, Lieutenant JN Fletcher, of the Army Air Battalion, whom Cody had agreed to train for his test for free while he awaited the arrival of the £75 grant.

On an early evening in April, Cody accompanied Fletcher for his final lesson. His pupil had just completed a figure of eight and was gliding steadily to earth with the engine off towards a small

A new innovation. Cody proudly shows off his monoplane, 1912.

pavilion when Cody suddenly intervened. 'Cody, fearing I was going to hit the pavilion, leaned over my shoulder and pushed the control column,' Fletcher recounted. 'But he pushed it too much.'

The plane hit the ground at seventy-five miles per hour, throwing Cody and Fletcher out. As he left the plane, Cody's foot accidentally hit the engine switch and the plane staggered on, bouncing along the ground, pilotless, until it ploughed into a tree near the Basingstoke Canal. Fletcher was unhurt but Cody took a heavy blow from the tail wheel as the plane went by him. He was found on the ground concussed and suffering from a fractured shin bone.

As usual he asked to be taken home rather than to hospital. Lela, in particular, would never forget his arrival back at Ash Croft. No sooner had she helped carry Cody upstairs than another ambulance had pulled up outside. In his rush to get back to the house to tell his mother of his father's accident, Frank's bicycle had collided with a dog. He had been thrown and had also picked up severe head wounds. It took Frank weeks to recover from his bicycle crash. According to the family, Lela never fully got over the day and remained a nervous shadow of her former fearless self from then on.

Cody was inspecting the wreck of his machine the following Monday morning. Once more he faced a long and expensive rebuilding job. Once more he fell back on the Cathedral that had carried him around the Circuit of Britain as his main plane. In May, with Cody back at the controls, it entered – and won – a minor race for a cup presented by the actress Marie Tempest. The fact he was back in the air at all was worth far more than the trophy and the kiss he received from the picturesque star of London's West End.

O N 12 JUNE 1912 CODY CLIMBED THE STEPS OF THE TREA-sury building in Whitehall flanked by a team of pinstriped solicitors. He was shown into an inner chamber, where he was greeted by the leonine figure of David Lloyd George, the Chancellor of the Exchequer.

Seven years after he had first set out his terms for the sale of his man-carrying kite, Cody had finally won the right to have his case heard. Lloyd George sat in arbitration in the case billed as *Cody v. The War Office*.

Cody had already made one appearance before Lloyd George in February that year. Giving evidence, Cody had blamed himself for exercising poor commercial judgment when he first agreed to join the Army as Kite Instructor.

The Army had insisted he give up his *Klondyke Nugget* business – at the time a profitmaking enterprise worth £1,800 a month, he claimed. On top of this he had been obliged to hand in every one of his fifty kites to the Army when he joined up. They were then broken up and he was given a 'paltry sum, rag value' for them. 'My reason for doing what a real businessman would term unbusinesslike, to accept less pay from the government than I got in my theatrical enterprises, was the hope that within two or three months they would pay me £8,000 . . . or £5,000 and a continuation of employment,' he said. 'That failing, I had a rather bad deal.

'We learn as we live,' he added philosophically.

As his financial situation was examined in more detail, it was not difficult to understand why he had frequently run into trouble over the years. He admitted that he had only recently acquired his first chequebook. 'I have never kept books,' he said while being questioned about the expenses he had run up. 'Even today I do not.'

Cody's lack of accounts turned out to be the crux of the case as far as Lloyd George was concerned. He had adjourned the case while Cody went away to put together a more detailed breakdown of the £3,500 he claimed he had spent developing the man-lifter before joining the Army.

Cody's barrister ensured he kept his replies to simply statements of yes or no in the main. His evidence under examination offered a few intriguing insights nevertheless. He had, for instance, gone so far as to volunteer to fight for the British during the Boer War. Significantly Cody claimed that until 1900 he had spent 'very little' on kiting. He also revealed that he had been involved in a dispute with an impresario who had claimed a percentage of his profits during *The Klondyke Nugget* days. 'Rather second-rate theatrical companies,' Cody called his touring troupe. 'But never mind, they paid, they made money.'

Even the starchy Attorney General, Sir Rufus Isaacs, had recognised the dramatic quality of Cody's story. Cody's counsel, Edward Hemmerde, divided his time between the Inns of Court and the West End, where his popular plays included *A Maid of Honour* and *Proud Maisie*. 'I am sure the end of it will be Mr Hemmerde will write a play and Mr Cody will act in it,' the Attorney General joked. 'If it is as successful as some of Mr Hemmerde's plays he will have great reason to congratulate himself,' Lloyd George agreed, leavening an at times tense atmosphere.

As the hearing moved to its conclusion, it was clear where the Chancellor's sympathies lay. Witnesses, including a Lieutenant

Waterlow from the Balloon Factory, attested to the value the Army was still getting from the man-carrying kite. The suspicion that the War Office had simply hoped Cody would quietly disappear was inescapable. 'There is really nothing between us except the question of how much you think that Mr Cody ought to have,' the Attorney General told Lloyd George at one point. When his colleague for the defence, Mr Rowlatt, justified the War Office's position, claiming, 'We have slipped into the position, we have not exactly deprived him of anything,' Lloyd George seemed offended on Cody's behalf. 'I do not see why the State should treat a man more shabbily than an ordinary commercial concern would.'

The former solicitor even exercised a paternal hand here and there. At one point Cody joined in a conversation about the weakness of the language used in his patent. 'The patent does not divulge the secret,' he said. 'You had better not say too much about that,' Lloyd George added quickly. (As the original architect of the 1907 Patent Act under which Cody had brought his action, he must have known, it is safe to suppose, what he was talking about.)

Lloyd George's only concern was that Cody did not sell the kites to foreign governments. Cody and his solicitors agreed that he would sign a declaration to that effect immediately.

As the hearing drew to a close, and Lloyd George agreed to make his decision known in a few weeks' time, his affection for the inventor shone through. 'I was frequently to my own knowledge dubbed an absolute madman, but . . . I paid no need to my critics,' Cody said in one exchange. 'That is the right spirit, Mr Cody,' said Lloyd George, no stranger to slander himself. 'To pay no heed to your critics.'

CHAPTER TWELVE

THE ARM
OF THE NATION

O N 23 JULY 1913, LLOYD GEORGE BROUGHT SEVEN
years of acrimony and argument to an end. Announcing
his adjudication in the case of *Cody v. The War Office*, he
found in favour of the claimant and awarded compensation. 'Taking into consideration Mr Cody's written guarantee not to communicate the secret to Foreign Governments, we award the sum
of £5,000, inclusive of the £1,000 already paid by the War Office,'
he wrote in his official adjudication. Amid the chaos of the aeroplane shed, there was barely a moment to savour the victory.

The sense of anticipation with which he left the Treasury in
June had been erased by the disastrous events of early July. Cody
had begun the month with hopes high for the Military Trials. It
was a measure of his confidence in his two entries that, on the
evening of 3 July, he had agreed, for the first time, to have the
biplane and monoplane in the air together. At the controls of
the newer machine, Cody had not been able to resist demonstrat-
ing its superior speed by skimming smoothly over the top of the
Cathedral's pilot, another pupil from the Army Air Battalion, a
Lieutenant H.D. Harvey-Kelly. Minutes later Cody touched
down to see the aftermath of Kelly's landing ahead of him. The
Englishman had misjudged his approach, clipped the Cathedral's

wing on a tree and crashed so violently that the biplane was a write-off.

Cody's despair was as nothing compared with that of five days later. Two thousand feet up in the monoplane he suddenly heard his engine cut out. He was forced to glide, or 'vol plane', down and picked out a landing on seemingly open ground on Laffan's Plain. As he hit the ground he suddenly saw the propeller shatter, then felt the monoplane crumpling all around him. Cody emerged badly shaken and confused. At first he imagined he had hit a tree stump. The sight of the bruised and bleeding carcass of a cow revealed the more bizarre truth. The animal had, according to witnesses, charged towards the monoplane, collided with it head on and died instantly. One look at the monoplane's mangled wreckage told Cody it too had suffered terminal injuries.

To the press it was all faintly amusing. 'MR CODY KILLS A COW. NEW ADVENTURE AT ALDERSHOT', ran a typical headline. Another saw Cody's miraculous escape as 'further evidence to the superstition that he bears a charmed life'. To Cody it marked the nadir of his fortunes. In April he had been able to call on three working aeroplanes. Three weeks away from the Military Trials he did not have one.

A CCORDING TO VIVIAN, HIS FATHER RESPONDED AS HE had in all the defining moments of his life. Vivian later described how Cody's depression had been deep, dreadful to witness and dispatched to history within one night. The next morning he had watched Cody head for the aeroplane shed, take stock of the material available to him, begin making furious drawings and summoning up his most trusted volunteer helpers on the telephone.

If it is hard to believe Cody could have recovered so quickly it is tougher still to credit that he set out on the course he then did. Even today aviation historians shake their head in disbelief at the task Cody set himself. He had three weeks to effectively design and build a new plane.

Cody's idea was to incorporate some of the successes of his monoplane in a new version of his most reliable surviving plane, the Mk III Circuit of Britain Cathedral. While some of the additions, such as twin triangular rudders, were his idea, other requirements were dictated by the Trials rule book. Entrants were, for instance, required to provide their pilots with protection from the wind. Cody replaced the cockpit of the monoplane with a piece of fabric 'fairing'. Most significantly, Cody was determined to use the Austro-Daimler engine – even though he had to reinforce his chassis to carry its extra heft. A familiar mantra was soon ringing out. 'Work will do it,' he told his helpers. And – miraculously – it did.

The rules of the Military Trials required Cody to present himself and his plane at Salisbury Plain by the evening of 31 July. As his small team of helpers set off by car – and in some cases bicycle! – he took off from Laffan's Plain, crossed from Hampshire into Wiltshire, headed west until he saw the distinctive outline of prehistoric Stonehenge, then dropped towards the semicircular, corrugated-roofed hangars of the Larkhill aerodrome on Salisbury Plain.

Cody's entrances were rarely devoid of drama. His touchdown an hour or so later was a particularly irresistible piece of theatre even so. Cody was one of nineteen entrants – ten British, nine European – and his plane one of thirty-two entered in the trials. Every one of the rival machines had arrived on Salisbury Plain, carefully packaged on the back of a lorry. With the arrival of his War Office compensation still weeks away, Cody had neither the time nor the money for such an outlay. He was the only competitor to risk flying all the way there.

One glance at the crowd gathered at Larkhill was enough to confirm the Trials were the most important aviation gathering Britain had yet staged. Indian potentates and assorted ambassadors, government ministers and senior Army figures mixed with the great names of European aviation, including Bleriot, Farman, Deperdussin and Ducrocq of the Hanriot company, who had all come to supervise their entries. Europe's best pilots were there too, including Valentine and Vedrines, and the new French sensation, Prevost, hired by Deperdussin to show off its much-fancied monoplane.

Cody again revelled in his role of maverick, outsider and underdog. 'Cody went through the trials in a manner that was fascinating to watch,' wrote the *Telegraph*'s CC Turner. 'He was a lonely figure, unsupported, as everyone knew, by the resources of a big factory with mechanics and pilots.'

Even his most powerful rivals were unsure just exactly what the trials judges were looking for, however. The judging panel, a collection of senior military aviators including Major Sykes, head of the Military Wing of the Royal Flying Corps, and Mervyn O'Gorman, superintendent of the Army Aircraft Factory, were certainly offering few clues. 'The judging committee have wisely kept their method of classification secret,' wrote the air correspondent of *The Times*.

Their vagueness was, to him at least, understandable. 'At the present moment "tactics for the air" are in an unformed state. There are few experts who would hazard a definite opinion as to what will rule for supremacy in an aerial contest.'

As the trials got under way, it was soon clear that only the most durable machines would even manage to complete the exhaustive testing.

Each machine was to be evaluated in two areas: first construction, then performance. In the first discipline each pilot had to prove he could start his engine from his seat and then run his machine at low revolutions without moving forward. The view from his seat was then evaluated by a judge. (Reconnaissance, it turned out, was still the only real use the Army saw in aeroplanes.) By far the most difficult construction test was the so-

Maverick, outsider, underdog. Cody draws a crowd at the Military Trials,
Salisbury Plain, August 1912.

called 'quick-assembly' trial in which each plane had to be first
presented in a dismantled form in a packing case, then assembled,
loaded on to a lorry, reassembled, then flown, before being dismantled again.

Cody could not compete with Parke and the six-man Avro
team, who during their test put the biplane together in a staggering 14.5 minutes. Cody and his six-man team put the Cathedral
together in an hour and thirty-five minutes, the thirteenth best
time in all. (The test was too much for one team who – watched
by a stopwatch-wielding judge – spent more than nine hours finishing the first assembly stage of the test alone.)

The flying tests were, in comparison, a piece of cake.
Entrants were required to climb to 1,000 feet with a full load, fly
at a height of 4,500 feet, complete a duration test of three hours,
and fly into a twenty-five-mile-an-hour headwind. On top of all
this they would have to prove they could take off from a

ploughed field. The War Office's decision to allow an entire month for the trials was vindicated by the appalling weather that descended on Salisbury Plain almost as soon as the testing got under way. Cody was the second competitor to begin testing and passed the duration and height tests comfortably despite the weather. The Cathedral performed well again in the climbing test, reaching 1,000 feet in the fourth quickest time after two Hanriots and the Deperdussin of Prevost. Cody's long experience at improvising landings proved invaluable. He was one of only six who passed a test in which flyers were required to glide, or 'vol plane', to earth with their engines switched off.

The Austro-Daimler engine proved his second greatest asset. Its huge power range meant his plane could fly at a far greater variety of speeds than the other, mainly sixty- to eighty-horse-power-engined machines. As a result Cody easily won a test to measure the range of speeds at which each plane could function. The Cathedral's maximum flying speed was 72.5 miles per hour, its minimum 48.5 miles per hour, a range of 24 miles per hour. The Bleriot, in comparison, could vary its speed by just two miles per hour.

The awful weather conditions took their toll. The Mersey aviation company's monoplane crashed on 13 August, killing its pilot, Fenwick. Cody's old protégé Parke, now of the Royal Navy but employed by AV Roe's Avro, was lucky to escape a similar fate when he made his landing after his attempt at the test of flying into a stiff, twenty-five-mile-an-hour wind. Parke landed on a particularly bumpy piece of land, hit a huge molehill and turned a somersault. Only his elastic safety belt saved him.

As the trials entered their final phase at the end of the month, Cody's Cathedral, a Hanriot piloted by the Frenchman Sippe and the Deperdussin monoplane of Prevost had emerged as the clear leaders. Prevost's display of acrobatic flying so impressed the panel of judges, three of them went for a ride in his plane after his tests were complete. It was an exercise in public relations Cody

Boy's Own hero. A popular Cody cigarette card, circa 1912.

would undoubtedly have loved to copy. Until he finished the trials, however, he steadfastly refused every request for recreational trips over Salisbury Plain.

Of all the tests, none suited Cody better than the ploughed-field take-off. He had been taking off from the equivalent all his flying life. 'The Bleriot had difficulty in getting away but Cody was little affected,' wrote the *Times* correspondent. With the pattern of the trials now established, the reporter was convinced the smallest manufacturer could easily leave Larkhill with the biggest prize. 'Cody is well placed for the ultimate consideration of the judges,' he speculated as the trials entered their final week.

The biplane performed badly in some areas, petrol consumption in particular. Only one plane used more than the nine gallons an hour Cody consumed, hardly a surprise given the size of his engine. Yet the engineering excellence of the Austro-Daimler also made it easily the most efficient in oil consumption, using only 0.42 of a gallon an hour.

By the time he completed his trials on 23 August, Cody completing his testing with the shortest 'emergency stop' of the trials, thirty yards, his hopes were justifiably high. At this stage only the Cathedral and three other planes, a Bleriot, a Deperdussin and a

Hanriot, had completed all elements of the trials. No British plane had completed its set of tests at all.

Cody celebrated by giving passenger rides to a group of young officers from the RFC. The wait was a long one, a week in all. The trials came to an end officially on 30 August. At the end Cody had been the only British plane and pilot to complete the tests.

The decision came surprisingly swiftly. Cody had just given a Captain Hamilton of the RFC a ride in the Cathedral when he was approached by Major Sykes, commandant of the Military Wing of the RFC. His immediate reaction to the result listed inside the envelope Sykes gave him is not recorded. It is not difficult to imagine, nevertheless.

Later that afternoon the results were announced officially. Three British planes – two Bristol monoplanes and the British Deperdussin Company's monoplane – had been awarded £500 each despite having failed to complete the trials. Six other planes, two Hanriot monoplanes, one Farman biplane, two Bleriot monoplanes and AV Roe's biplane were awarded £100 each for at least submitting themselves to all the tests.

Only two planes were worthy of the main prize money, however. In the international division, the second prize of £2,000 went to the French Deperdussin company for Prevost's plane. The first prize of £4,000 and the £1,000 for the best British entry both went to Cody.

The result provoked a mixture of delight and disgust. Many could not believe Cody's cumbersome Cathedral had outperformed the products of hundreds of thousands of pounds' worth of research and development. 'The judges displayed an astonishing lack of intelligent criticism,' grumbled one aviation historian afterwards. The Hanriot in particular had seemingly outperformed every other plane. Yet to others it had been increasingly obvious that Cody's strengths – visibility, power and flexibility – made it the most solid and serviceable machine, and by far the best bet in the demanding conditions of war, whatever they may

Weighing in. Cody takes to the scales during the Salisbury trials.

be! In this respect, as a military plane maker first and foremost, Cody had been working along the right lines for years. Only now had the qualities of his unfashionable work been realised.

No one outside Larkhill could begrudge him his win. 'For years he has been a regular "mother in law joke" to certain papers; he and his kite and his plane have been the constant theme for essays on derision and ridicule. Throughout it all, Samuel

Franklin Cody has preserved the marvellous conceit of himself which yesterday was rewarded,' read a leading article in the *Daily Dispatch* the next morning.

The three-column eulogy in *The Times* was even longer.

Because of his confidence in his own inventions and designs he may have been charged occasionally with too much promise and too little performance. But the time when such charges can retain currency has now passed and he has given the world assurance of his merit. He has defeated the best that the world could bring into competition with him. In spite of ridicule, misadventure, calumny and all, he has persevered and proved that he possessed not only a genius of conception, but also a genius of consummation. There will be few in the country who will not be proud of the old man's achievement, since he has done it all himself.

The surge of pride his win had produced among his country-men was evident at a reception at Salisbury Town Hall the follow-ing day. Thousands lined the streets to watch Cody drive by, a Union Jack fluttering from the back of the car. He almost broke down during an impromptu speech. Casting his eyes to the por-trait-filled walls of the room, he said, 'I have spent my life in a hard struggle against long odds in the hope that hundreds of years from today, when the history of aviation will be written, my photograph may be among those of the pioneers,' he said.

Cody could not help reflecting on the irony of his win. 'The aeroplane I built was built while I was in British service, but some people thought I was wasting a lot of the taxpayer's money, so the government gave me the aeroplane and told me to go away and practise on my own account,' he said to laughter. 'Yesterday morning that same government gave me £1,000 for the aeroplane [and] I won two prizes amounting to £5,000. The bargain was a very good one for me and I hope it will be a very good one for them,' he added to shouts of 'hear, hear'. Cody ended by promising the audience he would build on his triumph. 'I . . . assure you of my intention of trying, during the rest of my days, to build up the success you accuse me of being entitled to now.' He had to dab at his eyes as the entire audience broke into a rousing chorus of 'For He's a Jolly Good Fellow'.

His reception was similar back at Farnborough and then Aldershot, where he and Lela were given a standing ovation when they attended a musical at the Theatre Royal. The entire audience sang along with the show's star, Jamie Dallis, as he sang an impromptu verse:

> Three ringing cheers for our Cody who flies,
> He's wiped out all foreigners high,
> Stand by him and you'll see that he'll try,
> To make England the boss of the skies.
>
> If you'll just take a wrinkle from me,
> You'll find that our Cody will be,
> The arm of the nation, to lick all creation,
> A wrinkle with which you'll agree.

His finest hour lasted the rest of the summer. The Royal Aero Club awarded him its highest honour, the Gold Medal, and King George ordered a command performance at the Army's manoeuvres at Cambridge. George had passed on his congratulations by telegram via the new head of Aldershot Command, General Sir Douglas Haig, the day after the trials. He had asked to see Cody fly the winning plane at first hand, however. Once more Cody obliged – once more he landed, with a flamboyant flourish just a few yards from the monarch's feet.

———

AT THE FLYING CAMP.

King Congratulates Col. Cody.

AN EXHIBITION FLIGHT.

His Majesty arrived at Hardwick Camp about ten o'clock, and was met by Major Sykes, Commanding the Flying Corps.

After a few minutes' conversation with Major Sykes, the King walked towards the aeroplane tents, where Colonel S. F. Cody was standing, and greeted the famous designer and airman with a cordial "Good morning," and a hearty handshake, congratulating him again on winning the two first prizes in the recent military trials.

Shortly afterwards Colonel Cody withdrew, hurrying towards the tent where his famous biplane was housed, the Royal party following.

I N THE SPACE OF THREE MONTHS, CODY'S FINANCES were transformed. His new account at the London County and Westminster Bank was swollen even more when, three weeks after the trials win, he won that year's Michelin prize, this time for the fastest time around a 186-mile circuit. Cody's course took him from Laffan's Plain to Larkhill, Newhaven, Brooklands and back. He ran into fog at sea and ended up travelling twenty miles. It was still good enough to win him another £600.

'I am not going to spend it on building machines, but shall invest it in good securities,' he said when asked what he planned to do with all the money. True to his word he spread the money among $2,000 (£700) worth of Canadian Pacific Railway shares, $5,000 (£1,750) worth of Union Pacific Railway stock, £2,000 in the London County and Westminster Bank and another £1,010 worth of five-per-cent debentures in Cordoba Light Power & Traction Company Ltd.

Predictably he was soon fending off those who wanted to separate him from his new-found wealth. In November, Cody found himself standing before the local magistrate defending an action brought against the farmer whose cow had been killed during the monoplane accident, Mr Maynard.

Even the judge regarded the case as something of a joke. 'I suppose it is not disputed that the cow met its death at the hands of the monoplane?' he asked Cody's solicitor, Ernest Jackson, as the hearing began. 'Committed suicide,' Jackson corrected the judge, to laughter. 'We say the aeroplane did not run into the cow but that the cow —' he added before the judge interrupted. 'Then I am very surprised at the cow,' he said to even more howls of laughter.

Cody did not find the proceedings funny at all, however. Eventually the judge found him not guilty of negligence but liable to compensate Maynard. He was ordered to pay the farmer £18 for his loss.

CODY'S FIRST TASK THAT WINTER WAS TO HAND OVER THE trials-winning Cathedral to the Royal Flying Corps and begin work on the new version for the War Office. His imagination was now being fired by far grander schemes, the downfall of the dreaded Zeppelin for instance.

Cody's colourful presence was by now a boon to any newspaper's circulation. He used the columns of the *Daily Mail* to explain the technique he believed could bring the lumbering German airships to their knees. 'Airmen ought to be trained in fishing for dirigibles,' he wrote, proposing aeroplane pilots take to the air armed with lines fitted with explosive hooks with which they could puncture the airships. Cody had even worked out an attack pattern in which three planes would attack the Zeppelin, two distracting it from below while the third pounced from above. The plane would feed out a long wire, up to 4,000 feet in length, with an explosive device at the end. It would either have an explosive shell or even a firework — 'just as efficacious' — at the end. Needless to say, he

'The world's first aerial omnibus'.
Cody and a colourful passenger,
circa 1912.

added that he had an aeroplane near completion that would have the stability necessary to allow the pilot to 'devote himself to angling'.

Cody's success had brought him an even wider international following. Shortly after the trials he confirmed he had been approached to train a new Australian air force for six months. He was considering a trip 'to the old country' on the way back, he told one newspaper. Even more intriguing were overtures to produce aeroplanes for Russia.

Cody had by now employed an agent, a Yorkshire salesman called Oscar Andren. Andren had begun working as Cody's representative and general assistant in March. He found Cody a demanding taskmaster and had moved from Yorkshire to Fleet, near Farnborough. In the space of the following months he would claim to have written 700 letters to assorted governments, agencies and associations who might have been interested in the plane. As he said later, 'All this necessitated very hard work on my part so that not only the days but also the evenings and Sundays were fully

With the hunt. The Aldershot Beagles greet Cody at Laffan's Plain, 1912.

occupied on Mr Cody's business, at whose beck and call I was throughout.' Despite Andren's repeated requests for a formal arrangement, Cody neglected to pay him for his work.

Andren was close to concluding a deal in St Petersburg with a representative of the Russian government, Charles Richter. At the same time he had put together a prospectus for the planned flotation of the Cody & Sons Aerial Navigation Company. Investors were invited to apply for a stake in an issue of 50,000 £1 shares in the company. Cody was presented as managing director. The company's aims were to establish an aerodrome, a factory and flying school somewhere in the south of England. Within six months, Andren projected, two planes a month would be rolling off its production lines. Andren's job was to capitalise on what he later called Cody's 'inventions and schemes'. As ever, there was no shortage of material.

His simplest idea was the air ambulance he had been developing with a Lieutenant JDF Donegan of the Royal Army Medical Corps, inventor of a patented portable operating table, complete with equipment. In early trials the Cathedral had been able to carry the table, along with a three-man medical team – doctor, assistant and anaesthetist – across country with ease. In early August its future was strengthened by a photograph in the august *British Medical Journal.* Donegan told the British Medical Association he expected the machine would be 'of extreme practical value' when it was inevitably taken up by the medical wing of the War Office.

Cody's proudest boast was that no one had ever perished in one of his planes. By April that year, however, he was forced to remove that line from his sales pitch. Since the RFC had taken delivery of the trials-winning Cathedral in December, Cody had become friendly with its most frequent pilot, Lieutenant Lancelot Rogers-Harrison. On the morning of 28 April, Cody heard the plane's engine 'fluttering' as Rogers-Harrison flew over Ash Vale. Sensing something was wrong, he ran out of the house, jumped on a bicycle and headed in the direction of Farnborough. The first two Royal Flying Corps men he met said they had seen the Cathedral passing overhead and 'flying splendidly'. Minutes later he met a mechanic on a motorcycle. 'It's all up, he's dead,' he told him.

The following morning Cody appeared at the inquest at Farnborough's Connaught Hospital. 'I viewed him as a very promising and careful pilot,' he told the coroner. Cody concluded that Rogers-Harrison had come in too steeply, put too much pressure on his elevator and broken up. Had Cody warned him about coming in too fast? 'It was my intention to warn him the next time I saw him,' he said sadly.

A day later, Cody joined a large group of soldiers and airmen in accompanying Rogers-Harrison's coffin from the Connaught to the North Camp railway station. He watched as the Union

Cody's waterplane on the Basingstoke Canal, 1913.

Jack—draped coffin was placed on board and saw the train head off for Cheltenham, where the pilot was to be buried.

Rogers-Harrison was the latest victim of an annus horribilis for British aviation. In recent months Cody had learned of the deaths of the young Lieutenant Hamilton he had taken for a ride at Larkhill and Wilfred Parke, who had died flying a Handley-Page monoplane at Wembley in December 1912. The sudden and seemingly inexplicable deaths – along with that of yet another young pilot, Lieutenant Bettington – had led to the temporary banning of all monoplanes by the War Office.

Lela, the boys and Cody's colleagues knew Cody's luck could not continue. They knew too that the emerging entrepreneurs of the industry – Sopwith, Roe and Handley-Page, in particular – had all retired from flying to concentrate on building their business. For Cody, however, a permanent place behind his desk at the new Cody & Sons Aerial Navigation Company offices in Princes Street in the City remained unthinkable, particularly with a new wave of challenges on the horizon.

The ultimate aviating test presented itself in April 1913 as Northcliffe announced a new, £10,000 prize to the first flyers to cross the Atlantic. The crossing became an instant talking point, with opinion divided on whether the prize would be won by stealth or speed. As *The Car* put it, 'the very big machine with perhaps two or three engines, to do the journey without a stop, and the smaller, very fast type, which will alight every 500 miles or so to pick up the fresh fuel, and for lightness' sake have only one engine'. Any doubt as to the path Cody intended taking was dispelled by the accompanying photograph of him, dwarfed by a whale-sized propeller almost twice his height. His was, apparently, the second name to appear on the list of declared runners. A naval officer, Albert Bates, wasted no time in volunteering his services as Cody's wireless operator and met Cody to began planning the trip.

Northcliffe had provided the ideal preparation for the Atlantic challenge with another £5,000 prize, this time for a Coastal Circuit of Great Britain. The race was due to begin on 15 August, with entrants allowed seventy-two hours to complete a circuit from Southampton to Dover, then Aberdeen, Inverness, Oban, Dublin, Falmouth and back to Southampton again. The 'hydroplane' Cody had begun building for the race would, he hoped, be the prototype for a larger model for the Atlantic crossing the following year.

E VEN BY CODY'S STANDARDS, THE PLANE WAS A LEVIATHAN. Its sixty-foot wingspan exceeded anything he had built before. Cody practised floating the plane on water at the Naval Wing of the Royal Flying Corps at Calshot, near Southampton and on the Basingstoke Canal on the edge of Laffan's Plain. He was particularly proud of the floats he had designed and had already submitted a patent application.

That summer he posed for photographs balanced precariously on the end of the hydroplane's albatross wings. Newspapers, as ever, rushed to print the picture first.

July 27, 1912. **THE SCOUT.**

DODGING DEATH.

My Most Trying Times in the Air. By S. F. CODY.

Before I had time to realise what was happening, I was hurled from my seat and dashed against the turf.

Cody's innate gift for public relations ensured his face was rarely out of the papers for long. *Boy's Own* adventure comics frequently ran articles on his adventures. 'DODGING DEATH: MY MOST TRYING TIMES IN THE AIR' ran the headline to one hair-raising account of his flying life in *The Scout*. Not every publicity stunt worked out so well, however.

Cody had fallen foul of the local constabulary when he had pioneered a new way of advertising by dropping hundreds of flysheets over Farnborough one evening. The clergy too were less than impressed when Cody had suggested Vivian and Eva Copeland could marry on board the hydroplane. The idea had come from Grahame-White, who had captured the headlines the previous month by arriving at his wedding by plane. Cody, naturally, wanted to go one better. The ceremony went ahead on 2 August, on terra firma instead.

The most misguided stunt of all had come earlier that year, when Cody invited a troupe of American Indians for a ride in the Cathedral. (It is unclear who they were. They may have been friends of Edward, who had joined the troupe of the hugely popular Mohawk actress Go-Won-Go in her play *Wep-Ton-No-Mah*. They may have been connected to another popular performer JO Brant-Sero, 'the brightest Iroquois ever born on a reserve', with whom Cody had been friendly.) With photographers present to record the moment, the chief of the troupe, resplendent in his feathered headdress, proudly climbed on board with Cody. The sound of the huge, Austro-Daimler engine being started up sent his band of not-so-braves running for their lives. They did not stop until they reached the Basingstoke Canal, where they duly dived headlong into the water.

CHAPTER TWELVE A

'SWIFT AND SUDDEN'

T HIS MACHINE IS A BEAUTY, AND AS STEADY AS A ROCK.'
Midway through the morning of Thursday, 7 August
1913, Cody could be forgiven for crowing a little. A week
before the start of the Coastal Circuit of Great Britain, he had
just completed a successful first passenger flight in his hydroplane. He had intended taking Leon up, but had given the honour
to Lieutenant Charles Keyser of the 20th Hussars instead. Keyser
and a friend, WHB Evans, a former county cricketer home on
leave from a stint with the Civil Service in Egypt, had arrived at
Laffan's Plain early that morning offering to pay for their debuts
in the air. 'I may as well make a little pocket money before I go,'
Cody had smiled. He had agreed to take first Keyser, then Evans,
on a twenty-minute circuit of Farnborough Common.

Keyser's first experience of flight was everything he hoped.
'The machine behaved splendidly. Colonel Cody was delighted
and felt very optimistic as regards his chances in the *Daily Mail*
race,' he said later. As Evans climbed into the seat, raised at shoulder height behind his pilot, Cody told Leon to be ready to head
for Southampton and Calshot on his return. Leon headed inside
the shed to make a final phone call. Frank was among the crowd
watching from the doorway as the hydroplane taxied away.

On a clear day the first part of the flight went smoothly. As

Cody and Evans turned back home, Cody had begun skimming up and down over the trees, 'steeplechasing', as he liked to call it. The plane was passing over Ball Hill at a height of about 500 feet when, without any apparent warning, the hydroplane's wings suddenly closed in on each other. It was, as one witness put it, as if a sword had been driven into the middle of the plane. Another witness described how pieces of wood and fabric then began falling to earth. Amid the debris, the only clearly distinguishable object was Cody's white coat, tumbling towards the ground. The shape of his passenger following immediately behind him was less obvious. 'Something that looked like rags,' one of a party of boys camped out on the common called it.

Even away from the scene, the silence that followed was eerie. Geoffrey de Havilland was inside his house on the edge of the common. 'I heard the unmistakable note of Cody's open exhaust as he flew round Laffan's Plain. Suddenly the sound was cut off, as cleanly as if by a switch, and never restarted,' he remembered years later.

To the pockets of onlookers around Ball Hill and Laffan's Plain, the dreadful reality of what had happened was immediately apparent. The first to the scene was a gunner from the Royal Field Artillery, Harold Maxted, who had been watching the flight through field glasses on Ball Hill itself, 300 yards away. He jumped on his horse and galloped in their direction even before he had seen where the bodies had landed.

Maxted found the hydroplane in a clump of trees, a tangled mess of metal, wire and canvas. Cody and Evans were lying within three feet of each other. Both were on their backs, both motionless. He immediately galloped off to Puckridge Hill Camp, where he asked the staff to telephone for a doctor.

By the time Maxted had ridden back it was obvious there was little the medical men could do. Leon and Frank had by now arrived on the scene. Leon had flung himself across his stepfather's broken body. 'Dad, oh, Dad, Dad,' he had sobbed incessantly.

Aftermath. The scene following Cody and Evans' fatal crash
at Laffan's Plain, August 1913.

As the boys were led away by officers from the Royal Flying
Corps, the bodies were covered with blankets and a cordon was
placed around the accident scene. It was already too late to prevent the souvenir hunters taking the propeller and other parts of
the plane away.

Minutes later Cody and Evans were taken to the Connaught
Hospital, where they were pronounced dead on arrival. Leon was
asked to perform the formal identification of Cody's body and
belongings.

Lela had sensed the truth the moment she saw her sons coming through the door at Ash Croft. 'I knew what had happened
before they spoke,' she said years later. 'I knew he was dead.'

As the day dragged on, Leon continued to deal with the for-

All the Best Photographs of Colonel Cody's Funeral.

DAILY SKETCH.

LONDON, TUESDAY, AUGUST 12, 1914. ONE HALFPENNY.

HUNDREDS OF WREATHS SENT TO COLONEL CODY'S FUNERAL, AS TRIBUTES FROM A NATION THAT USED TO SNEER.

malities. 'My mother is prostrate with grief,' he told the reporters who had gathered outside. It seems he and Frank had promised Lela none of them would ever take to the air again. 'It has been a sad day for us,' Leon said. 'We shall retire from the business and look after her. We shall also try hard to do well in other walks of life.'

Leon's main concern by then was Vivian and Eva, on honeymoon in London that week and unaware of what had happened. The newlyweds had spent the morning at Westminster Abbey and had gone on for lunch in the West End. They learned of the morning's events when they saw the *Evening Standard* newsstand outside their hotel on the Strand. The front-page headline read,

COL. CODY'S FATE

DASHED TO EARTH FROM A WATERPLANE

FALL OF 300 FEET

AVIATOR AND OFFICER KILLED TO-DAY

That night and the following morning, the newspapers reflected the genuine shock Cody's death had provoked. Seemingly every airman in Europe paid tribute to their father figure, Papa Cody. 'This is the biggest blow, sentimentally at any rate, that aviation has yet suffered,' said Sopwith. 'By the death of Colonel Cody, England loses her first and foremost aviator. His was a gallant soul,' said the new hero of French flying, Salmet.

Every newspaper carried lengthy pictorial tributes and personal recollections. A florid piece by H Hamilton Fyfe, another *Daily Mail* man who had got to know Cody well, typified the sentimental tone:

Four years ago, when I saw him crawl out from beneath his overturned aeroplane at the Doncaster meeting, I said, thinking of his many accidents: 'you are the unluckiest man alive'. 'If I weren't the luckiest,' he replied, mopping at the blood which ran down his face, 'I'd be dead' . . . It was this happy temperament, breezy and buoyant, bobbing up again the instant after a blow, that made him a national figure, one of the few men of whom everybody knows and whom everybody thinks of with a feeling that is almost affection. 'Good old Cody!' That was the universal comment when he pulled off an Army prize. 'Poor old Cody!' one heard on all sides when he 'took a toss'. That was the sentiment in all hearts yesterday: 'Poor old Cody!' Millions who had never seen him felt they had suffered a loss almost as if they had lost a friend.

The sympathy was deepened by the knowledge that Cody had finally found himself in a position of strength. 'It is a sad thing that when, after years of striving, he had grasped success, when for the first time he was freed from the constant worry of money matters, death should have claimed him,' said the *Daily Mirror*.

Two days later — and only weeks after the inquest into the death of Rogers-Harrison — the Connaught Hospital became a courtroom again. Outlandish theories had already begun circulating in the press about Evans. According to one he was a German or Russian spy hired to eliminate Britain's best-known airman. The rumour had been fuelled by the testimony of two Grenadier Guardsmen who had seen the plane pass over Cove reservoir. One told the *Daily Mirror* how 'the passenger appeared to be suffering from great agitation. He was clinging to Cody with both arms around him.' The coroner wasted no time in summoning evidence to dismiss this as an optical illusion, caused by Evans sitting above Cody in the plane. (He did not dignify the other theory about Evans with a mention. According to the most morbid joke in circulation, Evans had been wearing green socks.)

Lieutenant Ivor Huddleston of the Royal Army Medical Corps confirmed that Cody's wishes had been fulfilled and that death had been 'swift and sudden'. Both men's 'injuries were so severe' they must have fallen from a great height, he said. 'Evans had every bone in his body broken.' On the cause of the accident, however, there was little sign of consensus.

In his evidence, Leon suggested it was a burst propeller. Gunner Maxted was adamant that he saw the tail come away from the main body of the plane. 'The bodies fell out after the rear part had gone,' he said. 'They were thrown out by the jerk.' His evidence was contradicted by the secretary of the Royal Aero Club, Harold Perrin, who had conducted an inspection of the wreckage. 'I think he must be mistaken because I found the tail under the wings,' he said.

Perrin's inspection had found that the two seats were 'very little damaged'. 'The fall was undoubtedly broken very much by the

Funeral of the Late Colonel Cody. Carrying the coffin from the house to the Gun Carriage.

trees. I think that had Cody and his passenger been strapped in they might not have been killed.'

With witnesses even divided on the height from which Cody and Evans had fallen – estimates varied between 100 and 500 feet – it was agreed that a full inquiry should be conducted by the Royal Aero Club.

Leon used the inquest as an opportunity to advertise the sale of Cody's equipment already being planned for Laffan's Plain a few weeks later. He explained that Lela had been left in 'poor circumstances' and that he and his brothers intended to 'hang together and see our mother through'. The sale was sad but necessary. 'It is not likely to fetch much,' Leon said solemnly.

News of Lela's 'straitened circumstances' brought a flood of donations from friends and admirers. The contributions were part of a tide of cards and messages of condolence arriving daily at Ash Croft. The messages came from every corner of Cody's life. An old theatrical friend, JF Elliston, managing director of the Bolton Theatre Royal, wrote telling Lela how he had 'a strange presentiment that what has happened would happen' and had earlier that year offered Cody a return to the stage if he gave up flying. 'He only laughed at me, and described how careful he was,' he wrote.

Many had only ever met Cody once. 'It was him that shot a ball off my head at the Exeter Theatre Royal while I was but a lad and I have followed his daring and brave career from that day with a lad's love for his hero,' wrote one such fan.

Even those who had locked horns with him in the past were moved to write. 'Not many would have had better opportunities that I had of observing the straightness and independence of character under what must have been to him very trying circumstances,' wrote Major General RM Ruck, who as a lower-ranking head of the Army's Director of Fortification and Works had negotiated Cody's original contract with the Army.

George V's telegram arrived on the day after the accident via General Haig's office at Aldershot. The full text was reproduced in newspapers all over the world, including the *New York Times*.

By the weekend Haig informed Lela and the boys of the decision to offer Cody a place at the Military Cemetery at Thorn Hill. The Royal Flying Corps were soon overseeing the arrangements for the funeral and the preceding procession.

On the afternoon of 11 August, Leon, Vivian and Frank managed to march the mile or so to Thorn Hill in the overwhelming heat. Lela was too weak and distressed to contemplate joining them and was comforted in a carriage by her daughter Liese on the way there and back.

CODY

Crank of the crankiest, ridiculed, sneered at;
Son of a boisterous, picturesque race.

Butt for the ignorant, shoulder shrugged, jeered at:
Flint-hard of purpose, smiling of face.
Slogging along on the little-trod paths of life;
Cowboy and trick-shot and airman in turn!
Recklessly straining the quick-snapping lath of life,
Eager its utmost resistance to learn.
Honour him now, all ye dwarfs who belittle him!
Now, 'tis writ large what in visions he read.
Lay a white wreath where your ridicule riddled him,
Honour him now, he's successful and – dead.

— J Poulson

L EON'S FEARS WERE CONFIRMED WHEN CODY'S STOCK WAS put up for sale at the shed on 8 September. Grahame-White bought much of Cody's equipment. His three Green engines fetched the highest prices, the one fitted to the hydroplane getting £100, two others fetching £75 each. The remains of the mono-plane fetched a paltry £14. In all the auction raised just £700, a fraction of what had been expected.

The disappointment made the contributions to the official Cody Fund being run by the Joint Committee of the Aerial League all the more welcome. Money had been sent by the highest and lowest in the land. Edward VI's widow Queen Alexandra sent £50, Salmet collected £25 by charging a penny for each autograph he signed, around the country paper boys donated their pocket money. By October, a cheque for £1,375 had been sent to Lela.

There were, by now, those who wondered why the family needed such support in the first place. 'Only a builder of aero-planes knows the frightful expense which is attached to the build-ing of flying machines and my dear old dad was absolutely alone and had no one to finance him,' Leon explained in an open letter in response. 'I cannot describe the numerous expenses there now are – bills and otherwise – they are too many to mention.'

By now his statement hid an even more painful truth.

Cody had, in fact, left a substantial estate worth in excess of £6,000. Even allowing for the dizzying list of creditors who claimed Cody owed them some £1,800, a residue of £4,000 would be due to his legal heirs. Unfortunately, Cody had died intestate. If Lela and Frank's claims had been weakened by the lack of a will, they were undermined even more by the reappearance of a ghost from Cody's distant past.

Cody's death had been mourned around the world. (In France reports on the 'Mort du colonel Cody' had in many cases been run with obituaries of Buffalo Bill.) The news made it even as far as Iowa, where the *Davenport Democrat & Leader* ran a story on the Sunday after the funeral. 'In the death of Colonel Cody,' its report began, 'the life of a true "soldier of fortune" was brought to a close.' It went on to suggest that Cody had 'left a snug fortune' in England.

A similar report seems to have made its way to Camden, New Jersey, where Joseph and Lilian Lee had been as intrigued by the money as the news of his English 'wife'. Within a fortnight of Cody's death Mrs Lee had paid a visit to the courthouse where she had greeted reporters brandishing photographs of Cody and declared that she was taking steps to secure his estate for his legal widow, her stepdaughter, Maud.

Even if he had wanted to divorce Maud to marry Lela, Cody's prospects would have been bleak. In the aftermath of their marriage break-up, she continued a peripatetic existence herself, seemingly performing in a parachuting act back in America. Her luck had run out in 1905 or so when, according to her stepmother, she had fallen. 'She was so badly injured about the head that her mind became a blank,' Mrs Lee had told reporters. She was now under the care of the State Hospital for the Insane at Norristown.

Her parents had told her of Cody's death that week but she had been unable to comprehend. 'She does not realise it,' Mrs Lee explained.

The Lees placed the case in the hands of a local solicitor, David Goff. He immediately set about getting Maud recognised as Cody's lawful widow on both sides of the Atlantic.

IN MOURNING CODY'S DEATH, THE BRITISH PEOPLE had been mourning the passing of an era. No one had better epitomised the self-confidence, perseverance and eccentricity of the pioneer age. He had, more than any other man in Britain, made flying popular and widely accepted. It had been the English critic, essayist and aviation historian Sir Walter Raleigh who said 'the engine is the heart of an aeroplane, but the pilot is its soul'. Cody had seemed the heart *and* soul of the new air age. Within a year of his death, however, aviation – and the world – had entered a darker epoch.

It is tempting to think that Cody's fortunes would have blossomed in World War One. With luck, better management and the right financial backing his big biplanes and flying ambulances could have played their part in the aerial war, just as de Havilland, AV Roe and Sopwith would do with their prototype warplanes, the Army Aircraft Factory's BE2C and SE5A, Avro's 504 biplane and Sopwith's famous Tabloid and Pup. As it was, Cody & Sons Aerial Navigation Company remained nothing more than a prospectus and the memory of the last great hero of the prewar era faded all too quickly.

The loose ends of his life were, in truth, best forgotten in any case. The cause of his accident was never satisfactorily resolved. The Aeronautical Society's eventual conclusion that a front spar had broken because of the 'inherent structural weakness' of the hydroplane left the family deeply unhappy. Speculation as to the cause continues to this day. The most plausible explanation was raised only in 1998, in a lecture to the Royal Aeronautical Society on the ninetieth anniversary of Cody's first flight. Paul Chapman, a distinguished engineer, had discovered the tendency of bamboo to expand and crack violently in heat. The hydroplane's flight had coincided with a heat wave.

The unseemly scramble over his estate dragged on endlessly too. On the morning of 27 October 1914, Maud made a brief appearance at a court in Camden. Doctors from the asylum testified that she was incapable of managing her estate and 'would be likely to be imposed upon by designing persons'. From the stand, Maud told the judge she understood it was 'necessary' to have someone look after her interests and recognised her father and stepfather as her guardians. The judge agreed she was 'a person of unsound mind'. Joseph Lee had told the court he expected the estate to be worth about $5,000. Within weeks he saw that figure shrink as it emerged they would have to share Cody's estate with the brother and sisters-in-law Maud had never known she had. Cody's Davenport connections had been discovered by a London firm acting for the Treasury. The report in the *Davenport Democrat & Leader* had identified Cody as the brother of Martha Cowdery Meckel. She said she had not heard from him in seventeen years. All four of his siblings had survived. Charles, Amanda, Martha and Elizabeth all swore affidavits. The case would drag on for seven years. By the end of the dispute Maud would be awarded £1,000, while Charles, Martha, Amanda and Elizabeth Cowdery received £250 each. Lela and Frank would receive not a penny piece. By the time the process had finally been worked through the biggest beneficiary of Cody's estate would be David Goff, the solicitor to whom Lily Lee had gone running. In her haste to pursue the case, she had signed an agreement granting half of any proceeds to him.

VIVIAN FOUGHT HARDEST TO KEEP HIS FATHER'S achievements alive. While Leon returned briefly to show business, he remained at Farnborough, eventually becoming head of the Fabrics Division when it became the Royal Aircraft Establishment. (Despite the mountain of evidence to the contrary he stuck to the story that he was Cody's American-born son and even went through the bizarre process of applying for British citizenship in 1923.) He reacted angrily when, in 1929, Cody's first flight in Britain was effectively written out of history by the specially appointed Gorell Committee of the Royal Aero Club. The committee had decided that since Cody had not been a British citizen at the time of his first flight the honour should go to Moore-Brabazon for his first flights at Shellbeach in April of 1909.

With Cody's most loyal helper, George 'Broom' Broomfield, Vivian campaigned for a memorial to the events of 16 October 1908. Their efforts ended in controversy. By 1949 Broomfield had persuaded the flying establishment that Cody had flown even earlier than imagined, in May rather than October 1908. (The date had been chosen to scupper AV Roe's renewed claims for his 'powered hops' of June that year.) The claim was exposed as a hoax during the fiftieth-anniversary celebrations in 1958, forcing Farnborough into a humiliating rewriting of its history.

The complex story is encapsulated in an inscription that can still be seen on a plaque attached to Farnborough's sole link to its flamboyant founding father: Cody's Tree. It reads,

S.F. Cody measured the thrust of his first aeroplane in 1908–9 by tying it to this tree. Near by he made his first tests with his powered aeroplane on 16th May, 1908, and his flight of 1,390 feet on 16th October, 1908, was the first powered and sustained flight in Great Britain.

The last remaining pine of a clump that once stood outside the Balloon Factory, the tree's origins are almost as uncertain as those of the man it remembers. According to official history it was here that Cody used to tether his first aeroplanes while he tested the thrust of his Antoinette engine. Some think it acquired the name Cody's Tree when he used to fix his plane while sneaking into the premises 'on the scrounge' for supplies after his exile to Laffan's Plain. Others wonder whether it played much of a part in his story at all.

Its almost mystic importance to the airmen of what is still Britain's most important aviation establishment is unquestioned, however. When the original tree withered and died many years ago, a team of apprentices at the Royal Aircraft Establishment forged an exact replica of the original, this time in all-weather aluminium. Today the tree stands outside the gleaming new Cody Building, at the heart of the R.A.E's successor, DERA, the Defence Evaluation Research Agency. Its gnarled and knotted branches make for an unconventional, incongruous and slightly surreal sight. As a memorial to the life and times of Cody it seems altogether perfect.

PREDICTABLY IT WAS CODY'S ONLY BLOOD SON WHO FOUND it hardest to resist the pull of his father's life. Frank disobeyed his mother's wishes and joined No. 41 squadron of the Royal Flying Corps at the outbreak of World War One. He distinguished himself in action over the fields of France. On the morning of 23 January 1917, he learned of the birth of his second son, Leslie Helier Cody, born five days earlier in Farnborough. Later that day he was shot down in a dogfight with four German planes. His death bestowed the Cody name with its last and least welcome aviating distinction: it was the first recorded instance of two generations of the same family being killed in the air.

The pain Lela would have felt at the loss of her only child by Cody is too hard to contemplate. According to one legal letter, she was paralysed for a time. She withdrew into a reclusive life with her grandchildren at Ash Croft.

She made only one public appearance again, as far as can be

ascertained, when an enterprising reporter from the *Daily Sketch* beat a path to her door in 1932. The gloom lifted momentarily as she spent the morning recalling her time as his assistant. She recalled how she had once flown in his man-lifter. 'My husband, in his excitement, momentarily forgot that I was flying on his kite right up in the clouds – so high that my clothes were wet with moisture. When someone reminded [him] that I was still up in the air he exclaimed: "Good God, yes" and hauled me down,' she laughed. 'Afraid? No, I was not a bit afraid. I never knew what nerves were in those days, especially with *him*. When they buried him that day my world was ended. He was my King – my all.'

It was another seven years before she was finally reunited with him. When she died in February 1939 at the age of eighty-seven, the Army broke with protocol once more and allowed Cody's grave to be opened up. She was laid to rest alongside him, beneath a statue of Christ the Redeemer and an epitaph made even more fitting by her arrival: I put all my trust in thee.

ACKNOWLEDGEMENTS

M Y INTEREST IN THE STORY OF SAMUEL Franklin Cody took shape almost a decade ago. At the time I was researching the stirring, if less spectacular, lives of the first men to fly in Wales, Howard and Herbert James. The brothers had taken to the air in the fields below my childhood home, in the small village of Clynderwen in Pembrokeshire, in the year of Cody's death, 1913, and had been utterly obsessed by the Anglo-American pioneer. Their passion rubbed off – and the journey that led to the completion of this book began.

Ten years ago the material available on Cody was scant. The accepted wisdom regarding his life was based on two short biographies, one written in 1953 by his faithful assistant George 'Broom' Broomfield and another, a decade later, by Arthur Gould-Lee, based mainly on the colourful testimonies of the age-ing Vivian. Both perpetuated the mythology about Cody's origins in America and his marriage to Lela. Neither had access to the volumes of official documentation relating to Cody's turbulent public and private life.

It was my good fortune that I came to write this book at a time when much of this material emerged into the public domain. In the course of my writing and researching I have been able to gain access to a wealth of previously unseen material, private and public, in particular at the Public Records Office in London.

The availability of much of the private material was made possible by the auction of Cody's archives held at Sotheby's in London four years ago. With the help of Stephen Maycock at Sotheby's I was able to trace much of the most important mate-rial disseminated around the world during the sale. In Seattle, thanks to Ali Fujino and Elizabeth Snodgrass at the Drachen Foundation, a charity devoted to kite history, I was able to gain access to many of the legal files relating to Cody's action against the War Office as well as his curious early kiting diaries. In Los Angeles, Marva R. Felchlin and Alison Poulsen at the Gene Autry Museum were helpful in supplying me with a wealth of material on Cody's early days as a showman and travelling horse v cyclist champion in continental Europe. In London, Leonard Lewis and his estimable assistant Carmel allowed me access to his fascinating archive of clippings, postcards and ephemera.

By far my most important source, however, was Jean Roberts, the present occupier of Cody's old home in Mytchett, Pinehurst. Jean's diligence in collating and researching Cody's life is only surpassed by the generosity she displayed in sharing her material with me. Her contribution to this book has been immense and I owe her – and her husband John, who supplied two wonderful illustrations to the book – a debt of gratitude beyond calculation.

Jean's research allowed me to open up new avenues, in America in particular, and I am indebted to a number of people who moved Cody's early story on. In Montana I am grateful to Brian Shovers of the Montana Historical Society in Helena, Fulton Castleberry at the old 'hash knife' ranch at Box Elder Creek, in Norristown, Pennsylvania, Michael Tolle at the Historical Society of Montgomery County and Joan Barborak at the San Antonio Public Library's Hertzberg Circus Collection. In England I am grateful to Ian Mayne at the Rushmere Borough Museum, Jane Rushton and Harvey Moseley at DERA in Farnborough, and Jay and Fiona Aleander for translating the arcane French cuttings I accumulated during my digging.

Forming Cody's complex – and frequently exasperating – story into a book was always going to be a challenge. Here I must thank my agent Mary Pachnos, as well as Gillon Aitken, for their early enthusiasm for the story. I must also thank the supportive voices of Martyn Palmer and Tony 'Radar' Downes, both of whom encouraged me to believe this was a story worth telling and in the latter's case, that I was telling it in a way that might appeal to a wide audience.

At Simon & Schuster in London, Helen Gummer caught the Cody bug early on as did George Witte at Picador in New York. As I brought the book to its close, however, no one offered a better barometer than my editor, Katharine Young. Energetic, efficient and enthusiastic at all times, she was also good enough to cry at the right places! I must also extend thanks to a too often unsung hero of publishing, the designer. Peter Ward's grasp of the material and the manner in which it should be presented has, I believe, brought Cody's remarkable story to life even more vividly than I could have hoped.

The final thanks must be personal ones. The birth of this book coincided with that of my son, Thomas William Jenkins, born a few weeks before this manuscript was delivered. The manner in which she coped with him, our daughter Gabriella, as well as their deeply distracted father only served to reinforce my belief in my wife Cilene's right to some form of semi-sainthood. My gratitude to her extends beyond mere words.

INDEX

aeroplanes:
air ambulance, 247
Atlantic crossing, 248–9
Britain's first flight, 165–6
Circuit of Britain Challenge, 207–21
Coastal Circuit of Great Britain,
  249
Cody's 'British Army Aeroplane
  No. 1', 146–7, 149, 153–67
Cody's 'Cathedrals', 192–3, 199–200,
  208, 210, 224–5, 227, 231, 233,
  243
Cody's gold medal, 241
Cody's 'hydroplane', 249, 253–4
Cody's injuries, 184, 200, 226
Cody's monoplane, 224–5, 231–2
Cody's second army plane, 171–3
Cody & Sons Aerial Navigation
  Company, 246, 248
distance record, 183
Dunne's, 135, 143–5, 154, 156, 174–5
fatalities, 199, 210, 247–8
first flight expunged, 265
first passenger, 180
military trials, 232–9
prizes, 184–5, 188–9, 197–8, 202–4,
  208, 219–24, 227, 238, 242,
  248–9
shows, 190–5, 197
tapioca, coating of, 147
airships, 136–43
  Baby, 178
  La Patrie, 136, 138
  Nulli Secundus, 136–45
  Nulli Secundus Mark II, 149, 152–3
  Zeppelin, 136, 138, 243
Albert, Frank, 38–40
Alexander, Patrick Young, 102–3, 131
Andren, Oscar, 244, 246–7

army contract, 126–8, 130–1
  end of, 173
  reinstatement, campaign for, 176
Axelby, George, 21

Baden-Powell, Colonel B.R.S, 82, 85,
  90, 103, 105
Baldwin, Professor Charles, 38
balloons, 90–1, 122, 223
Bartleson, Frederick, 14
Belgium, 59–60
Belle Island prison, 13–15
bicycles, 51–6, 58–60
Birdville, Texas, 5
birth, 8, 15
Bleriot, Louis, 184–5, 188, 201
Bradford Exhibition, 125
British citizenship, 195–7
Brooklands motor-racing circuit, 145
Buffalo Bill *See* Cody, WF
bullocks, riding, 17
Butler, Frank, 33
Butler, Lieutenant-General Sir William, 122

Capper, Colonel John, 103, 122–5, 132–5,
  148–9, 172, 187–8, 223
  attempt to block Cody, 176
  circulars to news organizations,
    156, 161
  Cody's contract, 130–1
  hair-raising first aeroplane flight, 180
  Nulli Secundus, 138–145
  reports and memos on Cody's
    progress, 127–8, 162–3, 174–5
  support for Cody, 126
  Wrights' plane, 151–2
Carver, 'Doc', 1–3, 32–3, 71–2
cattle, 19–24
chariot racing, 60–2

INDEX

Civil War, American, 11–15
Cody, Frank (son), 60
  bicycle crash, 226
  Cody's death, 255–6
  Cody's estate, 264
  death, 266
  first aeroplane flight, 182
  Royal Flying Corps, 266
Cody, Lela Blackburne *See* Davis,
  Lela Blackburne
Cody, Maud (wife) *See* Lee, Maud
  Maria
Cody, Samuel, Sr and Phoebe
  (parents) *See* Cowdery
Cody v. The War Office, 227–9, 231
Cody, WF ('Buffalo Bill'), 3–4, 37
  family-connection claims by SF
    Cody, 4, 38, 40, 71
  role model to Cody, 4
  'Wild West' name controversy, 37, 39–40
Conneau, Lieutenant ('Beaumont'), 208,
  210, 212, 214
Cook, James H, 27
Cowdery, Amanda (sister), 11, 16, 264
Cowdery, Charles (brother), 15–16, 264
Cowdery, Jabez (uncle), 10, 16
Cowdery, Lillie Elizabeth (sister),
  15–16, 264
Cowdery, Martha (sister), 11, 264
Cowdery name and line, 8–10
Cowdery, Phoebe (mother), 4, 8
  divorce, 16
  marriage, 11
Cowdery, Samuel Franklin, Sr,
  (father), 5–6, 9–11
  captured, 13
  Civil War, 6, 11–15
  death, 16
  divorce, 16
  marriage, 11
  postwar illness, 15

Davis, Lela Blackburne, 44–7, 226–7
  car accident, 169
  Cody's estate, 264
  'damsel in distress' in shows, 62
  death, 267

death of Cody, 257
  first aeroplane flight, 180–1
  marriage to Cody, 41–42
  races against bicycles, 60
  straitened circumstances, 259
Deadwood Dick, 33
death in air accident, x, 254–5
  aftermath and reaction, 257–61, 263
Defence Committee on Aerial
  Navigation, 151
de Havilland, Geoffrey, 223, 225, 254
Delagrange, Leon, 147, 190–2, 194,
  199
Dodge City and Wild West legend, 24
Dunne, John William, 134–5, 143–5,
  154, 156, 158–9, 173–5

fame spreads, 56
Forepaugh, Adam D, Jr, 1, 36
Forepaugh, Adam D, Sr, 1–2
  criminal proceeds, 32
  death, 35–6
Forepaugh show, 1–2, 29, 32
  Cody leaves, 34
  scout discovers Cody, 7
France, 49–59, 62–3, 113, 135
Franklin, Benjamin, 80–1
funeral, *vii–xi*, 260
  military honours, *xi*

Gallon, Monsieur, 57–8
Germany, 59
gold strike, 26
Grohmann, W Baillie, 36
guns and gunmanship, 3, 37, 46–7, 70–1
  British Army, offer to, 64–5
  rapid-fire handgun, 64–6

Hadden, CF, 144
Haldane, Richard Burdon, 145, 173–4,
  185
Hargrave, Lawrence, 82, 85
'hash-knife' cowboys, 21
horses and horsemanship, 18
  bicycles, competition against, 51–6,
    58–60
  mustanging, 26–9

walker, competition against, 57–8
horse-thief lynchings, 3, 37

Italy, 59–61

King, Edward (stepson), 42, 44, 85
  acting abilities, 80
  becomes 'Leroy', 57
  departure, 127
  'stock Redskin', 62
King, Leon (stepson), 42, 44, 85, 97,
  183, 264–5
  Cody's death, 255–6, 258
  kite maker, 127, 132
  races against bicycles, 60
King, Liese (stepdaughter), 42, 131
King, Vivian (stepson), 42, 44–6, 50,
  85, 97, 183, 265
  campaign for memorial, 265
  Cody's death, 256
  first aeroplane flight, 182
  glider-kite accident, 132
  kite maker, 127, 132
  races against bicycles, 60
  star billing in shows, 46
kites 80–7, 147–8, 153
  accidents, 95–7, 100–1, 124, 132,
  153
  army contract, 126–8, 130–1
  Calais-Dover crossing, 113–8
  Dover-Calais crossing, 115
  glider, 132
  man-lifting, 87, 89–100, 105–11,
  119, 124–6, 223
  meteorological survey, 100
  'motor kite', 132–3
  novelty, 103
  signal, 119
  thrills and chaos, 98
  see also Chapter 5

Last Days of Pompeii show, 63–4
Latham, Hubert, 190
Le Blon, J, 191, 194
Lee, Maud Maria, 34–6
  claim on Cody's estate, 262–4
  marriage to Cody, 35

marriage collapses, 41
  performances with Cody, 37
Leroy, Edward See King, Edward
Lloyd George, David, 151, 185, 227–9,
  231
Loste, Henri, 56, 62
Louis of Battenberg, Prince, 105,
  108, 110

Malta, 60–2
marriage:
  first collapses, 41
  to Lela, 41, 42
  to Maud, 35
Meckel, Frederick, 16
Meyer of Dieppe, 52–4
Moore-Brabazon, Charles, 197, 202,
  265

Oakley, Annie, 33

Parker, Lewis, 40

Ridgeley, Albert Newton, 37
Roe, Alliott Verdon, 145, 154, 185
roller-skating mustangs, 37
Rolls, Charles S, 103, 185, 200–1
Ross, Jake, 19, 28–9
Royal Flying Corps, 223, 243
royalty, friendships with, xi
Ruck, RM, 144

Sabre, GE, 13–4
Savage, William W, Jr, 17
shows and showmanship, 62, 69
  Alexandra Palace, 69
  cruelty-to-animals claim, 72
  France, 49, 56
  The Klondyke Nugget, 70–80, 85,
  124, 126, 160, 227
  Malta, 62
  Royal Aquarium, London, 44–6
Simpson, Colonel John N, 20
Sioux raid on Cody homestead, 6–7
stagecoach attacks, 3
stories, myth and hokum, 4, 7–8, 17,
  24–5, 35

stories, myth and hokum, (*continued*)
Boot Hill, 24
gold strike, 26
'hash-knife' cowboys, 20
horsemanship, 52
mustangs, 28
superstitions, 199
Swinburne, James, 110

Taylor, Buck, 33
Templer, Lieutenant Colonel James
Lethbridge Brooke, 97–8, 136
Trollope, Major Frank, 97, 103
Tunisia, 62
Tupper, Reginald, 105, 110

Turner, Frederick Jackson: *The Frontier In
American History*, 84
Tussaud's 'Lenin' likeness, 205

Valentine, Jimmy, 208–9, 212, 214, 220–1
von Zeppelin, Count Ferdinand, 102–3,
138

Walker, Percy, 144
weightlifting, 61–2
Wright, Orville, 103–4, 133–4, 146
Wright, Wilbur, 103–4, 133–4, 146,
149–50, 172
Wyndham, Charles, 40
Wyndham, WG, 185